Witness to War Crimes

Witness to War Crimes

The Memoirs of an Irish Peacekeeper in Bosnia

Colm Doyle

Edited by Kenneth Morrison

First published in Great Britain in 2018 by Pen & Sword Military

First published in Ireland in 2018 by
Merrion Press
An Imprint of Irish Academic Press
10 George's Street
Newbridge
Co. Kildare
Ireland
www.merrionpress.ie

ISBN 978-1-78537-189-9

British Library Cataloguing in Publication Data
An entry can be found on request

Library of Congress Cataloging in Publication Data
An entry can be found on request

Printed and bound in the UK by TJ International Ltd, Padstow, Cornwall

This book is dedicated to my wife Grainne and our children Elaine, Mark, Sheena and Shane, who endured my many absences on peacekeeping tours of duty abroad. Thank you all for your enthusiastic and constant support.

Contents

Acknowledgements

My thanks are due to all the following people: Dermot Cogan for his friendship, loyalty and sage advice; Pandelis Botonakis and the late Jean-Loup Eychenne for being great teammates; Vitor Ferreira for being an outstanding deputy; Darko Ivić for being the perfect interpreter and someone whose good humour was infectious; Lieutenant Colonel Slobodan Dimitrijević of the JNA, an officer and gentleman; Professors Zoran Pajić and Borisa Starović of the University of Sarajevo for their insightful knowledge and support; Lord (Peter) Carrington for selecting me as his Personal Representative in Bosnia; Ambassador José Cutileiro for believing I could make a difference; Martin Bell for a special friendship between journalist and soldier and for starting me on this memoir journey; Annette McElligott for crossing the t's and dotting the i's; and Professor Kenneth Morrison, who gave so generously of his time to bring my Bosnian memoir from draft to book form. Thank you one and all.

I pray that my grandchildren will never have to experience the brutality of war and hope that this memoir will encourage them to work in their adult lives towards a peaceful, just and inclusive world.

Abbreviations

ADL: Armistice Demarcation Line

AO: Area of Operations

APC: Armoured Personnel Carrier

DFF: De Facto Forces

DPKO: Department of Peacekeeping Operations

EC: European Community (now the European Union)

ECMM: European Community Monitor Mission

FCA: Forsa Cosanta Aitiul (Irish Reserve Defence Force)

FCO: Foreign and Commonwealth Office

HDZ: Hrvatska Demokratska Zajednica. The Croatian Democratic Union – Bosnia

HOM: Head of Mission

HQ: Headquarters

HVO: Hrvatsko Vijeće Obrane. Croatian Defence Council

ICA: Israeli-controlled Area

ICRC: International Committee of the Red Cross

ICTY: International Criminal Tribunal for the Former Yugoslavia

IDF: Israeli Defence Force

IFOR: Implementation Force

JNA: Jugoslovenska Narodna Armija. The Yugoslav People's Army (Yugoslav Federal Army)

MOU: Memorandum of Understanding

NATO: North Atlantic Treaty Organization

NCO: Non-commissioned Officer

NGO: Non-governmental Organization

OGG: Observer Group Golan

OGG-D: Observer Group Golan-Damascus

OGL: Observer Group Lebanon

OP: Observation Post

OSCE: Organization for Security and Cooperation Europe (formerly CSCE)

PfP: Partnership for Peace

PLO: Palestinian Liberation Organization

RAF: Royal Air Force

RCC: Referendum Coordinating Committee

ROG: Referendum Observer Group

RS: Republika Srpska. The Serbian Republic of Bosnia Herzegovina

RSK: Republika Srpska Krajina. The Republic of Serbian Krajina

RTE: Radio Telefis Eireann. Ireland's national broadcasting organization

SAR: Serb Autonomous Region

SDA: Stranka Demokratske Akcije. The Party for Democratic Action (Muslim)

SDS: Srpska Demokratska Stranka. Serbian Democratic Party (Bosnia)

SLA: South Lebanon Army

SPO: Srpski Pokret Obnove. Serbian Renewal Movement

TDF: Territorial Defence Force

TO: Teritorijalna Odbrana. Territorial Defence

UN: United Nations

UNDOF: United Nations Disengagement Observer Force

UNEF: United Nations Emergency Force

UNFICYP: United Nations Force in Cyprus

UNHCR: United Nations High Commission for Refugees

UNIFIL: United Nations Interim Force in Lebanon

UNMLOY: United Nations Military Liaison Officers Yugoslavia

UNPA: United Nations Protected Areas

UNPROFOR: United Nations Protection Force

UNSC: United Nations Security Council

UNTSO: United Nations Truce Supervision Organization

VBL: Vehicule Blinde Legar (French light armoured vehicle)

VRS: Vojska Republike Srpske. Army of Republika Srpska

Foreword

The Irish Defence Forces, to their credit, are not primarily a fighting but a peacekeeping organization. They are used to taking part in what is sometimes termed 'Operation Sitting Duck' – caught in the middle of others' wars. They have served with distinction in many conflicts, from the Congo to Lebanon. The Army, more than any other, has punched beyond its weight, and it has paid the price: eighty-six of its soldiers have lost their lives on United Nations peacekeeping duty.

One of its most remarkable soldiers was Colm Doyle, a quiet man from Drogheda, who rose from Cadet to Colonel in a 43-year career. He served under the United Nations flag in Lebanon, Syria and Cyprus. But for his most prominent exploits he was not in army uniform. In 1991, as Yugoslavia was beginning to disintegrate, he was seconded from the Irish Army to serve as a European Community Monitor in Bosnia. He started in the northern city of Banja Luka, and then very quickly became the European Community Monitor Mission's Head of Mission in Sarajevo. He was widely and uniquely seen by all groups – Serbs, Muslims and Croats – as being a fair, unbiased mediator. He earned their trust more than anyone else did, and after Lord Carrington became President of the Hague Conference, set up by the European Community in an attempt to avert the wars in former Yugoslavia, he was appointed Carrington's representative on the ground.

So it was that a middle-ranking Irish Army officer (a Commandant, meaning a Major) spent his year of living dangerously, crossing front lines under fire, drinking *slivovitz* with warlords and mixing with generals, presidents, prime ministers, foreign ministers and others. This is where I got to know him. We developed a relationship closer than is usual between a reporter and a soldier/diplomat. Sometimes I knew what was going on, sometimes he did (though he more often than I). I was definitely out of order in April 1992, when I met him for the first time and urged him to do something to stop the ethnic cleansing that I had witnessed. I could even have told him what a Khe Sanh landing was, but I don't remember him asking me. I had been in Vietnam and he had not. Our friendship was both personal and professional.

The Bosnian war began in April 1992 and ended with the signing of the Dayton Peace Agreement in November 1995. It was the most consequential conflict of the late twentieth century. So the war deserves to be studied in detail: how it started, who was responsible for it and whether it could have been pre-empted or ended before it was. For a whole year as Bosnia slid into war, from October 1991 to October 1992, Colm Doyle was a prime witness – perhaps even *the* prime witness – to how the war began and how it developed. That was why he was called on seven times in war crimes trials at the Hague, including those of Slobodan Milošević and Radovan Karadžić.

This book is an account of it all. We are lucky to have it.

Martin Bell

Editor's Note

That I was able to contribute to the editing of this book was a matter of both chance and good fortune. Having invited the renowned former BBC correspondent, Martin Bell, to give a lecture at De Montfort University's Cultural Exchanges Festival in February 2017, we met in advance of his lecture, drank coffee and discussed the themes he would be focusing on throughout his talk. During this short discussion the name 'Colm Doyle' was mentioned. I knew of Colm Doyle as the Head of the European Community Monitoring Mission in Bosnia and Herzegovina and as Lord (Peter) Carrington's personal representative thereafter (the only person ever to have held the latter role). I was acutely aware, from my own research, that he had played a central role in the diplomatic efforts, particularly on the ground, that sought to halt the slide to war. Martin told me that Colm (whom he knew well from his own time covering the early months of the war in Bosnia) had written memoirs, but that they were, as yet, unpublished. I immediately expressed an interest in reading them, and Martin was kind enough to assist me in establishing contact.

It is rare indeed that one simply stumbles upon memoirs that are of genuine historical significance, but that is precisely what happened. Even upon my first reading of the draft I realized that these memoirs simply had to be published and I thus put myself at Colm's service to ensure that this happened. As editor my interventions were relatively limited and largely focused on stylistic changes. The final text, based on Colm's extensive personal archive of letters, diaries and reports, does not deviate in any way – in either form or content – from the original draft; my role has simply been to help maximise the potential that was already there and to help ensure that these memoirs would be available to students and scholars of European and

Balkan history, particularly those researching the important events that took place in Bosnia during the first six months of 1992.

I would like to thank Henry Wilson at Pen & Sword for his enthusiastic response to the manuscript and his willingness to commit to publication; Martin Bell for encouraging me to pursue the project; and, primarily, Colm Doyle for his willingness to spend whole days and late evenings poring through the text with me, and Colm's family for making me so welcome in Limerick during the latter stages of the editing process.

Kenneth Morrison
Professor of Modern Southeast European History
De Montfort University

Introduction

'I solemnly declare that I will speak the truth, the whole truth, and nothing but the truth.'

As I spoke these words at the witness stand of the United Nations Criminal Tribunal for the Former Yugoslavia (ICTY) in the Hague in May 2010, I glanced across at the face of Radovan Karadžić, the former leader of the Bosnian Serbs, at whose trial I was to appear as a witness for the prosecution. I had been very apprehensive at the prospect of having to undergo cross-examination by Karadžić himself, who seemed determined to prove that he was an innocent victim of the Bosnian conflict. I had earlier been informed that the trial judges were granting him fifteen hours to cross-examine me, and I feared that this experience would greatly challenge my memory. This trial was for me the culmination of events which had begun in 1991 when I was seconded by the Irish Defence Forces to serve with the European Community (EC) in Yugoslavia.

The first indication that I would face him in court came when I received a request through the Irish Department of Foreign Affairs some eight months previously asking if I would be willing to testify at his trial as a prosecution witness. I had known Karadžić very well throughout my service in Bosnia as a member of the European Community Monitoring Mission (ECMM) in 1991 and thereafter as the personal representative in Bosnia of the Chairman of the International Peace Conference (for Yugoslavia), Lord (Peter) Carrington in 1992. I didn't see myself specifically as a prosecution witness but rather as a witness to a war that destroyed or changed many lives. Accordingly, I had agreed to meet personally with Karadžić prior to my trial appearance.

My agreeing to meet with him at the United Nations Detention Centre in the Hague had come about following a request by his American legal adviser, Peter Robinson. Karadžić's legal team had sought and been given a list of prosecution witnesses who were scheduled to testify at his trial. His defence team was anxious that he should have the opportunity to meet with some of these witnesses individually prior to their testimonies. The tribunal judged that it was appropriate for such a list to be supplied but also ruled that it was at the discretion of the witnesses whether or not they were willing to accede to this request. Having given it a lot of consideration, I informed his defence team that I would meet with Karadžić, albeit under certain conditions. Among these were that I would only discuss with him the content of my original witness statement given to the tribunal in July 1995 and my testimony at the trial of Slobodan Milošević in August 2003. I also stipulated that there should be no electronic recording or written record of our meeting, and I insisted on there being a member of the prosecution team present. Robinson readily agreed.

I checked into my hotel under a number rather than a name. The protection of witnesses is a serious matter for the tribunal, and each witness is allotted a number by which he or she is referred to. I remember being rather nervous on my way to the Detention Centre and being, on reflection, very glad to have insisted on a member of the prosecution accompanying me. I feared that Karadžić might somehow seek to take advantage of my lack of knowledge about legal issues and I wondered if I had made the correct decision in agreeing to the meeting.

Having gone through the usual security measures on entering the building, we met in a small room close to his cell. Karadžić was accompanied by two of his defence lawyers. We had not met for eighteen years, but he looked much as I remembered him. Although his face was a lot thinner, he still had his characteristic mop of long hair, though now white rather than the familiar grey. We exchanged the usual pleasantries. He was courteous almost to a fault, even offering me some chocolate, which I diplomatically declined. The meeting lasted for about three hours, most of which was taken up by him questioning me on the content of my testimony at the Milošević trial. Much of that testimony centred round the events in Bosnia of which I had first hand knowledge. I was informed by his legal team that they had sought and been granted fifteen hours to cross-examine me. In court time this meant three days. I drew a deep breath. I had not expected this and suspected that however cordial he might appear to me within the confines of this prison, his cross-examination of me in court over the next few days would be anything but pleasant.

Colm Doyle

Map of Bosnia

Chapter 1

Under the Blue Flag

It was 1963 and I was in the car with my father coming home to Drogheda when he asked what I intended to do when I finished school. I hadn't a clue so I said nothing. He suggested banking, insurance, even the priesthood. Finally, he asked me if I had ever considered a career in the army. This was more appealing. He suggested that I visit the Local Defence Force – Forsa Cosanta Aitiul (FCA) – to see if it might be something I was interested in. So a few weeks later I headed up to the Sluagh Hall on the North Road in Drogheda, and before I knew it I was signing for a brand new pair of brown army boots and being given a Lee Enfield rifle. My platoon Sergeant, Mickey Bell, informed me that I should iron the toecaps of the boots and apply some 'spit and polish'. He also told me to do a hundred arm stretches holding the rifle every evening and to keep the rifle under my bed. The following day, I went to my local shop and asked the shopkeeper for some spit and polish. When I explained what it was for he just smiled, took out a tin of oxblood polish and promised that it would do the trick. I really enjoyed the FCA, never missing a single training night.

And so I became a member of the 39th Cadet class in October 1964. Training was pretty demanding. Each minute of our day was organized with typical military precision. We were instructed about what to do and how to do it, where to go and how to get there, what to learn and how to learn it. In fact, we had hardly had time even to think for ourselves, because, as we were told, we would have to do it ourselves soon enough. We learned about marching and tactics, shooting and weapon skills, peacekeeping, conflict and the principles of leadership. The school motto was 'Truth, Honour and Loyalty', and we came to respect and practise each. There were thirty-six of us in the class and we endured two years of constant supervision and assessment.

This proud class marched through Dublin as part of the military parade on Easter Sunday 1966, commemorating the 50th anniversary of the Easter Rising, and giving our salute to the distinguished gathering of VIPs in front of the General Post Office in O'Connell Street. The following day, twenty-two of our class formed a guard of honour for the opening ceremony of the Garden of Remembrance, a memorial garden near Parnell Square dedicated to the memory of all those who gave their lives in the cause of Irish freedom (the site of the garden is where the Irish Volunteers were founded in 1913). Receiving our Presidential Commissions and unit designations in September of 1966 was very special as we were presented with sword, Sam Browne (belt) and a bar on each shoulder. I was posted to B Company, 12th Infantry Battalion in Clonmel as a platoon commander, and it was there, under the supervision of very experienced non-commissioned officers (NCOs), that I learned about real soldiering. While I loved every minute of it I was, like every young officer, hoping for a chance to serve an overseas tour of duty with the United Nations (UN).

My first taste of UN service came in 1968, when I was appointed a platoon commander with B Company, 11th Irish Infantry Group, United Nations Peacekeeping Force in Cyprus (UNFICYP). I was still in my second year as a commissioned officer with the rank of 2nd Lieutenant, and I would command thirty troops. I was reminded more than once of the responsibility involved in leading men in an area of conflict over a six-month period. While thrilled to have the opportunity to serve overseas, I knew this would be my first test as an officer on active service. I was to have command of a full strength and fully equipped platoon abroad, something I had aspired to since entering the cadet school.

Cyprus is a beautiful island, but we, as soldiers of the UN peacekeeping force, had little opportunity to enjoy its tourist draws. The peacekeeping force was deployed along a 'Green Line' drawn between warring Greek Cypriot and Turkish Cypriot factions since 1964. The island had been a British protectorate and the British still retained a considerable presence there with two large military bases in Dhekelia and Akrotiri in the south of the island. The Greek Cypriots were in the majority and most of them supported a policy of unification with Greece. UNFICYP's mandate was to prevent the recurrence of fighting, help maintain law and order and promote a return to normal conditions. Operationally the situation was very quiet, with no major incidents to disturb our daily routine. It was a sort of 'hands on' learning curve for me without too much interference. Boredom was the greatest challenge, and we had to ensure the men were kept busy, be it at sports, in training or on operational duties. By the time we left, the unit had participated in a wide range of sporting activities, become very fit and developed a good operational reputation.

That first tour of duty taught me to appreciate the importance of 'public diplomacy': genuine interaction between peacekeepers and the local population. While this might appear pretty obvious, it was only when serving in Cyprus that I realized just how beneficial such dialogue could be. It is vital to treat people with dignity and respect, regardless of their culture, religion or beliefs. A UN presence, however well intended, which shows no understanding or appreciation of these factors will only damage the credibility of the organization. Part of a unit's role is to build confidence within the community by its presence, and this can be achieved by actions such as carrying out patrols in areas where locals are fearful of working and giving them protection as they tend to the sowing and harvesting of crops. In addition to this, the morale of troops is often heightened by their involvement in humanitarian work. This is crucial if units are to make confidence-building contributions to communities which can help win the 'hearts and minds' of local populations. It has since become an important element of Irish peacekeeping.

Summoned by my commanding officer in 1978, I was excited to be informed that I had been nominated for UN service with the United Nations Truce Supervision Organization (UNTSO). I was delighted with this news – UNTSO was an unarmed military observer mission covering most of the Middle East (it remains an unarmed mission to this day). Established in 1948, it was the first peacekeeping operation set up by the UN. Its military observers monitor cease-fires, supervise armistice agreements, prevent isolated incidents from escalating and assist other UN peacekeeping operations in the region to fulfil their respective mandates. Selection for service with UNTSO meant two years abroad, with the added bonus of having the family accompany me. By this time I had been married to Grainne for five years and we were living in Limerick. We had three small children, the eldest being four, the youngest just ten months.

Having successfully completed my medical I expected to be selected within a few weeks. Some time later, however, I was ordered to report to my headquarters in Cork. I duly reported to the barrack adjutant, who congratulated me on being selected to serve with the first Irish unit heading for Lebanon. I was knocked back on my heels. I told him that I had been nominated for UNTSO, but he responded by informing me that I had been selected as a deputy company commander for the United Nations Interim Force in Lebanon (UNIFIL). While I was thrilled at being selected for this newly established mission, I knew Grainne would not be very enthusiastic, particularly as it meant the family would not be accompanying me. However, she took the news in her usual good spirit, assuring me they would be fine in my absence. She had no wish to influence my decision, but I knew it must have been disappointing for her, facing a period of over seven months with three very small children while her husband was working in the Middle East. So I found myself heading to Lebanon with the advance party of the 43rd Battalion within two weeks of my selection, feeling somewhat guilty at being away from the family for so long.

Lebanon was a steep learning curve and a more challenging mission than Cyprus. On the night of 11 March 1978 the Palestinian Liberation Organization (PLO) mounted a commando attack, encroaching into Israeli territory. Eleven Palestinian fighters landed on a beach next to the Ma'agen Michael nature reserve, south of the Israeli port of Haifa. Nearly forty Israelis were killed and many more wounded. All eleven Palestinians died. Attacks on Israel had increased following the relocation of Palestinian armed elements from Jordan, whence they had been expelled, to Lebanon. In response, Israeli forces invaded Lebanon and within a few days had occupied the entire southern part of the country as far north as the Latani River, with the exception of the city of Tyre and its environs. The United Nations Security Council (UNSC) was convened after the Israeli invasion and Resolution 425 was passed calling for the establishment of a peacekeeping force. A key word in the title of the force was 'Interim', which implied a temporary operation on the presumption that the Lebanese government would soon re-establish its authority. The force was mandated with three objectives: confirming the withdrawal of Israeli forces, restoring international peace and security and assisting the government of Lebanon in ensuring the return of its effective authority in the area. The first UN troops arrived at the end of March 1978, with Ireland offering to supply an infantry battalion.

B Company of the 43rd Infantry Battalion (of which I was now the deputy commander) assembled at Kilworth Camp and underwent intensive training in preparation for our deployment. There was great excitement at the prospect of this new mission, given that we had not been part of a peacekeeping mission since 1974 – our last deployment had been as part of the United Nations Emergency Force (UNEF) in the Sinai Desert (though as a consequence of the internal security situation in Ireland at that time, the unit was repatriated by the Irish government). Now we had the chance to return to peacekeeping, and there was no shortage of volunteers. The unit was deemed to have been the best equipped of any in UNIFIL, and nothing had been spared in terms of arms and equipment.

Shortly after arriving at Kilworth I was informed I would be travelling to Lebanon with one of my corporals as members of the Battalion advance party, of which C Company would form the main element. The deputy commander of A Company, Captain Dermot Cogan, who would later play a key role in the EC Monitoring Mission (ECMM), would also be in the advance party. We had little time to prepare and after some frantic last minute preparations were soon en route to Tel Aviv. After a few restless days in a makeshift transit camp our convoy headed towards the border crossing with Lebanon. Taking no chances as we entered Lebanon, we were ordered to be armed and prepared. Within a few kilometres we arrived at UNIFIL's headquarters in Naqoura without incident. Geographically, Southern Lebanon is characterized by numerous hills separated by valleys and deep, dry gullies. The road network was very limited and all roads were in a bad state of repair with enormous potholes.

After arriving at Naqoura it was decided that while the main convoy of trucks and troops would proceed immediately northwards to the battalion's designated area, about an hour's drive north, we would head towards the village of Haris, which was to be the temporary headquarters of the Irish Battalion (IRISHBAT). We made contact with the village headman or *muktar*, who was delighted that the blue helmets were coming to protect his village. We were allocated an area of operations and soon the entire company was busy erecting tents, cookhouses, perimeter defence positions, shelters and 'long drops' (deep trench latrines). Within a short time we were pretty well established. Water was, however, a real problem as our supply had to be drawn from the Latani River, a considerable distance from our base and a challenge for our drivers.

Lebanon was as different to Cyprus as chalk is to cheese. Here we were faced with numerous warring factions who were ready to use force against the UN. These ranged from the Israeli Defence Forces (IDF) and its surrogate allies the Lebanese 'De Facto Forces' (DFF) to fighters of the PLO. Initially, UNIFIL was to be 4,000-strong, but it was later increased to 6,000. Before long, infantry battalions from France, Nepal, Iran, Nigeria, Norway, Senegal and Ireland were in the mission area. In addition, support units were supplied by Sweden and Canada. Forty-two military observers from UNTSO were permanently attached to UNIFIL where they became known as 'Observer Group Lebanon' (OGL).

Within a week or so of our arrival, Israeli forces conducted a phased withdrawal from Southern Lebanon. There were several exchanges of fire between UNIFIL and elements of the PLO and between UNIFIL and the DFF. In the final phase of their withdrawal, the Israelis turned over control of the border area to the DFF, thus forming a security zone, soon known as the 'Enclave' and later as the 'Israeli Controlled Area' (ICA). At its edge stood the village of At-Tiri, which the Israelis had planned to hand over to the DFF but, much to their surprise and rage, found the Irish Battalion occupying with a platoon of troops. The village was located at the forward edge of our battalion's area and in a valley running east to west dominated to the north by a range of hills, the highest being 'Hill 880', also occupied by B Company. It would have been a serious military and political setback if the village and the surrounding high ground had fallen under DFF control, as this would have allowed them to dominate the entire Irish battalion area. This fact was not lost on us, and it is little wonder that the area became the target of numerous shootings during our tour of duty and for many years thereafter.

A serious problem during that first tour was the danger from cluster bombs (subsequently banned under the Convention of Cluster Munitions of 2009). These munitions had been dropped from Israeli aircraft during the invasion in large artillery shells. On hitting the ground the shells would break open, scattering dozens of bomblets in all directions for some unsuspecting villager or child to pick up. Not much more than the size of a tennis ball, they could be lethal if touched. That they could have severe and indiscriminate effects, especially in populated areas, seemed to cut little ice with the Israeli authorities. In the second week of my tour of duty I was on my way to battalion HQ when a teenager appeared in front of my jeep waving at me to stop. When I got out of the vehicle he indicated I should follow him, and on reaching the front of a house, down a roadside path, we came upon a small boy of about eight years old sitting on a wall. I noticed blood on his hand, and when I took my arm away from his back after helping him stand up, it was covered in blood. He had picked up a cluster bomb nearby and it had exploded just as he threw it. He never spoke a word but was in obvious pain, and I felt a rage inside me that an innocent child should have been injured in such a cowardly and callous way. We lifted him into the jeep and took him to the local hospital in Tibnin.

It was gratifying to see how well received our battalion was by the local population and the appreciation they expressed for the contribution of our unit. We had brought a degree of stability to their lives in an otherwise desperate situation. Nevertheless, the Irish battalion's 'area of operations' (AO) was in one of the most volatile portions of UNIFIL – in particular, our platoon area around At-Tiri. One never knew when or where trouble might arise. Lebanon was yet another practical chapter in my military education. It was there I learned how to 'duck for cover'; it was the first time I had ever been shot at and it was the first time I had seen our soldiers perform under fire. I was impressed by the way they operated under stress and much provocation, particularly those based in At-Tiri. We soon learned that most of the dangerous harassment was coming from the DFF, who were acting as proxies for the Israeli Army. We were determined to hold firm, but unfortunately UNIFIL's mandate was not achieved. There was no full withdrawal of Israeli forces from Southern Lebanon, nor was there any restoration of Lebanon's 'effective authority' in the area – so much for the 'compliance' of all parties to the conflict. It would be many years before the UNSC resolution on Lebanon was in any way implemented.

My selection for UNTSO finally arrived six years after I was first nominated. At least I could now look forward to having the family accompany me and to giving them a taste of life in the Middle East. The HQ of UNTSO was based in Jerusalem, with regional HQs in Lebanon, Tiberias, Damascus, and Cairo, as well as liaison offices in Beirut, Amman and Gaza. My initial posting was to Damascus, from where I would be carrying out 'observation post duty' in strategically located observation posts on the Golan Heights. My first priority was to find suitable living accommodation for my family in Damascus. This was a challenge, but fortunately I managed to rent a ground floor apartment, not far from the HQ, with a small patio both in the front and rear which would provide ample space for four young children. My family settled well into their new surroundings, soon becoming used to the change in climate, culture and environment. What they might have lost in terms of a traditional Irish education was more than compensated for by meeting the children of observers from so many different countries as well as by learning much about Syria. We were also fortunate that they could attend an international school close by. We found Damascus, with more than 1.7m people and thought to be the oldest continuously inhabited city in the world, a great place to live, and during time off we got to visit many of the city's attractions. The famous Umayyad Mosque located in the old city is one of the largest and oldest mosques in the world, and a street named 'Straight', mentioned in the story of Paul's conversion to Christianity, runs for 1,500m from east to west in the old city. A visit to the famous al-Hamidiyah Souq was a must for every tourist.

'Observer Group Golan-Damascus' (OGG-D) was based in Damascus. Its observers manned a number of observation posts on the Syrian side of an 'Area of Separation' (AoS) on the Golan Heights that was put in place as part of the 1974 'Disengagement Agreement' between Syria and Israel following the 1973 Yom Kippur War. In addition, the observers carried out fortnightly inspections inside an 'Area of Limitations' (AoL) to verify that both sides adhered to limitations on troop levels and military equipment within 10km, 20km and 25km zones. As it was an unarmed body, liaison and negotiation were crucial to the settling of disputes.

A striking feature of the area was the amount of war debris, a legacy of the earlier conflict (the Yom Kippur War of 1973). The wreckage of battle tanks and artillery, with long forgotten fragments of military equipment, was a stark reminder of the war fiercely fought some ten years earlier and the dangers that confronted us. The area was infested with unexploded mines that were a constant threat to shepherds looking after their flocks. During one of my stints on observation post duty the quiet was shattered by the sound of an exploding shell, which sadly killed a young boy herding goats not far from our position. His body was extracted by members of the United Nations Disengagement Observer Force (UNDOF).

There were no official border crossing points between Israel and Syria. However, an unofficial one existed at Quneitra, referred to as 'the A-Gate', which was used frequently by UN personnel crossing to and from Israel. We were warned to be cautious when returning to Syria from Israel, and to be sure that anything we might purchase had no Israeli markings. The Syrian border guards would take great delight in searching UN vehicles looking for such goods, which, if found, were confiscated. Observation Post (OP) duty comprised officers manning five observation posts along the 1949 Syrian Israeli 'Armistice Demarcation Line' (ADL); these posts were strategically placed on the Golan Heights, affording good visibility of the cease-fire lines and within sight of the Israeli border. Each post was manned by two officers from different countries for a week, with each officer rotating 'inside' (cleaning, cooking and free time) and 'outside' (observing and reporting on aircraft overflights and border incursions). Conditions could be pretty harsh, particularly in winter, when snow would cover the area for weeks at a time. UN colleagues taught me how to manoeuvre a jeep to and from an elevated observation post on the Golan in heavy snowfall.

Towards the end of my period in Syria I saw an example of how much President Hafez-al-Assad, in power since 1970, was revered by the citizens of Damascus. He had not been seen in public for many months during 1984 and was rumoured to be ill, so his sudden appearance in the city was a cause of great celebration. I could hear bursts of gunfire from my apartment window, and television was covering his motorcade as it headed towards the parliament. As his car neared the building it was surrounded by throngs of followers, who suddenly lifted the vehicle and carried it forward to the edge of the entrance. Celebratory shooting took place for hours afterwards and it was reported that about forty citizens were accidentally hit by stray bullets. It was a strange and unsettling feeling for me, particularly with my family living in the city.

It has been the policy for UNTSO officers to serve in two stations during their tour of duty, normally on either side of Israel (if not within Israel itself). In my case, after six months in Syria I was transferred to OGL, returning to Lebanon six years after my first tour of duty there. OGL came under the operational control of the UNIFIL Force Commander, and having already served a tour of duty with UNIFIL I had an advantage over those observers who were serving in Lebanon for the first time. UNIFIL had from its inception the co-operation of UNTSO unarmed military observers. Before the arrival of the first troop contingents, UNTSO observers filled selected staff positions at the force HQ at Naqoura and made the necessary arrangements for the arrival and deployment of the first units of the force. Now the observers were performing various tasks under the operational control of the Force Commander. Our tasks included manning OPs along the armistice demarcation line outside the control of UNIFIL and conducting patrols within UNIFIL's area of operations. In order to help fulfil both the UNTSO mandate and that of UNIFIL, OGL provided six mobile liaison teams, of which four lived with and worked directly in support of the battalions of UNIFIL. The other two worked outside the UNIFIL AO, one of them in the Tyre coastal area and one in the 'Enclave'. Having a team in the latter was important in keeping UNIFIL informed of developments within the ICA.

Not much had changed since my tour of duty there in 1978. The Israeli invasion of 1982 had produced a new pro-Israeli militia, the 'South Lebanese Army' (SLA), which took up positions inside the Enclave or ICA formerly controlled by the DFF. The SLA contained many Shias who were armed by the Israelis. The invasion had greatly curtailed the operations of the PLO in Southern Lebanon and caused great suffering among the Lebanese population. This, in turn, led to the growth of the resistance group Amal and, subsequently, Hezbollah. Meanwhile, the Israeli Army still occupied much of the area inside Lebanon close to its own border.

I spent my initial two months as a member of 'Team Sierra', attached to the Norwegian battalion based in Ebel Es-Saqi in the eastern sector. They carried out patrols throughout the AO and their vehicles were clearly marked with team names in Arabic for easy identification. I was partnered with an Austrian, Major Johan Kantzler, and we patrolled throughout the Norwegian AO, as well as being available on call to the battalion commander should he require us. On one such occasion we were urgently called to a stand-off between members of the SLA and a heavily armed Norwegian patrol. When we arrived on the scene the Norwegians had taken up firing positions at an SLA armoured half-track which had its mounted machine gun cocked and directed at them. It was a potentially dangerous situation in which a sudden unprovoked move could have had fatal consequences. Johan drove our jeep very slowly to a position on the road midway between the Norwegian unit and the half-track and stopped. Because our vehicle had the markings 'Team Sierra', the SLA would immediately have known that we were unarmed and as such did not pose any threat. I slowly dismounted, held my hands in the air and slowly approached the half-track. Luckily I recognized one of the SLA soldiers, having attended a meeting with his unit the previous day. After I greeted him with the words '*Salam, kaifa haloka*' ('Hello, how are you?'), he said something to his trigger-happy comrade, who immediately eased off. The tension was suddenly broken, and after a brief discussion through an interpreter both sides withdrew. It was an occasion where being unarmed helped to defuse what might otherwise have been a dangerous impasse.

For most of my 18-month stint in OGL I served as the operations officer based with the force HQ at Naqoura. My family were now living in the Israeli town of Naheriya, six miles south of the border, where Grainne took over as teacher to the children. I commuted each day to and from Naqoura, and the only downside to this was suffering the daily routine of having my vehicle closely checked by the Israelis at the border crossing of Rosh Hanikra. This crossing was only open to UN personnel and, of course, the Israeli Defence Forces (IDF). Naheriya was a popular place to live, being very close to the beach and having all the facilities of a modern city. OGL had its administrative rear HQ there, which was very beneficial for the families of military observers.

The years 1984 and 1985 were a tense period in South Lebanon as Israel was implementing its 'Iron Fist' policy. This consisted of imposing curfews on villages throughout much of South Lebanon with the objective of curbing resistance to its continued occupation of the region. The Israeli National Security Service (Shin Bet) had many operatives working alongside its army during this period, openly defying UN checkpoints and causing many casualties among the Lebanese population. This was countered with an increase in suicide attacks on Israeli convoys by the Lebanese resistance. Our observers witnessed many operations carried out by the Israeli Army during this period. They usually commenced with a heavy build-up of forces on the Lebanese side of the border, and these would then head northwards to a selected village, cordon it off and force all male inhabitants to a central holding area for questioning. Meanwhile, selected homes were identified and destroyed. Escape routes were covered by fire, and this caused many casualties. Our observers were limited to witnessing such events and submitting reports. Their efforts at intervening on behalf of the inhabitants were routinely ignored.

My tour of duty finished in January 1986, and within a few days, with family in tow, I was driving towards the port of Haifa for the long journey home. I assumed I had seen the last of Lebanon and the UN's 'interim' force. Yet nearly twelve years later, in 1997, I would be back once again wearing my blue beret, this time as commander of the Irish 82nd Battalion. By then, the 'interim' force would be entering its twentieth year and I had experienced the slide to war in Bosnia and Herzegovina, a conflict that was part of Yugoslavia's bloody disintegration. Bosnia was to prove the greatest challenge of my career.

Chapter 2

From Blue to White

In September 1991 I was serving as Adjutant of the Southern Brigade FCA, based at Sarsfield Barracks, Limerick, when the call came from my Brigade headquarters in Cork informing me that I had been selected to serve a tour of duty in Yugoslavia with the European Community Monitoring Mission (ECMM). I was somewhat taken aback at the suddenness of the call and hardly had time to register its import. However, as my name had been on the volunteer list for overseas service I immediately intimated my willingness to serve there. The ECMM had been established in 1991, and its legal right to exist can be found in the Brioni Agreement signed on 7 July 1991 by the Foreign Ministers of Luxembourg, the Netherlands and Italy, collectively referred to as the 'Troika', and the six republics of Former Yugoslavia, namely Slovenia, Croatia, Bosnia and Herzegovina, Serbia, Montenegro and Macedonia. The Brioni conference had been held with the objective of finding a solution to what was seen as a dangerous development within Yugoslavia when the assemblies of both Slovenia and Croatia declared independence unilaterally on 25 June 1991. Within days the Yugoslav Federal Army (JNA) deployed troops to Slovenia. Although the JNA was a conscript army drawn from all nations and ethnic groups in Yugoslavia, its officer corps was Serb-dominated. Fighting was limited as the Slovenes had prepared by blocking routes with mines, covered by gunfire. Despite the JNA's yielding in this case, it seemed inevitable that conflict would spread to the other republics.

The parties agreed that a monitor mission (the ECMM) would become operational as soon as possible. Its aims were to stabilize the cease-fire in Slovenia and to monitor the lifting of a blockade of JNA units and bases, the clearing of roads, disbandment of the Slovenian territorial troops, an exchange of prisoners and the gradual withdrawal from Slovenia of the JNA.

As the ECMM was already active in Croatia to monitor this withdrawal it was natural that its tasks would follow the fighting in Croatia. Accordingly, the mission was extended to include Croatia, Serbia and, shortly thereafter, Bosnia.

The Mission's exact role was contained in the Memorandum of Understanding (MoU), which detailed the ECMM's status, area of responsibility and assignments in each republic. These would initially include monitoring and reporting on the political, military and humanitarian situations, investigating and reporting breaches of the Brioni agreement, using 'good offices' to settle disputes and monitoring the implementation of agreements. Further assignments would follow as the situation developed in the various republics. The head of the ECMM and the headquarters staff were appointed by the Presidency of the EC for a period of six months. Whichever country held the Presidency took over responsibility for the mission, which would report back to it. The mission headquarters would oversee its various regional and coordinating centres and, in due course, establish liaison officers. In 1991 the ECMM brought together the then twelve EC members and four additional countries, Canada, Sweden, Czechoslovakia and Norway, all of whom were member states of the Conference for Security and Cooperation in Europe (CSCE) – the title changed to the Organization for Security and Cooperation (OSCE) in 1994. The mission initially comprised about 200 military officers, diplomats and civilian staff of the EC Commission. About 100 of these were monitors, and the remainder were drivers, signallers and administrative staff. The mission was headed by a senior diplomat of ambassadorial rank, referred to as Head of Mission (HoM) and coming from whichever country held the EC Presidency. All monitors were unarmed and all dressed in distinctive white clothing, wearing armbands and caps with the distinctive EC emblem. All ECMM vehicles were painted white, bore the EC emblem and flew the EC flag.The headquarters of the mission was in the 'Hotel I' in the Croatian capital Zagreb, with regional centres in Ljubljana in Slovenia, Split in Croatia, Belgrade in Serbia and later in Bosnia's capital, Sarajevo.

The ECMM was quickly established, with Ireland supplying two experienced military officers, Lieutenant Colonels Colm Mangan (later

Lieutenant General) and Michael Mullooley (later Colonel), to the mission headquarters. The monitors were recruited from both civilian and military members of OSCE member states. The head of Ireland's delegation was Michael Gaffey from the Department of Foreign Affairs. A few weeks later a further three officers were added, of whom I was one. The others were Commandants Mick Nolan from Cork and Dermot Cogan from Cavan, both of whom I knew very well. Mick and I were from the same Southern Brigade and had previously worked together. I knew Dermot (or 'Der' as he was known) well as we had both served with the UN in Lebanon in 1978 and again in 1980 with the 29th Infantry Battalion in Cavan, where I was the barrack commander.

Following completion of the mandatory overseas medical examinations the three of us were summoned to Defence Forces HQ in Dublin for some hastily arranged operational briefings. These included a briefing on the MoU signed by the EC and the then federal authorities in Yugoslavia. We were informed that monitors would be wearing white civilian attire. This posed some logistical problems because the normal procedure for obtaining overseas dress and equipment involves reporting to the Defence Forces clothing stores at Clancy Barracks and being issued with the standard schedule of clothing such as uniforms, boots, berets, flak jackets, helmets and so forth. However, on this occasion 'whites' were to be the order of the day, and so our briefing officer suggested we take time to go shopping for said whites in the city. This proved to be no easy task in mid-September, especially when it came to buying white slacks, shoes and anoraks. One shop assistant suggested we try a sports shop, which might stock cricket gear, or maybe a medical supply outlet, while another looked rather dubiously at the three of us, no doubt wondering if we were joking. Finally, after trudging in and out of several shops we managed to acquire an assortment of white shirts, slacks and socks and off-white shoes.

There is always a great sense of anticipation when going overseas which seems to take over everything else; the need to get out there to the mission area becomes all-encompassing. Unanswered questions cram the mind: what will it be like? Where will I end up? Who will I be with? Will it be dangerous? However, there are also questions like: is this fair to my family? Am I being selfish and irresponsible? Is this a proper time to serve abroad? How do my family really feel about me going abroad? Am I being totally irresponsible in leaving my wife and four children, aged between nine and eighteen at this time? Will they cope in my absence? So the sense of adventure and challenge is tempered by pangs of guilt, something which, I'm sure, applies to many soldiers about to depart on overseas service.

This particular mission would be unlike those I had previously experienced. Hitherto I had always imagined overseas service as taking place somewhere outside Europe, but this assignment would be in the heart of it. The mission was, moreover, the first conducted by the EC. Having had previous experience of serving abroad with the UN in both troop-contributing and observer missions, I was reasonably confident of being able to tackle whatever tasks the ECMM might throw at me. I had no idea, however, that I was about to face momentous events that would prove both extraordinary and challenging.

I flew with Mick and Der to Amsterdam on 1 October 1991 and then via Milan to Trieste, where we arrived in the evening and in darkness. Meeting us at the airport was an Italian driver of the ECMM with an Iveco truck. Having identified ourselves to him, Mick enquired as to the form of transport that would be provided to take us to Zagreb. The driver nodded towards the truck. Mick was quick to decide that as the 'senior' he should take the passenger seat, so Der and I travelled with the luggage in the back. We started out on a long and, for us in the back, quite bumpy drive across Slovenia and headed into Croatia. We spoke little, each of us keeping our own thoughts to ourself and no doubt wondering what might lie in store. It was very quiet entering Zagreb, with little traffic about, and it was only after reaching the hotel which housed the mission headquarters that I was informed that a blackout was in operation. Welcome to the Balkans.

The first few days were occupied with meeting other monitors, being briefed on the numerous aspects of the mission, learning different operational procedures and generally 'bedding in'. My previous service with the UN gave me a distinct advantage in this regard. One of the first monitors I met was Jan Rusjink from Holland, a colleague with whom I had served in Damascus back in 1984 with UNTSO. Much of what was expected of us followed more or less a similar pattern to any other mission area. The ECMM would observe, report and, crucially, remain strictly impartial – very much like any UN observer mission.

I was used to staying at a military camp on my overseas tours of duty. However, for now we were based in the suburbs of Zagreb, in the Hotel I, which was partially occupied by ECMM personnel. Frequently, upon leaving my room, I would find an package placed on the floor just outside the bedroom door by staff from an information office manned by Croats, located on the ground floor of the hotel. These packages contained reports and photographs of what I can only assume to have been incidents of violence carried out by the JNA against Croat civilians. I suspected that this was an attempt to convince us of the sufferings being endured by Croats at the hands of the JNA and authorities in Belgrade. I remember Croat television showing coverage of federal tanks crushing civilian cars and their occupants. While there was much conflict taking place within Croatia, a lot of the footage was from the limited conflict earlier in Slovenia; but it suited the Croats, nevertheless, to use this material for propaganda purposes.

The atmosphere in Zagreb was tense. It became normal for blackouts to occur at night, when sirens were sounded over the city and all power was cut off, though I do not recall there being any aerial threat during my stay there. It seemed the population was being prepared, psychologically, for war. The situation within Croatia was deteriorating rapidly, but trouble seemed far enough away from Zagreb not to affect us directly. The ECMM teams operating out of the city were chiefly concerned with monitoring developments in places like Eastern Slavonia, where fierce fighting was being reported. It would appear that the agreement recently signed, which required the JNA to withdraw from Slovenia, was creating great turmoil in Croatia. Military developments shadowed the rising political temperature. As the Croats formed their own National Guard, the forerunner of the Croatian Army, the Serbs of Krajina, which had formed its own Serb Autonomous Region (SAO), created their own militia, backed by the JNA. The towns of Osijek and Vinkovci were being bombarded, the city of Vukovar was being systematically destroyed and the old city of Dubrovnik, the 'Pearl of the Adriatic', was targeted by the JNA and Montenegrin irregulars. Daily reports coming in to the ECMM headquarters from monitors based in these regions gave a stark picture of what was happening, as well as the distinct impression that the conflict could spread to the other republics.

'Hurry up and wait' is an order often directed at soldiers while their superiors work out various courses of action. Our stay in Zagreb was no different. We soon learned that many of the arriving monitors were expecting to be sent to Belgrade in Serbia and others to Sarajevo in Bosnia, where regional centres were already in the process of being established. First, however, there was the question of peace talks with Yugoslav federal authorities, which were taking place at our hotel. The HoM was the Dutch ambassador Dirk van Houten (as the Netherlands was holding the EC Presidency at that time, the monitor mission came under Dutch control). It appeared that the further deployment of additional monitors to Serbia and Bosnia was conditional on the success of these talks, and so we hoped for a positive outcome. In the meantime, I met some of the other newly arrived monitors, including Peter Innes from Scotland, a diplomat who had worked for some years with the British Embassy in Dublin, Jean-Loup Eychenne, a naval officer from France, Frank Bognar from Canada, Pandelis Botonakis from Greece and Alan Winters, who worked for the British Foreign and Commonwealth Office (FCO).

While the peace talks were ongoing we took time out to visit Zagreb and get a 'feel' for the city. Outwardly things seemed pretty normal. Shops and restaurants were open, public transport was operating to schedule and people appeared to be going about their daily routines as they would in any other city. It was difficult to believe that there was fierce fighting taking place in other parts of the country. However, late in the evening of 8 October 1991, under the auspices of the ECMM, agreement was reached at the hotel between the Yugoslav federal authorities and the Croatian government on a cease-fire throughout Croatia. Blockades imposed by land and sea of the Adriatic Coast were to be lifted, as were the blockades on military barracks occupied by units of the JNA.

Early the following morning, a convoy of monitors including Der Cogan and I started out on the long journey by way of Hungary to Belgrade. We had been at the mission HQ for seven days and were anxious to receive our operational orders. We were told that we would receive our assignments after arriving in Belgrade. It seemed a very circuitous route but it was deemed the safest, given the outbreaks of fighting throughout many parts of the country. As we crossed the border into Hungary at Letenye Granicni we were joined by a police car which was to escort us through the country. This was my first experience of this type of escort and I found it both ludicrous and embarrassing. It would appear that if you were deemed important enough you owned the road, and everyone else had better get out of your way. It was obvious that our escort was taking this task very seriously, with each civilian car which happened to come from the opposite direction being forced to 'give way' by the police officer in the passenger seat frantically waving a hand-held lollipop-type sign out the window. Clearly, the police wielded significant authority, and civilian cars practically drove into the ditch to avoid disobeying their signals. The police seemed to take particular pleasure in turning on the car's siren as we passed through sleepy villages en route, despite the distinct absence of traffic. They cheerfully bade us farewell by sounding their horn and waving the lollipop stick as we crossed over from Hungary into Serbia. It was a welcome relief when we finally reached the ECMM regional centre in Belgrade after some fourteen hours on the road.

There was quite an assembly of monitors gathered that evening in Belgrade. Those of us who had journeyed from Zagreb were joined by others who had deployed directly to Belgrade and were, like us, anxious to determine where they were to be ultimately stationed. Monitors were representatives of all the EC countries except for Luxembourg, with additional representatives from the OSCE countries of Norway, Canada, Poland and Czechoslovakia. It was quite an experience to meet up with so many military officers from other countries for the first time, and we looked forward to working with them as colleagues over the next six months. That evening, a bottle of Jameson's whiskey which I had brought with me from Ireland went down a treat, and it played a significant role in establishing the foundations of a strong bond of team spirit and friendship.

It was the following day that I learned Der and I would be moving to Sarajevo as part of an expanding regional centre in Bosnia. With about eight others we were to be ready to leave at short notice. The Sarajevo centre had only been established a few weeks earlier and was in need of monitors to be deployed throughout the country. The centre was headed by a British FCO diplomat, Tony Abbott, who was focused on initiating contact with the political heads and government officials based in Sarajevo. Having set up meetings with regional military commanders of the JNA throughout the country, he and his team were considering where to station ECMM monitor teams when they arrived. It was the following day, Friday, 11 October 1991, that our convoy departed Belgrade for Sarajevo and the beginning of what was for me the most dramatic and demanding assignment of my military career.

While Croatia was going through the pains of war in 1991, Bosnia remained peaceful, though tense.The republic contained twenty different ethnic communities and nowhere in Yugoslavia was the ethnic, religious and cultural mix more complex. According to the 1991 census, 44 per cent of the population of 4.3 million considered themselves Muslim (Bosniak), 32.5 per cent Serb and 17 per cent Croat, with 6 per cent defining themselves simply as 'Yugoslavs'. In the first multi-party elections in November 1990 most seats were won by the three largest nationalist parties: the (Muslim) Party of Democratic Action (SDA), the Serbian Democratic Party (SDS) and the Croatian Democratic Union (HDZ). These parties were thus established firmly along ethnic/national lines. They created an unwieldy governing coalition in which each pursued its own narrow national interests. The Serbs looked to Belgrade and insisted on remaining within Yugoslavia. They feared that within an independent Bosnia they would become a minority, a scenario they were determined to avoid at any cost. The Croats, concentrated in both central Bosnia and western Herzegovina, largely looked to Zagreb. As for the Muslims, they saw Bosnia as their homeland.

Relations between the three ethnic groups had been generally cordial, with a few notable exceptions. During the Second World War Bosnia was the scene of many of the worst atrocities committed in the war of occupation and resistance between 1941 and 1945, when Yugoslavia was dismembered by the Axis powers and different domestic groups fought both the occupiers and each other. During this period, Serbs were massacred by the Croatian Ustasha, while the Serbian Chetniks carried out their own brutal killing of many Muslims. The long rule of Josip Broz Tito and the Communist Party of Yugoslavia did much to bury these resentments, but in towns and villages across Bosnia everyone knew who had done what to whom during the war.

During our briefing sessions in Zagreb we were reminded that of all the republics of Yugoslavia, Bosnia was the one which had the greatest ethnic mix and was likely to provoke the greatest amount of turmoil. Reference was made to an agreement that had been reached between President Milošević of Serbia and President Tudjman of Croatia in March 1991, known as the 'Karađorđevo Agreement', by which the two had agreed to a carve-up of Bosnia between them. If this were to become a reality it would mean an uncertain future for the Muslims, the largest ethnic group in Bosnia.

As we drove through the city of Sarajevo that Friday evening all eyes seemed to follow us. Many citizens stopped to watch our white vehicles. They were as unsure of us as we were of them. It was raining, and the streets seemed drab and dull. One could not help but notice that the city was almost entirely surrounded by heavily forested hills and mountains. It was easy to see why it was chosen as the venue for the 1984 Winter Olympics, but I wondered if the topography of the city might have any bearing on its future fate. We proceeded through the centre by the Miljacka River, which is spanned by several bridges, one of them named after Gavrilo Princip, close to the spot from where he shot Franz Ferdinand of Austria on 28 June 1914, the deed that initiated a chain of events leading to the outbreak of the First World War. We carried on towards the western part of the city to the suburb of Ilidža and our headquarters, which was located at the Hotel Srbija (Serbia). It seemed a good location, close to the city yet providing some privacy with its tree-lined avenues and extensive parkland. Ilidža is famous for its spa, known as Vrelo Bosne (The Spring of Bosnia) at the foot of Mount Igman. There to meet us, with a relieved expression on his face, was Tony Abbott.

We had little time to familiarize ourselves with our new surroundings before Tony summoned us for initial briefing. Over the next hour he gave us a broad outline of the developing situation within Bosnia, expressing some concern at the entrenched positions of each of the three main political parties. He was anxious to deploy three-man monitor teams to cover the major population centres of each ethnic grouping, in order to 'monitor and report on' developing situations. This would, he said, enable the team based in Sarajevo to obtain a clearer understanding of the main issues of concern for the different ethnic groups and to include these in our reports to the mission HQ in Zagreb. It was essential we acted in an impartial manner so as to be accepted by all three sides. His briefing was very much in tune with similar briefings I received on tours of duty with the UN. Initially, the mission teams were to concentrate on preventative mediation and on contacting and engaging with local representatives within the various municipalities. English would be the working language, and local interpreters would be engaged to assist at meetings. The MoU clearly stated that the 'host parties' would be responsible for the full protection, safety and security of the ECMM, and that its personnel would enjoy unrestricted freedom of movement in the mission area.

Two monitor teams were to be deployed to the area of Banja Luka, Bosnia's second largest city. The municipality had a population of about 140,000, of which over 50 per cent were Serbs. Both teams would reside within the city, one team focusing on the Doboj region and the other around Banja Luka itself. I was assigned to the Doboj Team (known as 'Team 3') along with Pandelis Botonakis and Jean-Loup Eychenne. Der was assigned to the Banja Luka team ('Team 4') and joined by monitors from Spain and Denmark. Each team was assigned transport with an Italian driver, and our vehicles were painted white, with the EC logo prominently displayed, and flew the EC flag.

While Der and his team departed for Banja Luka, I had a weekend in Sarajevo. I met up with Tony Abbott and on hearing me inquire as to where I might attend mass he offered me a lift in his staff car into the city. We attended mass in the Catholic Cathedral of Jesus's Sacred Heart, which is situated on the main pedestrian street close to both the Serb Orthodox Cathedral and the sixteenth century Gazi Husrev-beg Mosque in nearby Baščaršija (also nearby was the Ashkenazi synagogue). Sarajevo was famous for its religious diversity, with adherents of Islam, Orthodoxy, Catholicism and Judaism co-existing there for generations. How ironic that a place renowned for this co-existence would fuel hatred and suspicion and inflame the population towards an ethnic conflict of proportions not seen within Europe since the Second World War. That Sunday after mass we drove through the city and toured the surrounding hills and mountain peaks. On this occasion they looked both bleak and bare. During our tour I had the chance to listen to Tony give his views of the situation in Bosnia as he saw it, and he was not very optimistic about its immediate future. He was interested to hear that I had served with the UN and, in particular, that I had experience of serving with a military observer mission in the Middle East. He was confident that this experience would be of considerable benefit to our monitoring duties, which were about to commence. From the briefings I had received, both in Zagreb and in Sarajevo, I was of the view that the duties we would be expected to perform as monitors differed little from those I had carried out some seven years previously.

That evening, I met up with my new team mates, Jean-Loup and Pandelis. Both appeared relieved that an English speaker was to be part of their team, particularly someone who had previous experience in peacekeeping operations. I suspected, in the light of this, that I would be the one compiling the daily situation reports. As neither of them had previously served on a 'peace support' mission, they were happy to defer to me for some procedural guidance. Jean-Loup was an engaging personality, who had only recently been on a tour of duty on the French aircraft carrier *Clemenceau* (during the First Gulf War). He was determined to learn as much of the Serbo-Croat language as he could and always had a phrasebook and dictionary close to hand. Pandelis was a major in the Greek army on his first overseas tour of duty. Married to an Englishwoman, he was fluent in the language, and he was delighted to hear that I was, like him, a father of four children, two boys and two girls. The three of us hit it off straight away and we looked forward to working together as a team.

We departed for Banja Luka, and the journey took about four hours. We passed through some very rugged but picturesque countryside and we encountered some pretty hilly terrain, much of it covered by forest which seemed to close in on the winding roadways. For much of the journey we passed along the Vrbas River valley, the source of which is about 90km to the south of Banja Luka. Our distinctive white vehicle with its EC markings and fluttering flag provoked some curious glances from locals in the many towns and villages we passed through, and we wondered how our relationship with these people would fare over the next few months. Banja Luka was a predominantly Serb city, but in addition to the local population many thousands of Serb *izbeglice* (refugees) were arriving there, having fled the conflict in Croatia.

We checked into the Hotel Bosna, which had been selected as our accommodation and office headquarters. Despite the usual problems of space, security, communication and so forth, we simply set about establishing our presence and deciding upon our modus operandi. Initially, we decided to visit each municipality in our designated area and make contact with the political party representatives, mayors, police chiefs and military commanders, in order to 'observe and report on' the developing situation. These municipalities were situated north of Banja Luka, with many of them bordering on Croatian territory. In order to achieve this we would require the cooperation and assistance of the local authorities to provide for our safety, security and freedom of movement. We were anxious to make ourselves available to any group wishing to meet with us and to listen to their fears and concerns.

We were given the services of a local Serb, Radomir Košić, who would act as our interpreter. He was director of an electronic export-import firm based in Banja Luka. I asked if we could meet with him prior to starting out on our series of visits to the different municipalities. He explained that he was happy to assist us in meeting with the various municipality leaders, and he explained that he had volunteered to act as interpreter as an alternative to being 'mobilized' for military service, something he had no desire to do. He seemed pretty excited about his forthcoming role. However, I explained to him that it was essential he confine himself to translating verbatim everything said to us in Serbo-Croat and that he should not 'interpret'. I had enough experience on peacekeeping operations to know that translating was very different to 'interpreting', and I needed him to be under no illusions about what was expected of him. The last thing we needed was somebody who might decide to interpret rather than translate exactly what was actually said. In other words, we did not want anything 'lost in translation'. He seemed to understand exactly what would be required of him.

Later that evening we met with Der's team, who gave us a quick update on their first day of meetings in Banja Luka. He advised us to be prepared for long-winded lectures by party representatives hoping to impress upon us how much they had suffered at the hands of the other ethnic groups. This was to be a regular feature during almost all of our subsequent meetings, before we realized that such references to history were blocking any progress towards tackling more immediate concerns. I soon learned that to most Yugoslavs history is a living part of their present life and everything in the present is related to the past. However, for now, we decided to tolerate their every word, if for no other reason than to listen and learn.

Chapter 3

Three Men in a Boat

In order to obtain a broader understanding of the fears and concerns of the various ethnic groupings in Bosnia we needed to visit as many municipalities or *opštine* as possible in our area of operations. We decided to visit a broad cross-section of municipalities which reflected different ethnic majorities. Operating in this way would also be an indicator of our impartiality, an essential element in successful peacekeeping. To achieve this we selected a list of municipalities which we planned to visit over the next few weeks. As the conditions of the ECMM to Bosnia included a guarantee of freedom of movement as well as safety and security, we requested a daily police escort from the regional capital of Banja Luka to accompany us. Throughout that first week we established a pattern and routine for each visit. As soon as the escort arrived at our hotel we would drive to a pre-arranged municipality, where we would pay a courtesy visit to the mayor, followed by a meeting with the local police chief. Then we would meet with the various party representatives and listen to whatever they might wish to say to us. For the sake of balance and objectivity, we made it known that we were willing to meet with any other group that wished to talk to us.

The visits over these first few days gave us a general idea of the issues which were of concern. We visited some municipalities north of Banja Luka in the areas of Kobas, Doboj, Gračanica and Srbac. Kobas, like many other border towns situated between Bosnia and Croatia, was divided by the river Sava, and the portion of the town on the Croatian side was known as Slavonski Kobas while the Bosnian side was called Bosanski Kobas. On the whole, we were always very well received and made to feel welcome. There seemed to be a general desire to cooperate and a feeling of appreciation by all parties of what we were trying to achieve. For our part, we would endeavour to explain the role of the ECMM and then invite party representatives to have their say on matters that were of concern to them, with each side then giving us the background to the situation from their perspective.

Prior to arriving for our first meeting, Jean-Loup and Pandelis requested that I lead the talks, given that my spoken language was English. I readily agreed. We arrived in Doboj around 10.00am and were cordially received by a delegation including representatives of the three main parties. They insisted on us having coffee and a small glass of *slivovitz*, a type of colourless plum brandy common to Yugoslavia and often home-brewed. Having explained the purpose of the ECMM we invited the delegates to respond. Unfortunately, the team was soon reminded of what Der had been telling us a few days before. We were bombarded with history lectures from the various representatives.

From our first meeting we came up against the intransigence of the parties in the conflict, a pattern that was to be repeated in meetings over the subsequent weeks. There was a ritual of sorts to these encounters: each side would begin by welcoming us, expressing their belief that we were there for the greater good and pledging their willingness to cooperate. Very soon, however, voices would be raised, with one side accusing the other of all manner of misdeeds. Atrocities from the Second World War were often recalled and each side would become increasingly inflexible, entrenched and stubborn. This seemed to be in stark contrast to what we had heard from some Bosnians we had met earlier on our arrival in Sarajevo. They told us that they were proud of the claim that they defied outsiders' belief that there was chronic ethnic tension in Yugoslavia. But this was not Sarajevo, with an urban culture that had, to some extent, transcended the ethnic rivalry that was more acute in rural areas.

Here we were, seeing the deep-rooted and increasing tensions for ourselves, and it did not augur well for the future. From our meetings on those first two days we became acutely aware of the sources of friction between the communities and the potential for conflict. With the Bosnian President, Alija Izetbegović (leader of the Muslim SDA party), declaring the recent 'mobilization' decision by the federal authorities to be invalid, only Serbs complied with the directive. Accordingly, the JNA had demanded voting register lists from local authorities, which, in the case of Muslim or Croat-dominated councils, were denied. In some instances the JNA allegedly broke into offices to obtain these lists. One consequence of Serbs being conscripted was that only Serbs were issued with weapons, which they were allowed to retain on completion of their period of military service. Muslims and Croats, on the other hand, were deemed disloyal to the federal government in Belgrade and slowly alienated. Having no access to weapons, they became increasingly fearful of the Serbs, who now enjoyed the support and protection of the army.

We also heard criticism of the behaviour of Serb conscripts in many towns and villages. One only had to visit the bar in our own hotel in the evening to witness the sometimes disturbing behaviour of many of them, mostly in uniform, drinking heavily and acting in an arrogant and threatening manner. Moreover, it confirmed our fears that these men were preparing for, and anticipating, armed conflict. Such a conflict had not yet broken out, but our role as mediators was brought into play a few days later during our visits to two towns near the Croatian border and divided by the river Sava. In the case of Bosanski Kobas, where the only means of crossing to the Croatian side (at Slavonski Kobas) was by a small river ferry, we were informed that the Croats had attached explosives to the underside of the ferry, which they then floated to the middle of the river to deter an attack from the Bosnian side. Urged by those on the Bosnian side of the river to do something to break this impasse, I discussed with Jean-Loup and Pandelis what the best course of action might be. I suggested that as a gesture of good faith we should attempt to cross the river to the other side and find out why the Croats were afraid of being attacked. It was important, however, that the Croat side should be aware of who we were and what we were about to do, lest they misinterpret our motives. As we made preparations to cross, someone produced a megaphone and shouted across the river to a group of inhabitants gathered on the other side. After numerous exchanges between the two sides, translated by Rade, a small rowing boat was produced and a local agreed to row us across the river, which was about 50yds wide. We maintained a safe distance from the ferry and by the time we reached the far bank the crowd there had multiplied. Far from the tense situation we had expected, both sides seemed to enjoy the spectacle of white-clad monitors (known to locals as 'ice cream men') sitting nervously in a small boat and trying carefully to avoid a potentially lethal collision with a ferry packed with explosives. In truth, I felt very vulnerable and exposed, but the banter exchanged between groups on each bank, none of which seemed threatening, gradually calmed me. They all seemed to know each other, and I wondered if we were being 'tested' in some way.

We were made welcome by the Croats, whose spokesman insisted on us visiting his house and meeting his family. Before we knew where we were, glasses of *slivovitz* were produced and toasts were proposed. We discussed the issue of the ferry and were assured that their actions were purely defensive and that the Bosnian side could rest assured that no action would be taken against them. They then suggested that we should take the matter up with the Croat authorities at Slavonski Brod, where we were due to visit the following day. We left hoping that our visit had made a positive impression on both sides, because we needed to earn their trust; only time would tell whether we had done so.

When we arrived in Bosanski Brod the following day we were faced with a similar situation. In this instance, a bridge divided the two sides of the town, and the Croats of Slavonski Brod had placed explosives and mines on the bridge, blocking it to inhabitants of the Bosnian side (Bosanski Brod). Again we were asked to mediate and in negotiations by telephone persuaded the Croats to allow us passage over the bridge. As we cautiously walked across I felt very vulnerable again. There were about four trucks strategically placed across it, each with explosives placed underneath. Additionally, any gaps were covered by mines all linked by fuse wire. I looked over at Jean-Loup and Pandelis, wondering if they felt as I did. The look on their faces confirmed that they almost certainly did. Nevertheless, we continued and after reaching the far side were met by some stony-faced officials, who escorted us directly to the office of the mayor.

Unlike our experience in Slavonski Kobas the previous day, there was nothing friendly about our meeting with the town's mayor. He was wearing uniform, spoke in a combative manner and made it clear to us that as far as his people were concerned they were at war. When we asked him to explain what he hoped to achieve by mining the bridge, we were subjected to a lecture on his views of recent events in Croatia. Bosnian Croats, he warned, would not be dictated to by either Serbs or Muslims. Upon hearing that I was Irish, he proceeded to suggest that the struggle of the Croats was similar to that of the Irish Republican Army (IRA). When I politely pointed out that I viewed the IRA as a terrorist organization he became rather angry. Clearly, it was time to leave.

Jean-Loup was of the view that the mining of both bridge and ferry by the Croats was being used as a political weapon, and while we could understand why the Croats might view Serbs with some suspicion, the same could not be said about Muslims. In any event, we achieved nothing from our visit despite our best efforts at explaining our role and our offers of mediation. When we returned to the Bosnian side of the town we reluctantly informed the residents that we had made no progress in finding a solution that would alleviate their concerns. They were appreciative of our efforts, but that was of little consolation to us. As it transpired, this was to be the first of numerous attempts, many of them frustrating, to broker agreements between the differing communities. I didn't know it then, but I would experience this same sense of frustration many times over the following months.

I had been very anxious to connect with Grainne, who I had not been able to contact since leaving home. Communications in Bosnia at that time were very poor, and international phone calls were almost impossible to make because of government restrictions, or so we were informed. However, our mode of transport (an Iveco truck) did have a phone. Our driver suggested that if we could reach an elevated location outside the city we might be able to establish a connection. So that evening, having consulted a map, we followed a route that took us into the hills on the outskirts of the city. After many failed attempts I succeeded in getting through to Grainne. It was such a relief that I hardly noticed the heavy snowflakes which had begun to fall on the hillside. Looking back down at the city was a spectacular sight, with lights shining through the thickening snow. As we drove back down, the snow-laden tree branches sagged low and seemed to create a series of curtains, which opened wide as we drove through them. The scene looked peaceful and serene, and I was not to know at that point that it was to be the beginning of a long and increasingly dangerous winter.

Upon our return we met with Der and his team for a debriefing; we gave him an account of our meeting with the Croat mayor of Slavonski Brod. He informed me that both our teams were scheduled to have two meetings at Banja Luka City Hall the following day. These had been arranged by the mayor's office, and we were to meet the leaders of the parties initially and thereafter the mayor and his officials. We discussed how best to approach the meeting with the mayor and decided we should just listen, take note of what was being said and confine ourselves to explaining the role of the ECMM. We had been briefed prior to arriving in Banja Luka that the Bosnian Serb leadership there was regarded as radical and that we should be prepared for difficult discussions.

When we arrived the following morning at Banja Luka City Hall there was a gathering of press outside. The mayor made a point of stressing that we were welcome guests, that he would ensure we were treated well and that the ECMM would have the full cooperation of the Serb population. We were given some time to meet religious leaders and spent some thirty minutes listening to their concerns. Both the Serbian Orthodox Church and the representatives of the Islamic Community of Bosnia and Herzegovina were particularly critical of Croats along the border causing damage to places of worship. However, within Banja Luka itself the local *mufti* alleged that the Serb leadership was making life increasingly difficult for Muslims. He informed us that there was a subtle campaign to oppress them: business rents had been increased and Muslims were being fired from their jobs to make way for Serbs. We promised that we would raise these issues with the mayor.

By the time we emerged from our meetings we had no doubts as to the considerable differences that existed between the three main parties. The mayor of Banja Luka, Predag Radić, while outwardly courteous, left us in no doubt as to why it was essential that the Bosnian Serbs should remain within Yugoslavia and what the consequences might be if Bosnia seceded from it. Once again he referred to the way in which the Serbs had suffered at the hands of the Croat Ustasha during the war and the threat that Muslims posed by, according to him, their desire for an Islamic state. We noted an increase in the use of warlike terminology and the tendency to use it in a derogatory manner. When we mentioned the alleged damage to Catholic and Muslim places of worship he replied that such matters were for local authorities to investigate. It was evident that Radić was not going to be easy to deal with. Moreover, we soon realized that meeting the three party representatives together simply did not work. Much time was simply wasted listening to one side accuse the others of breaking promises, intimidating citizens and perpetrating random acts of violence, rendering these meetings pointless. Though we were aware of the problems we came to fully appreciate the depth of divisions and mistrust that separated the political parties. I also began to realize that the hard-line positions being adopted by the parties within Bosnia, particularly Serbs and Croats, were largely influenced, if not dictated, by their 'sponsors' in Belgrade and Zagreb. In any event, we needed to find a better way to engage with these parties.

That evening, on return to our hotel, we reviewed the day's events, and both teams concluded that, contrary to our original instincts, it would be futile to continue meeting all parties together. Meeting them separately might allow us to control proceedings, consolidate our relations and make some progress. We therefore recommended this in writing to our headquarters in Sarajevo, though we had to be cautious in the language we used when compiling these reports. Our only means of communication with headquarters in Sarajevo was the hotel's fax machine. We had neither computers nor mobile phones at this early stage. This was, of course, hardly an ideal means of reporting, and we pressed the headquarters to provide secure means of conveying developments on the ground. However, these were the early days of the Bosnian mission and we would have to improvise until better facilities were established. In the meantime, we spent our evenings compiling operational reports, reviewing our own procedures and relaxing as best we could. These light-hearted moments were a relief from the tense meetings we attended during our working day.

Our team returned to Sarajevo on 23 October 1991 for debriefing and discussions, as well as some down-time. These periods were used to confer with other monitor teams that were deployed throughout Bosnia and to assist Tony Abbott and his staff in preparing situation reports (referred to as 'sitreps') for ECMM headquarters in Zagreb. Until such time as our communications improved it was prudent to conduct these meetings at our regional headquarters in Sarajevo. Tony was anxious to have our impressions on the overall situation in our area of operations. I suggested that we attempt to meet with the commander of the JNA in Banja Luka to discuss the behaviour of the reservists. Tony acknowledged this and said that he, too, had heard that this was a problem. He went on to explain that a meeting had been arranged for the following week in Banja Luka with General Nikola Uzelac, the commander of the JNA's V Corps at his headquarters, which was in the centre of the city. Tony also said that he had a special task for our team but would brief us when we arrived there. He didn't want to go into any further details.

Being in Sarajevo gave us a chance to unwind, write letters and meet with newly arrived monitors. The hotel complex in Ilidža, in the western part of Sarajevo, where we were based, was surrounded by wooded avenues which were ideal for daily runs. It was, in fact, a great relief to be able to go for long runs with fellow monitors, sharing with them our experiences and learning more about their lives. Friendships were quickly made and a sense of camaraderie was soon established. We could also call home relatively easily, and I had one important phone call to make. My eldest daughter, Elaine, who had just commenced studying at the University of Limerick, was due to attend her debutantes' ball, and I was determined not to miss wishing her well. Despite the long wait in trying to get through it was lovely to be able to talk with her for a few minutes. She had been hoping I'd call, so I was very pleased it was possible.

The weather had suddenly turned foul and very cold. I seized the chance of taking a tram into the city to buy some warm clothing and after following directions found myself in the old area of Baščaršija. Sarajevo's old town was charming. The residential quarter boasted a very picturesque bazaar with narrow cobbled streets flanked by houses with overhanging upper stories, minarets, hookah pipes and steep shingle roofs. Despite the cold I very much enjoyed roaming round the streets looking at the wide variety of wares on offer; it reminded me very much of my time in Damascus. Moreover, I was able to buy sufficient clothes there to keep me warm for the coming harsh weather.

On returning to Banja Luka I briefed Jean-Loup and Pandelis about Tony Abbott's impending visit the following week and made sure we had no other visit planned for that day. As the following day was Sunday, I decided to attend mass so slipped into the back of the Cathedral of St Benaventure. The celebrant was the Bishop of Banja Luka, Franjo Komarica, whom I had encountered at Banja Luka City Hall during a previous meeting. He recognized me and was waiting as I left the church, whereupon he insisted on inviting me to his residence, where we had a pleasant chat over coffee and the inevitable glass of *slivovitz*. A very mild-mannered man who did not wish to offend, he nevertheless raised concerns at the behaviour of the JNA reservists and expressed the view that the Serbs were becoming increasingly hostile towards both Croats and Muslims. There was a big increase in the number of Serbs arriving in Banja Luka, having been forced to leave their homes in the Krajina area of Croatia as a result of heavy fighting there. After this, the team were invited to a pleasant barbecue given by our translator, Rade Ćosić, who had invited us to his country retreat some distance from the city.

Tony Abbott arrived on Wednesday, 30 October 1991 with his Dutch deputy, Walt van Zueren. He lost no time in telling me that there existed credible information that the JNA operated a prisoner-of-war camp at Manjača containing over 300 Croat prisoners. He told me that he was meeting with General Uzelac to see if the ECMM could gain entry to the camp to check on the prisoners and assess whether they were being taken care of properly. He said that no one except the International Committee of the Red Cross (ICRC) had gained entry to the camp.

Before we arrived at the general's headquarters I mentioned to Tony the complaints we had received about the misbehaviour of the Serb reservists and asked if he might bring this up when meeting with Uzelac. The general was a heavy-set man who appeared outwardly charming. He greeted us at his headquarters, opened his desk drawer and took out a UN blue beret, telling us with some pride that he, too, was a man of peace and that he had served with the UN in the Middle East. I could see that Tony was anxious to get to the point, but Uzelac insisted we avail ourselves of the usual glass of *slivovitz*. Finally, Tony had a chance to speak and without preamble asked about the reports regarding the Croat soldiers being held as prisoners under the control of JNA troops at Manjača. Uzelac's reply was that he was responsible for the safety of all citizens in this area, and that the soldiers being held there were responsible for many atrocities against Serbs in Croatia. Many of these soldiers, he argued, were mercenaries from other countries. However, Tony was persistent in his demands that if these men were being held as prisoners of war, the ECMM should be given access to them in order to ascertain their condition. I was surprised when the general agreed to his request. Looking over in my direction, Tony informed Uzelac that my team and I would be leading the visit to the camp. General Uzelac stated that he would be happy to supply a military escort to accompany us to Manjača. I told him that we wished to go there immediately.

Tony and I had discussed this beforehand, agreeing that to visit the location immediately would give little time for the JNA to react before our arrival, so when the general agreed without argument I began to wonder if he had been made aware of an impending visit and had accordingly made provision for our arrival. Just before we left, Tony brought up the issue of the reservists and the complaints we had received about their general behaviour. Uzelac said that if he had any evidence of this he would certainly take disciplinary action against those involved. I doubted this would happen, but at least we had brought this very contentious matter to his attention.

Back at the hotel I assembled the team and quickly brought Pandelis and Jean-Loup up to speed. Doubtless they understood the significance of this, for which I was glad. Having picked up our JNA escort at the military headquarters we drove in convoy to Manjača. Located on a level plain on Mount Manjača, it is about 20km south-west of Banja Luka. We spoke little on the way, each of us probably nervous in anticipation of what may lie before us. Upon arrival we were met at the entrance by JNA security guards, who brought us directly to the commanding officer's room. An officer introduced himself as Major Fiperac, the deputy commander. While he was clearly not very pleased to see us, he indicated his willingness to show us around the camp and bring us to the location where 'detainees' were being accommodated.

In the camp there were 355 prisoners housed in three long barn buildings, each about 50m in length. Conditions were severe in the extreme. Each building held about 110 prisoners; there was no heating, electricity or furniture. Gaps were visible all along the walls and the only source of insulation was straw. Prisoners were lying in rows on the ground on beds of straw and wrapped in what looked like well-worn blankets. They all appeared gaunt, undernourished and demoralized. The sanitary conditions were crudely basic, open slit trenches running alongside each building. Prisoners were locked in at 8.00 pm every day. It was unquestionably a grim place and a scene of abject misery. I was appalled at what I saw and felt my anger rising, and as I made my way along the rows of prisoners I could feel their eyes following my every step. No one said a word. It was very unsettling.

Although we had been assured that there would be no restrictions with regard to asking prisoners questions, it was very obvious that none of them wished to talk to us, or were too frightened to do so – at least, as long as we were in close proximity to the security guards. Realizing this, Jean-Loup lingered behind the rest of us, and I could see him speaking quietly to one prisoner in French out of earshot of the guards. When I pressed the major to tell us how medical treatment was administered, he insisted that a local doctor was made available to sick prisoners and that each was given the very same food ration as a JNA soldier. Given the emaciated appearance of the prisoners, I did not believe this for a moment. The major denied my request to allow us to speak to the prisoners in private, and when we asked if he would provide us with a list of the prisoners by rank and name he said that this would be difficult, alleging that many had no form of identification and were suspected of having given false names. He also asserted that among them were mercenaries (for example, he made mention of at least two Germans, one Swiss and one Frenchman). He assured us, however, that no interrogation of prisoners had taken place, and when asked to indicate what measures were taken to provide heat he stated that it was hoped stoves would be made available 'very soon'. I knew he was lying. His arrogance was matched only by my anger.

On our way back to his office Jean-Loup whispered to me that the prisoner he had spoken with in French was a doctor. Jean-Loup was told that most of the prisoners had lost over 10kg in weight and that many had suffered beatings from the guards, though these seemed to have stopped about two weeks ago. The doctor also said that a smaller building behind the barns contained some prisoners held in confinement. As soon as I had the chance I confronted the major on this point and reminded him that General Uzelac had promised us full access. He nodded to one of the guards, who proceeded to bring us to a building set apart from the others. Inside were two prisoners dressed in uniform rags and manacled to a wall; they cowered in the corner not uttering a word. The odour of sweat and urine was overwhelming. The major informed us that these men had admitted to murder and would soon be charged with these offences. He went on to tell us that they would not form any part of a prisoner exchange and would not be released under any circumstances. We felt powerless to say or do anything, but I informed the major that we would be reporting on everything we saw and that his refusal to hand over a list of the names of the prisoners would be interpreted as an unwillingness to cooperate with the ECMM. He seemed unmoved by this and simply shrugged. After refusing his offer of *slivovitz* we left.

We drove back to Banja Luka in a sombre silence, each of us trying to absorb and process what we had just witnessed. My immediate thought was that it was of the utmost importance for us to report accurately on our visit to this awful place and to hope that our report might spur action to relieve the suffering of these prisoners. I asked myself the question, how could anybody justify treating their fellow human beings in such a way? Surely common decency would compel one to behave with at least a minimum degree of dignity? I had no answer, only a sense of frustration and rage. I wasn't alone. I glanced over at Jean-Loup and Pandelis, and both seemed lost in thought, just like me. Even our interpreter Rade had little to say. I kept picturing those two wretched prisoners chained in such crude and degrading conditions. This was something one sees in war films, but the reality of it was shocking. I was becoming more aware of a gathering darkness in Bosnia. The future, I feared, might prove pretty bleak.

We spent a long time that evening compiling our report. We were conscious of the need to make it hard-hitting and to make recommendations for urgent action. We also discussed the risks of sending the report via our hotel's fax machine, lest it be intercepted. To mitigate the risk, it was decided that our team would send the report back to Sarajevo with Der's team, who were returning to the mission HQ the following morning. Needless to say, he and his team members were equally shocked when we briefed them on our visit to Manjača. I could not ascertain what happened to the report after he handed it over, but we did learn that the prisoners were released a few weeks later. We were unable, however, to discover the fate of the two manacled men. I have often wondered what became of them and whether our report had any bearing on their eventual release. I would like to think it had helped in some way, but cannot be sure that it did.

In any event, our experience in Manjača was a glimpse into a location that gained further notoriety as the Bosnian conflict intensified. The camp was shut down in 1993 under international pressure but was re-opened in October 1995. Having been initially established by the JNA, it was later handed over to the control of the authorities of Republika Srpska and used to collect and confine thousands of male prisoners of Croat and Muslim/Bosniak nationalities. It became a miserable place, even by the standards of Bosnia, where torture and death were to become commonplace over the next few years.

Chapter 4

Welcome to Sarajevo

While our team continued to carry out surveys of the *opštine* in the areas where we had responsibility, news was filtering back of developments in neighbouring Croatia, where the conflict had been intensifying. In July 1990 the Serb SDS party in Croatia had created a provisional government of sorts – the Serbian National Council – which established the concept of Serb autonomy within Croatia. They laid claim to authority over all areas of majority-Serb populations in Croatia. One such area was the Krajina with its capital Knin, which, though small, was an important strategic crossroads in Yugoslavia. The Croatian leadership in Zagreb reacted to this by ignoring developments in Knin and pressing ahead with its pursuit of an independent Croatian state. There was in the new constitution, approved by the Croatian parliament in November 1990, no provision for any autonomous region in Croatia. So in February 1991 the SAO in Krajina proclaimed its separation from Croatia and declared the autonomous Republika Srpska Krajina (Serbian Republic of Krajina), which would, it was envisaged, remain within the Yugoslav state.

Military developments shadowed the rising political temperature, and attempts to halt the slide to war proved unsuccessful. As the Croats formed their National Guard, the Krajina Serbs created their own militia. This force received logistical and rhetorical support from Belgrade and, increasingly, from the JNA, whose officer corps was comprised, by then, almost entirely of Serbs. Thus when Croatia declared independence in June 1991 fighting began in earnest. A power base was consolidated in Knin, with the help of the JNA, who acted as the guarantor of Serb territorial gains, and by the autumn Serb forces controlled almost one third of Croatian territory. The JNA and Serb forces had superiority in both weaponry and equipment, and they used their advantage ruthlessly. Their military strategy comprised extensive shelling, at times irrespective of the presence of civilians. As a consequence, many Croat cities came under attack, most notably the pretty town of Vukovar on the banks of the Danube and the ancient port of Dubrovnik on the Adriatic coast.

The ECMM responded by sending monitor teams southwards and soon found itself working at full capacity throughout Croatia and the Krajina. There the work of the monitor teams revolved around the implementation of thirteen different cease-fires, all unsuccessful, and the agreed withdrawal of the JNA forces from Croat-controlled parts of the country. These forces were located chiefly around Zagreb and other regional towns where JNA military barracks were based. In many cases these barracks were blockaded (as had been the case earlier in Slovenia) but there was no withdrawal at this time from the Krajina. Both our teams in Banja Luka were informed that agreement had been reached in Croatia on the withdrawal of JNA forces from parts of the country. But exactly where they might withdraw to was anybody's guess. Der and I agreed that a further build-up of JNA forces in Bosnia evacuating from Croatia would only escalate the tension already existing, and in an increasingly febrile political context.

In the second week of November 1991 we learned of Tony Abbott's departure from the mission area. He had been reassigned by the UK Foreign Office, and we were about to meet his replacement, John Wilde, who like Tony was between assignments. We were surprised that this change was to take place so soon. After all, Tony had only been in the mission area a few weeks and had spent most of that time building up vital contacts, not only between the warring factions but at a government level as well. He had been very effective in a short period of time. However, the rotation of every monitor member was the exclusive responsibility of the contributing country. For a Chief of Station to be assigned for a short duration was not exactly ideal and would, to my mind, send out the wrong signals. From a military viewpoint it made no sense – most UN deployments are for a six-month tour of duty, and anything less, I thought, was not the most effective use of resources.

John Wilde had signalled to our Banja Luka station that he would meet with our team just south of Bosanski Brod. We were heading there to meet up with a JNA convoy scheduled to cross the border from Croatia and, presumably, heading to Belgrade. Our job was to escort it as far as Tuzla; thereafter, another team would take over and continue to monitor its route out of Bosnia towards Belgrade. The ECMM had been given the task of escorting these returning troop and equipment convoys through Bosnia in order to determine if their final destination was to be Serbia or elsewhere. So we met up with John later that morning as we waited for the convoy to arrive. Introductions were made, and Jean-Loup gave him a quick briefing on who we were and what we were about. We asked how long he expected to be assigned for. To my astonishment he replied that he believed he would only be in Bosnia for a few weeks and that, having returned from a stint in the South Atlantic, he would be deployed elsewhere very soon. He went on to tell us that word had been received from the ECMM Regional Centre in Split (Croatia) that a convoy was due to cross into Bosnia at Bosanski Brod shortly. He left us to await the convoy and drove back towards Banja Luka to meet with Der's team. Unfortunately, at this early stage in the functioning of the mission we had no means of communicating with our other teams, whether in Bosnia or Croatia. After about two hours' waiting we came to the conclusion that they weren't coming. We headed back to Banja Luka, and upon returning to our hotel we learned that the convoy had halted just prior to crossing into Bosnia and was expected the following morning. I met Der outside our office and he indicated he wished to have a word with me. He informed me that he had applied to take up the appointment of operations officer at our regional headquarters in Sarajevo. I was delighted for him, but it would be a loss to his teammates in Banja Luka.

The following morning, we heard that the JNA convoy had crossed over the border from Croatia and was en route towards Banja Luka. Having quickly assembled the team, we headed out to meet it north of the city and joined it as it headed east. It comprised about 300 vehicles with about 20 artillery pieces, anti-aircraft guns, troop-carrying trucks, medical supply vehicles, logistic support transport and communication jeeps. We estimated it to be of brigade strength, which is about 3,000-strong. However, we also passed another convoy heading in the opposite direction, so it was impossible to determine the exact destination of all these convoys. It did, however, lead us to suspect that not all JNA units withdrawing from Croatia were heading for Serbia. In any event, in the late afternoon we reached Tuzla, where the convoy was to remain overnight; from there it was scheduled to be escorted by another of the ECMM teams towards the Serbian border. After staying overnight in Tuzla we headed back to Banja Luka.

A visit to the municipality of Srbac, close to the Croatian border, was our next task. Here we were subjected to a diatribe from the President of the Assembly of the Krajina, Vojo Kupresanin. He was, frankly, a most unpleasant character, both loud and arrogant. He denounced America, the Vatican, the Jews, Britain, Germany, Austria and even the EC, blaming each and all for the current crisis. He was alarmed to hear that there might be monitors from Germany working in the mission area and expressed his total opposition to this. It was futile trying to reason with such an individual, and we made no further attempt to engage with him, much to his annoyance. It was certainly disheartening to think that such a man held an appointment of importance in the Krajina. It struck us that as long as radicals like him and the mayor of Slavonski Brod held these positions of responsibility, the future appeared pretty dim.

Our hotel base in Banja Luka was situated close to the location of the famed Ferhadija mosque. This was one of Banja Luka's outstanding buildings, dating back to 1579 and considered one of the greatest examples of the country's Ottoman and Islamic architecture (indeed, it was listed as a national cultural heritage site in 1950). Our team was invited to visit by Bedrudin Gušić, Chairman of the local Islamic Community and also vice president of the local branch of the SDA. We were met at the entrance by the *mufti*, who made us very welcome and gave us an account of the building's history. Following a tour of the building we had a short meeting, during which he conveyed his thoughts and concerns. He described in some detail what he claimed was a subtle campaign by the Serb authorities to make life difficult for the Muslim community. We were told of higher rents being levied on Muslim businesses, restrictions on applications to build premises and a high degree of intimidation – albeit largely psychological at this stage. We took note of these concerns and gave a commitment to raise these matters with the mayor on our next visit. Prior to our departure we were each presented with a prayer mat. I was shocked to hear later that this mosque was one of sixteen totally destroyed by Serb militia in 1993.

It was evident to us that the Muslim and Croat populations, particularly in Banja Luka, were becoming increasingly fearful of the Serb-dominated municipal assembly and, more broadly, the increasingly radicalized Serb population. With an increase in the number of JNA units in the area, attributable to the ongoing withdrawal of the JNA from Croatia, together with many armed Serb reservists, tension was understandably starting to rise. This was visibly manifest in a demonstration march which I chanced upon a few days thereafter. It was early November 1991 and I happened to be walking back towards my hotel in the late afternoon. As I rounded a corner I saw advancing up the street in my direction a sizeable group of demonstrators being led by a tall individual in military combat dress who was clearly the centre of attention. There was a lot of loud cheering and chanting, with many people rushing up to shake the hand of the leader. Wondering who this might be, I heard the name Vojislav Šešelj. In February of that year Šešelj had been appointed president of the newly founded Srpska Radikalna Stranka (Serbian Radical Party) and also elected a member of the Assembly of the Republic of Serbia. In daily rallies he used fiery rhetoric to call for Serb unity and war against Serbia's 'historic enemies', namely the ethnic Croat and Muslim populations. Now he was here in Banja Luka, parading in public and obviously rallying supporters to the Serb cause. It was difficult to believe that the leadership in Serbia did not know of Šešelj's forays into Bosnia.

When I arrived back at our office in the hotel I met with Jean-Loup and Pandelis, giving them an account of what I had witnessed. The hotel was packed, with many people hanging around in the lobby. We made our way through the throng and headed upstairs for dinner. However, as we climbed the stairs we were confronted by two heavy-set men who blocked our path. They informed us through a member of the hotel staff who spoke some English that we were not permitted to enter what they described as a private dinner function. We realized at once that the function was for Šešelj. We felt aggrieved that this had been arranged at short notice and that there was no provision for hotel guests to be fed elsewhere. I told Jean-Loup and Pandelis that it was 'time to make a stand' and, turning to the staff member, insisted on being permitted to enter the dining room, asserting that the hotel was our rightful place of work and residence. A tense few minutes were endured while the matter was discussed, but eventually we were allowed inside and escorted to a table at the end of the dining area. Although trying to put on brave faces, we were nervous, and I wondered if my actions had been the result of stupidity or stubbornness. Although we received a lot of stares and almost threatening looks we kept our cool and, having partaken of a hastily prepared dinner, quickly exited to the refuge of our office.

The overall situation was becoming very tense. The events of that week were a reality check for me and I began to understand that what we were endeavouring to achieve might have little chance of success. It would appear that the ECMM, despite our best efforts, had little influence over party representatives. While on the surface these people made us welcome and promised to support the monitor mission in what it was trying to achieve, the reality appeared very different. The more they promised, the less I expected. Entrenched attitudes seemed to be setting in, and the situation was steadily worsening. Moreover, I was shaken by the appearance of Vojislav Šešelj and his fellow radicals from Belgrade which convinced me that outside factors and players would largely decide the future of Bosnia.

A few days after Šešelj's appearance in Banja Luka both our ECMM teams took some time off to celebrate the birthday of one of Der's team. We got to talking with some local young men in the café we were in. We had asked them if they were aware of what we were doing in Bosnia and whether they wished to say anything to us or even to give us their views. At first they were hesitant, uneasy about talking to strangers. However, gradually they opened up and told us that they did not trust their political leaders. They looked upon them as old men who seemed to dwell on past events and animosities, had no vision for a future Bosnia beyond ethnic hatred and cared little for the younger generation. During our conversation one of them, a Serb, told us of a dramatic incident he had come across while serving with the JNA in southern Croatia. In graphic terms he described entering the destroyed home of a Serb family where, on reaching the kitchen, his attention was directed towards a cooker in the corner. On opening the oven he found a very young baby that had been burned to death. Attached to the cooking tray on which the baby lay was a scrawled message which read 'Dessert for the Chetniks'. Our celebration was abruptly ended. I have no way of confirming this young man's story, but it was another signal, among many, that we had entered a darker phase.

A few days later, I had just finished a pleasant meal with the head of the Serbian Orthodox Church in Banja Luka, who had invited both monitor teams to lunch, when I was told I should immediately contact the Deputy Head of the ECMM in Sarajevo, the Dutch General Elevelt. I didn't know him well and wondered what he might want, but I contacted him upon my return to the hotel. He wasted no time getting to the point, informing me that Ambassador van Houten, the head of the ECMM, would like me to take over as Regional Head of the Mission in Bosnia. I was speechless. I had only met the ambassador once, shortly after my arrival in Bosnia – so how could he have known anything about me? The only people who would have known me from Zagreb were two Irish officers working at the HQ, Michael Mullooley and Colm Mangan. The general mentioned that the ambassador had been quite impressed with the report I had submitted after my visit to Manjača camp and said that both Tony Abbott and John Wilde had spoken highly of me. I suspected that the mission was not very happy with having had two regional Heads of Mission made available by the British FCO for such short periods of time. Accordingly, they were looking for someone who would be spending at least four months in the mission area. Without too much thought I blurted out that I would be honoured to take over and promised to give my best efforts to the appointment. Up to this time the heads of the regional centres were diplomats, so I was to be the first military chief.

I immediately phoned Der in Sarajevo and asked him if there was any news on who might be in the running to take over from John Wilde. He told me there had been much speculation but that no one knew. I couldn't resist telling Der the news that I had been asked to take over. Somebody else was now speechless, and I was still finding it hard to believe that I would be taking over as the Head of Mission. Of course, I needed to let Grainne know of this development, and I succeeded in getting through to her later that evening which made this a good day for me.

On that same evening our translator Rade came to see me. I had not said anything to him but I was really surprised when he immediately offered to come with me to Sarajevo, where he would be 'honoured' to work with me for the duration. I found this offer not only surprising but somewhat disturbing. How had he known of my appointment so quickly? It seemed as if, somehow, there was a need for him or someone else to stay close to me in my new role. After all, Rade was a married man, living locally with a wife and family. Why on earth would he want to move to Sarajevo, a four-hour drive away, to be available to me as a translator? I wondered what or who might be behind this and it gave me an uneasy feeling. So I thanked him sincerely for all his help, wished him well for the future, but told him his services would not be required in Sarajevo.

Soon after, Jean-Loup and Pandelis came to my room as soon as they heard the news of my appointment. While they were both excited and pleased they also wanted to know who might replace me. We had a few celebratory drinks that evening, and early the following morning, after packing my bags and wishing my teammates well I headed for Sarajevo. While I was full of doubts and uncertainties about the future, I never imagined then that over the following few months I would experience at first hand the drama, political intrigue, danger and ferocity of a conflict that would turn out to be of such brutal proportions. In taking over as head of the Regional Centre for Bosnia I needed to quickly grasp the country-wide situation which prevailed at that time. Sarajevo was, after all, a microcosm far removed from Banja Luka, and although I had a general knowledge of what was happening at the local level, the situation in Bosnia's capital was very different. I needed to attain a quick understanding of the bigger picture.

In that same month, October 1991, the parliament of Bosnia passed a motion on the republic's sovereignty. This declaration resulted in the immediate withdrawal of the SDS members of the assembly, who then established their de facto headquarters in the nearby Holiday Inn hotel and organized their own referendum on remaining in a common Yugoslav state. A substantial number of Serbs participated and voted in favour of remaining in Yugoslavia. They then formed the 'Assembly of the Serbian Nation of Bosnia Herzegovina' within Serbian Autonomous Regions, similar in structure to those that had emerged in the Krajina in 1990. These were areas which had Serb majorities, apart from one of them, Brčko, which did not have a Serb majority but was deemed essential as it was of vital strategic importance – it was a land corridor between Serb heartlands in western Bosnia and Serbia proper. This gave me an indication of what exactly the strategic objective of the Bosnian Serbs was. The Serb political aim was that those parts of the republic inhabited principally by Serbs should remain in Yugoslavia, but that a corridor should be created that connected Serb-dominated regions with Serbia proper. This, of course, amounted to little more than a land grab and was, to my mind, the basis on which the SDS promulgated its constitution of the Serbian Republic of Bosnia in 1992.

The Croat position was different, though some within their leadership envisaged a similar outcome for Bosnia's Croats. The HDZ, the ruling party in Croatia, established a branch in Bosnia in 1990. Initially led by the moderate Stepjan Klujić, the more extreme elements of the party under the leadership of Mate Boban – who had the support of Croatia's President Franjo Tudjman and the powerful 'Herzegovinian Lobby' in Zagreb – had now taken effective control. This coincided with the Croatian War, which was now at its peak. It mooted the idea of the existence of the Croatian Republic of Herceg-Bosnia as a separate political and territorial entity on the territory of Bosnia.

If the elections of 1990 were to be a test of Bosnia's future stability, then they failed. As mentioned previously, nationalist parties had won the election and formed an inherently unstable coalition in which all major decisions had to be carried out by consensus. With the parties dividing power along ethnic lines, the president was a Muslim, while the leadership of the parliament was given to the Serbs, and a Croat became prime minister. The Presidency was established much along the lines of Yugoslavia's post-Tito system of rotating presidents from different republics. In Bosnia's case there were two places each for Muslims, Serbs and Croats, with one 'Other' (a 'Yugoslav'). Despite being a Muslim, originally from the Sandžak region, Ejup Ganić was elected on the Yugoslav ticket. The SDS's Biljana Plavšić and Nikola Koljević were elected as the Serb representatives, while Stjepan Kljuić and Franjo Boraš won the Croat seats. While Kljuić was supportive of preserving Bosnia, his colleague Boraš dreamed of autonomy for Bosnia's Croats which would lead to those Croat-dominated parts of Bosnia being eventually ceded to Croatia. The other two seats were for the Muslim SDA party, one of them filled by Fikret Abdić, a businessman from western Bosnia, and the other by the party leader, Alija

Izetbegović, who was selected as president. The leaders of the Croat HDZ party, Mate Boban and the SDS's Radovan Karadžić, were not members of the Presidency, though they possessed significant power nonetheless. Izetbegović became president, the Serb Momčilo Krajišnik was appointed speaker of parliament and Jure Pelivan, a Croat, was named prime minister.

It was hardly the ideal time for me to take over as head of the Regional Centre. There was little doubt that the immediate future was looking pretty grim and that the ECMM would be hard pressed to contain the country's fracturing structure. While it might be very difficult, if not impossible, for the mission to fulfil its primary role of assisting to maintain peace and stability within the republic, it was essential that it be effective in fulfilling, at the very least, its secondary role of assisting in establishing the facts to avoid further deterioration. Anyway, I had hardly had time to open my kitbag when Der came knocking on my door welcoming me to Sarajevo. John was also on hand to welcome me and introduce me to the operational, logistical and administrative staffs. I felt both honoured and apprehensive at the same time. Most of that day was taken up with briefings and learning our work routine. John Wilde gave me the benefit of his recently gained knowledge, apologising at the same time for his lack of experience. I had, however, the advantage of being able to draw on the knowledge of some experienced monitors who had been in Sarajevo since the start of operations there. Their main concern was the build-up of JNA units. Accordingly, a meeting was set up for me with the commander of the Army's IV Corps in Sarajevo, General Vojislav Djurdjevac, the following day. It was originally intended that John should attend, but he suggested that as I was in the process of taking over as chief it would make more sense for me to be there. He also suggested that as Der had taken over as operations officer he would be best placed to answer questions I might have on the day-to-day operational procedures of the HQ.

Der was concerned that, given a gradual increase in the monitor numbers and team locations, we ought to consider increasing staff numbers to keep pace with the developing situation. He also explained the relationship between the mission and the government, further explaining that the presidency had established a coordination team of four officials whose main function was to be a conduit between the ECMM and their representatives. These team members were to be available to us full-time and they would arrange meetings and any visits and trips we might wish to embark upon. I asked if we would have access to political parties and was both surprised and impressed with his answer. He told me that Izetbegović and members of the presidency would be available to meet at any time. They would also facilitate meetings with party leaders, both Karadžić and Boban, should I decide to seek a meeting with them.

The government coordination team was headed by Hajrudin Somun, a senior adviser to President Izetbegović, two interpreters, Vera Ljubović and Darko Ivić, and a security driver, Nijaz Fazlić. Vera and Darko were university graduates and both spoke very good English, as did Hajrudin Somun. Der informed me that Somun would accompany me to the meeting with General Djurdjevac the following day. I asked him what the relationship was like between the government and the JNA, and he told me that, as far as he knew, it was lukewarm at best. John Wilde then informed me he would be departing in two days time, as would his Dutch deputy, Walt van Zueren, but that another Dutch Reserve officer, Harry Brant, had already been appointed as his replacement. With Der recommending that we increase the number of staff officers, I decided to wait for about a week after taking over the reins before I considered making any changes in organizational or operational procedures.

Soon after, Somun arrived at our hotel to join me for the meeting with General Djurdjevac. We shook hands and he expressed his appreciation that I would be staying longer than a few weeks in the appointment. He was fluent in English and I found him to be diplomatic, sincere and gracious. He informed me that I would be introduced to members of the presidency the following morning at a cultural awards ceremony for Bosnia's national day, and that the Prime Minister, Jure Pelivan, had requested a meeting as a matter of urgency. On our way to the meeting I asked him how the government viewed the JNA and the level of contact that existed between the sides. I could see he was somewhat taken aback by my question, and he hesitated before telling me that there was 'a lot of concern about the JNA presence in Bosnia' and that 'some see it as an army of occupation, others a stabilizing influence'. I asked him if it was primarily Muslims who viewed them as an army of occupation, and he nodded knowingly.

The meeting with General Djurdjevac started off quite well. The usual pleasantries were exchanged and *slivovitz* was offered, followed by coffee. It was soon after this that Djurdjaevac got down to business. He began by expressing his displeasure that, as the garrison commander in Sarajevo, he had not been invited to the cultural event the following day. This, he stated, was an insult. Having vented his frustration, however, Djurdjevac suddenly switched tack and wished me success in my appointment, assuring me of his full support and cooperation. I had hardly had time to settle when he stated that he would like my help in finding a solution to a major problem which had arisen just a few days previously. He wished to inform me of a 'very dangerous development' which had occurred at the border with Montenegro: the Bosnian police had allegedly confiscated a consignment of armaments which were being transported on four trucks to Sarajevo. He raged that the police 'had no right to carry out this action' and that there would be consequences if the consignment was not returned with immediate effect. I was somewhat taken aback by this sudden development and wondered if this was some sort of ambush. I exchanged glances with Somun, who was translating, but I could garner little from his expression, so I asked Djurdjevac why the police would intercept a military convoy on a legitimate assignment and whether there was anything specific about the convoy that would have elicited such a response from the police. He declined to elaborate, simply stating that I should take up the matter immediately with the government. Again I looked across at Somun and from his expression I gathered he might have been aware of what exactly the problem might be. Anyway, I promised Djurdjevac that I would make enquiries and that since I had a meeting scheduled with the prime minister for the following day I would raise the issue with him personally. Back in the car, I turned to Somun and asked him if he could provide further clarification. He merely responded that such things 'happen for a reason' and that it was 'a question of whom one wants to believe'. He added that the prime minister would discuss it with me and that it was 'best that I leave him to explain'.

The following day was 25 November 1991, a national day for Bosnia and a day on which the republic was celebrating its cultural heritage. I was invited to a reception being attended by members of the presidency, party officials and prominent members of Bosnian society. It was the first time I had met President Alija Izetbegović and he made quite an impression on me. He had a gentle expression and twinkling eyes, and in the course of his speech he welcomed me as head of the ECMM in Bosnia and expressed the appreciation of the government for what we were trying to achieve. Afterwards, he made his way towards me and warmly shook my hand, saying that I would be welcome to visit him at any time. He was aware that I was shortly to meet with the prime minister and hoped that between us we could solve the question of the arms shipment raised by General Djurdjevac. I suddenly felt under some pressure to find a solution and became rather nervous. Here I was, a middle-ranking Irish Army officer, suddenly thrust from relative obscurity into the vortex of Balkan politics and expected to produce solutions to everyone's satisfaction.

Jure Pelivan had been selected as prime minister as part of the ethnic division of power. He was mild-mannered and courteous but also appeared somewhat nervous, which is something we had in common from the outset. I had noticed a TV camera crew waiting outside his office and wondered if they were waiting for the prime minister or someone else. Somun moved them aside and guided me into the room, and after the usual courteous exchanges the prime minister came to the purpose of our meeting. He said that he understood I had met with General Djurdjevac and asked whether he had mentioned that the consignment apprehended by the police had in fact consisted of weapons that were being smuggled into Bosnia from Montenegro. I told him that Djurdjevac had led me to believe that this was a legitimate military convoy bringing weapons to the JNA. If that was the case, I asked him, why should it have been stopped and the contents impounded by the Bosnian police? His response was sharp. He told me, in no uncertain terms, that Djurdjevac had been lying and that 'This was not a military convoy, but a convoy of four civilian trucks, driven by civilians, in which each truck carried rocket launchers covered over with tarpaulin.' He also said that when challenged by the police to produce the contents lists the drivers could or would not produce any. He queried why the JNA would resort to covertly importing weapons without lists and without the authority or knowledge of the Bosnian government, explaining that the consignment was now under their control and would be held until the matter was clarified. I asked him directly if there had been any contact between government officials and General Djurdjevac to discuss the matter. He told me there had not, and that the government saw the JNA not only as an army of occupation but as a force providing logistical support to the Bosnian Serbs.

As the meeting concluded, I told him that I appreciated the government's concerns but that dialogue with the JNA was vital, however unpalatable it might be to him. He acknowledged this and asked whether the ECMM might be able to provide some assistance. I mentioned to him that it was my intention to establish a liaison team from the ECMM to meet regularly with the JNA and discuss points of concern or interest, and I suggested that if this group could include a member of the government liaison team attached to our mission it might be very useful. He suddenly brightened and immediately agreed. I had the feeling that he had been hoping for any recommendation or suggestion that might solve the immediate crisis. We shook hands, and as I was about to leave I reminded him that the consignment would have to be returned to the JNA. The TV crew were waiting outside Pelivan's office to interview me. I confined myself to saying how proud I was to be taking over as the head of the ECMM and how much the other monitors and I were looking forward to working with all sides to help Bosnia though a difficult period.

The intensity of my new appointment was quite exhausting. Since arriving back in Sarajevo I had met the president, discussed the general situation with the prime minister, subjected myself to an earful from the commander of the JNA's Sarajevo garrison and conducted my first national TV interview; all this in just two days. John Wilde was on hand to meet me when I got back to the hotel. He thought the suggestion about establishing a liaison team was very sensible and suggested it should be led by the new Deputy Chief, Harry Brant. I took his advice and agreed. That night we had a farewell dinner for the departing staff. John wished us well and gave his view that the next few months would be very challenging. I got the impression he was relieved to be leaving, not having had much time to come to grips with the complex dynamics of Balkan politics.

Chapter 5

A Visit to Mostar

By early December 1991 I was settling in to my new role and becoming more familiar with the workings of the ECMM. My daily routine would begin with an early morning run, at about 6.30am, along a splendid tree-lined avenue for about four miles, just around the hotel. It was ideal for running, and the exercise provided a much needed escape from a demanding schedule. At that time of the morning it was pretty cold, which in itself was an incentive to 'get into the programme'. On these occasions I was frequently joined by some of my fellow monitors, including Der Cogan and Peter Innes, and I very much looked forward to these workouts, despite my general lack of fitness. I only learned later that the security police provided by the Bosnian Interior Ministry to guard our headquarters were constantly worried about protecting us on these runs and were kept pretty busy monitoring our progress without our noticing them. It was exactly along this stretch of avenue that the very first fighting of the war would take place within five months.

We now had a total of fifty-seven people working in Bosnia, mostly military personnel from countries who were members of the OSCE, though a few were diplomats and EC Commission officials. We divided these into eleven teams of three monitors each plus a driver, deployed in five locations covering Serb, Croat and Muslim centres of population. These included three teams based in Banja Luka and Mostar, with two teams each in Bihać and Tuzla and one in Sarajevo. Teams rotated every few days, with time spent back in Sarajevo for de-briefings and consultations. Der Cogan took over as senior operations officer and coordinated our teams' daily operational reports and analysis with two assistants. These daily reports were able to give us a pretty good picture of the developing situation throughout the country and an insight into the daily life of its citizens. A consolidated situation report was then prepared each evening for transmission to the Head of the ECMM, Ambassador van Houten, in Zagreb. Most of my own work was now centred on Sarajevo, meeting with members of the presidency, government and party leaders. Hajrudin Somun and his team occupied an office in the presidency where I would go, almost daily, to attend meetings. Harjudin was always impeccably dressed and ever ready to assist us. I would often request that he set up meetings for me which were aimed at learning more about the issues concerning the population. During these trips I would frequently meet President Izetbegović and other members of the government.

It was through this office that we managed to meet with a wide cross-section of Bosnian interest groups and institutional representatives. Sometimes the initiative would come from those wishing to meet with us. Having been somewhat concerned that our presidential liaison team were all Muslim, I asked Somun to arrange a separate meeting with each of the party leaders as well as each member of the presidency. This was to ensure that the mission was accepted as being impartial. One of the lessons I had learned from my previous UN service was that once impartiality is lost it's almost impossible to retrieve, and I was determined that we should be trusted to treat all sides equally and fairly. Over the following few weeks we met with politicians, religious leaders, the judiciary, business leaders, university professors, military commanders and many private citizens. We became an open forum for dialogue, listening to and learning from all parties. Many of our meetings were covered by local television and featured on nightly news broadcasts. We became a familiar sight throughout the country, wearing white clothing with blue EC caps and armbands and driving in white vehicles, each flying the EC flag. On many occasions we had police escorts, but my own preference was that we should move about unaccompanied, particularly in Sarajevo.

My first trip outside Sarajevo was to Sokolac, a town within the newly formed SAO of Romanija, to meet with the assembly. I was conscious that Somun seemed particularly nervous throughout this visit, and the state car assigned to us was driven by the liaison security driver, Nijaz Fazlić. I was almost certain he was armed. I knew I was taking a chance requesting this meeting but thought that the visit would give me an indication of how our organization was being perceived by a Serb community. In any event, and despite Somun's evident discomfort, the Serbs seemed very pleased to meet us. Shortly after the meeting started I could hear a lot of shooting nearby, and when I asked for an explanation of this I was assured it was only a few Serbs recently returned from active duty and letting off steam. The conversation was fairly general. I explained the purpose of our mission and emphasized the importance of mediation as a tool for finding solutions. It was important that the mission was seen as being impartial by agreeing to meet all sides. However, this was not to be taken to mean that the ECMM was giving recognition to the concept of SAOs. I needed to be careful that we avoided being accused of taking sides, which at times was difficult. The meeting was generally cordial, but Somun looked visibly relieved when we left Sokoloac.

In the first week of December I had planned to visit some of our teams based in Mostar in Herzegovina. Concern was growing at developments in the area, particularly as a result of the Croats proclaiming the existence of the 'Republic of Herceg-Bosna'. Western Herzegovina was a breeding ground of Croat nationalism, its Croat population being widely regarded as the most strident of nationalists. Indeed, its citizens had provided much support to Croatia in its conflict with Serbia earlier in 1991, and as a consequence the city of Mostar had gradually become divided – the western part dominated by Croat forces and an eastern part where the army of Bosnia was largely concentrated. Further south of Mostar, the Croatian medieval walled city of Dubrovnik was being blockaded by the JNA; reports were being received from the ECMM in Croatia that the city was being shelled from the territory of Bosnia, near Trebinje, and from Montenegro. Under the circumstances, I was keen to meet with the JNA commander in the area. Plans for this meeting were, however, put on hold when Ambassador van Houten announced his intention to visit Bosnia. We hastily prepared for the visit and set up meetings with President Izetbegovic, Vice President Ganić and General Djurdjevac. Briefing papers were prepared and a schedule made out to cover the duration of his overnight visit.

The ambassador arrived on the evening of 3 December 1991 at Sarajevo airport, accompanied by his advisers, who included two Irish monitors. The first of these was Sean Farrell, who had been seconded to the ECMM from the Irish Department for Foreign Affairs. An experienced diplomat, he had previously served with the Anglo-Irish Secretariat in Belfast. The second was Lieutenant Colonel Colm Mangan, who was a staff officer working at the mission HQ and had been deployed to the city of Dubrovnik. It was my first face-to-face meeting with the ambassador. Prior to taking up this post he had served as Dutch ambassador to Suriname. He had an impressive appearance, tall, slim but powerfully built. He was quietly spoken and immediately put me at my ease.

Our first meeting that evening was with the Deputy-President, Ejup Ganić. An accomplished politician, he had studied in the United States, had an excellent command of English and was, crucially, close to President Izetbegović. He expressed his gratitude for the presence of the ECMM in Bosnia and assured the ambassador of his full support and cooperation. This meeting was followed by the ambassador chairing a staff conference with all available monitors at which he was brought up to date on the latest developments in Bosnia, including my recent meetings with the Prime Minister and General Djurdjevac. We also gave him some briefing papers in connection with his meetings planned for the following day. He impressed on all the staff the importance of acting with professionalism, impartiality, vigilance and due care. Over dinner that evening he was anxious to hear my opinion on future developments in Bosnia. I told him I thought that the Bosnian Serbs would push to have their own entity and that they feared becoming a minority should Bosnia become independent. I also explained that the Croats in Sarajevo were more inclined towards a confederation but that the Croats of western Herzegovina might turn towards Croatia (as evidenced by the declaration of Herceg-Bosna). The Muslims, I told him, feared for their future if independence was granted to Slovenia and Croatia, and they might, in that event, have little option but to seek independence. I added that I believed the JNA to be the 'unknown factor'. Upon hearing my assessment he agreed that the situation did not look good and said that he feared an armed conflict.

After van Houten retired for the night I had a chat with Colm Mangan. I wanted to find out exactly how I had been selected for the role of chief and wondered how long the appointment would be for. I was aware the

Presidency of the EC would change on 1 January 1992 from the Netherlands to Portugal, as would responsibility for the ECMM, and I thought that the incoming Portuguese ambassador who would take over as HOM would want to select his own regional chiefs. Mangan said that he thought I should be allowed to continue, given the momentum that I had generated.

Over the next 24 hours van Houten met with President Izetbegović, Vice President Ganić again, who was also head of the 'Presidential Crisis Committee', General Djurdjevac and the Minister of the Interior, Alija Delimustafić. Izetbegović expressed a strong view that the only solution to the problems Bosnia faced was the deployment of a UN peacekeeping force or, as he called them, 'the blue helmets'. The UN Security Council had already passed resolution 721 in late November 1991, paving the way for such a deployment. However, Izetbegović wanted the force stationed in Bosnia to act as a deterrent against conflict and was now seeking the ambassador's support for such a call. Throughout this series of meetings the ambassador was closely followed by the media, all clamouring for interviews. His message at these meetings was much the same: explaining the role of the ECMM, the importance of negotiation, respecting the concerns of different parties and avoiding any form of conflict. As I accompanied him back to the airport for his return flight he was in no doubt that the next few months would determine Bosnia's future.

Following van Houten's departure on 4 December 1991, I continued with planning a visit to our two teams based in Mostar, about 120km south-west of Sarajevo. Rather than take the police escort offered by our presidential liaison team I settled on taking one of its members, Darko Ivić, who would accompany me in my own car along with Der Cogan, now our senior operations officer. Darko, who was in his mid-thirties, turned out to be a gregarious character. He spoke excellent English and informed us he had been an interpreter in Sarajevo during the Winter Olympics. A lawyer by profession, he had worked for the Ministry of the Interior (MUP) before moving on to a post with Bosnian State Security the following year. He was now working for the presidency as an assistant to Somun. He seemed to know just about everybody in Sarajevo and told me of his delight in being assigned to our mission. We got on very well from the moment we met.

Mostar, situated on the Neretva River, was so named after the bridge-keepers who in medieval times guarded the Stari Most (Old Bridge) over the river. This bridge, built by the Ottomans in the sixteenth century, was the city's most famous landmark. Our first meeting in Mostar was with the mayor, who spoke to us about recent incidents, including the burning of some shop premises, and the consequent rise in tension. He also expressed concern that the JNA, who maintained that one of their pilots had been kidnapped by unknown assailants and whose whereabouts were unknown, might adopt a more aggressive posture. The nearby military airport and barracks, where Montenegrin and Serb reservists were based, was causing unease in multi-ethnic Mostar, and sporadic shootings had been taking place. The recent declaration by Croats of the 'Croatian Republic of Herceg-Bosna' had only served to further divide the city and raise tensions.

When we had met with our monitor teams, Darko proposed that I should visit the coastal town of Neum. The small town and its coastline of 24km was the republic's only access to the Adriatic. It also connected the two parts of Croatia's Dalmatian coast. Croatian influence was everywhere to be seen: Croatia's flag flew prominently from many buildings, Croatian currency, the *kuna*, was being widely used and we saw troops wearing Croatian uniforms walking openly along the street. In short, it seemed that most of the town's citizens had more affinity with Croatia than Bosnia. While I was aware that the area was within the territory of the recently declared 'Croatian Republic of Herceg-Bosna', I was surprised at how little support there appeared to be for Bosnia. I asked Darko whether the Bosnian government knew how Croatian this place was. He told me that they were almost certainly aware of it, but it simply wasn't a priority for them at present. Their focus was on the Serbs, who posed a greater threat and thus received their full attention.

On our way back from Neum, Der, who was reading our map, mentioned that we were not far from Medugorje, a place of pilgrimage for many Irish Catholics because of alleged apparitions of the Virgin Mary there in 1981. It lies about half way between Neum and Mostar at 200m above sea level. The name Medugorje literally means 'between the mountains'. It was late in the evening when we reached it and it looked deserted. We posed outside the Church of St James to take a photograph and then returned to Mostar, where I dined with our monitor teams, before Darko took me, Der and a few of the team monitors for an evening walk through the city. We stopped at a small café in one of the side streets for a beer and Darko engaged a few of the patrons in conversation. Discussion centred around the ECMM presence, which they appreciated, but they also spoke of their collective concern for the future. They told Darko that they did not trust the JNA who, they claimed, were intimidating citizens. They also spoke of random shootings, mainly by Serb reservists, whom they also feared. Of course, I had heard such concerns before, but these stories were becoming all too familiar across Bosnia. Anyway, after these conversations we walked across the famous old Stari Most Bridge with Darko. Some 28m long and 20m high, its construction began in 1566 on the orders of Sulejman the Magnificent, the Ottoman ruler. It was a most impressive sight and had become the city's symbol. We arrived back at our hotel to find that the heating was not working and in fact had been out of action for some time. Fortunately, someone produced a bottle of whiskey, which was hastily consumed and helped to fortify us against the bitterly cold weather.

St Nicholas's Day, 6 December 1991, dawned sunny and bright, and we were soon en route to meet with the commander of the JNA's Second Operational Group, General Pavle Strugar, at his field headquarters near the town of Trebinje. As commander of this group he exercised authority over a considerable number of JNA units. We were aware that there was a corps headquarters in Nevesinje and another in Trebinje itself, where we were headed, though Strugar's own headquarters were in Bileća. Overall, we assessed that there must have been at least three JNA corps (about 10,000 troops) in the general area. Darko suggested we first meet with the mayor of Trebinje, an individual by the name of Božidar Vučurević, who had been a truck driver until 1990, when he co-founded the Trebinje branch of the SDS. Later elected mayor of the town, he was, to put it mildly, quite a controversial figure. Approaching Trebinje we could distinctly hear the sound of shells whistling overhead, though not the sound of any subsequent explosions. I looked at Der and asked him what was going on. His assessment was that this was definitely artillery, though he was unsure of the calibre, and that the sounds seemed to be coming from the east towards Dubrovnik. We suddenly became silent. Even Darko, normally full of chatter, had gone quiet.

We met the mayor of Trebinje in his office and I was surprised to see him wearing military uniform. As it turned out, he was not in the mood for a reasoned discussion and proceeded to rant about enemies all and everywhere. He reserved much of his invective for the citizens of Dubrovnik, declaring that he had often been verbally abused by them, though he proceeded to direct his tirade against Germans, Jews and even the Vatican. (I was immediately reminded of the earlier similar rantings of the mayor in Slavonski Brod.) On the few occasions I tried to interrupt he simply became louder and more animated. In the light of this, I realized that there was nothing to be gained from continuing to listen to him, decided that we should leave and promptly stood up. Apparently he was rather taken aback by this sudden move on my part, but I asked Darko to explain that I had heard enough and had no intention of listening to any more. Leaving his office in a hurry I felt sorry for the citizens of Trebinje who had such an individual as their mayor.

General Strugar's field headquarters were not far from Trebinje, and upon arrival we were met by a JNA liaison officer on his staff, who explained in good English that Strugar was otherwise engaged and that we should wait. I wondered if the artillery barrage we had heard earlier had anything to do with his being unavailable, but while we waited I tried to exact from the liaison officer information about where the units were deployed. He avoided giving me any specifics, which I could well understand. It was not our role to obtain detailed information of this kind, lest we appear to be on an intelligence-gathering exercise which was not part of our mandate. After about ten minutes of waiting with no sign of Strugar I began to become frustrated. Maybe I was still feeling angry from the meeting with Vučurević. In any case, I felt in no mood to be unduly kept waiting, so I turned to the officer and told him that I did not expect to be kept hanging on indefinitely and that if Strugar did not wish to meet with me then we would leave. The officer apologized for the delay and hurriedly left the office.

He returned almost immediately, closely followed by General Strugar. The general was quite a tall man of about sixty, heavy-set and with a large mop of grey hair. There seemed to be a good deal of consternation among his staff, as if the meeting had not been planned. He waited for me to speak, so I started by thanking him for taking the time from his schedule to meet with me. I explained what was becoming a familiar line, the purpose of the ECMM, our aims and so forth. With this basic explanation out of the way, I took the opportunity to ask him about the artillery fire we had heard earlier in the afternoon. My question was translated by the liaison officer rather than by Darko, and after a lengthy silence the general explained in a low voice that as a commander he had responsibility for the protection of his troops. He informed me that he had resorted to firing on the city of Dubrovnik because 'paramilitary forces' had attacked his troops on the territory of Bosnia and this was not acceptable to him. I was very surprised by his admission that he had fired on the city, and when I pressed him to explain the identity of these paramilitary forces he became somewhat vague and simply referred to them as 'enemies of the JNA'. After a few more minutes of conversation I decided it was best to thank him and leave. Just before doing so, however, I asked if he would be kind enough to stand with me for a photograph. He agreed and posed between Der and myself. Darko took the photograph with my camera. (This photograph would prove crucial at his subsequent trial, at which I testified.) I thanked him for his time and we left.

On arrival back at the office in Sarajevo I found a message had been left for me from Hajrudin Somun, inviting some colleagues and myself to join him on the Sunday at his holiday lodge in Pale, a small town located south-west of Sarajevo where many affluent and influential Sarajevans had *vikendicas* (weekend/summer homes). The nearby mountains of Jahorina, Trebević and Igman were venues for many events in the 1984 Winter Olympics. Though it seemed tranquil enough, this municipality had experienced much conflict going back to the time of the Ottoman rule and since then had had a Serb majority. Its inhabitants had suffered greatly at the hands of the Ustashe during the Second World War. It snowed heavily that night, which made the drive up to Pale the following morning quite a challenge. We were lucky to have Nijaz to take the wheel, and he manoeuvred his way through the heavy snow-covered roads that I would have been terrified to attempt. I had taken my Dutch deputy, Harry Brant, and our logistics officer, Hugo van Veghel from Belgium, with me, and having parked the car in a lay-by we proceeded to trudge along a narrow track until we reached Hajrudin's lodge. He was there with his wife to greet us and soon we were seated in the warm comfort of his holiday home drinking a hot punch. The views towards the mountains were simply spectacular and it was hard to imagine that anything could disturb this peaceful setting. The gathering winds of discord and conflict seemed far away, and in this comfortable and warm room we had no talk of war but of family, friendship and a desire for peace. It was a memorable occasion, made all the more enjoyable by the hospitality and graciousness of our hosts. I hoped that nothing in the future would interfere with this picture of tranquility. Subsequent events would prove me wrong.

The situation in Bosnia took a turn for the worse during December 1991, when Germany announced that it intended recognizing Slovenia and Croatia unconditionally on 15 January 1992. The EC had earlier offered to recognize each of Yugoslavia's six republics under certain conditions. The mechanism agreed on by the European Council of Ministers had been entrusted to the Commission headed by Robert Badinter, the chairman of France's constitutional court. His findings stated that of the republics requesting independence, only Slovenia and Macedonia had satisfied the conditions.The other two, Croatia and Bosnia, had not. Despite this, Germany's Foreign Minister, Hans Dietrich Genscher, pushed ahead with his government's announcement. This decision undermined the commission's findings and left Izebegović with an impossible choice: to remain in a Yugoslavia dominated by the Serbs or to go for secession. Accordingly, despite opposition from the two Serb representatives, the Bosnian presidency sought recognition.

With the three main political parties divided along ethnic and religious lines, I thought it might be a useful idea to meet with the leaders of the three main religious groups, to see if they might find some common ground. On 11 December I met separately with each of them. All three (Reis-ul-Ulema Jakub Selimovski, Patriarch Pavle and Archbishop Vinko Puljić) were very receptive, and when I suggested to each that an interdenominational service might be something to think about, they were in full agreement. To follow up on this I then met with the President of the Commission for Religious Affairs and discussed the issue with him. He readily agreed that such a move might prove beneficial and promised to consider the matter. I was both surprised and amused to hear a short time later that the French Government

Minister, Bernard Kouchner, had had exactly the very same idea and had gone ahead to organize the service.

Professor Borisa Starović was Dean of the Medical Faculty of the University of Sarajevo. I was invited to meet with him having suggested to Hajrudin Somun that I would like to listen to the views of a younger generation of Bosnians on the general situation and their hopes for the future. I was very impressed with Professor Starović. A Serb and a native of Sarajevo, he informed me that as an academic he preferred to stay out of politics and concentrate on educating his students to be good doctors. He made me very welcome and listened to my proposal to hold a forum with his students. He was somewhat taken aback when I explained that I wanted the views of students to be heard by those in power, if only to listen and learn, and that this could only be achieved by having TV coverage of the forum. He explained that normally he did not allow discussions of a political nature within his classes, but he appreciated what I was trying to do so eventually agreed on the condition that he himself would not take part in the event.

We arranged the forum to take place the following Friday. I took along Der Cogan, Hugo van Veghel and Vera Ljubović, who was to act as translator. We gathered in the university auditorium and, with about fifty assembled students, introduced ourselves and explained our mission and purpose. By this stage the TV camera was rolling. I should have realized, however, that this sort of dialogue in a country not long released from the grip of communism was uncommon, to say the least, and so, having invited anybody to comment, there was silence throughout. Not a word emerged from any of them. I (and I'm sure, my colleagues) started to feel uneasy. Hugo did his best to engage with the group, but still nothing. Finally, just when I was about to admit failure, the rear door to the auditorium suddenly opened, a middle-aged man entered and, without warning, started to speak in an aggressive tone. It turned out that this unknown individual was being very critical of the ECMM, declaring that we were only in Bosnia to make money and exploit the population. He went on to assert that we were not welcome in Bosnia and should leave. I began to feel very uneasy. Suddenly one of the students, a girl of about twenty, stood up, rounded on the man and declared, 'You do not speak for us. How dare you come in here and embarrass us in front of these people who are only here to help us?' With that, she turned in our direction and explained that students like her had never had the freedom or opportunity to express their views, particularly in public and certainly not on camera. She apologised and then spoke her mind. Before long, many more were anxious to talk with us, and we listened intently. They spoke of not trusting their politicians, who they said were of the older generation, bent on harking back to the Second World War and digging up old hatreds and grievances. They were also opposed to political parties drawn along ethnic and religious lines and expressed little confidence in the future. It was an extraordinary turnaround. I hoped the event would be covered on TV news broadcasts that evening, but I never expected it to be given the publicity it received. I was secretly grateful to the mysterious individual whose intervention ensured its success, something I presume he never intended. I hoped that representatives of the various political parties were watching the news that evening.

On 16 December 1991 the UN, by way of Security Council Resolution 724, approved the Secretary-General's report, which contained a plan for a possible peacekeeping operation for Yugoslavia. A small group of military officers, civilian police and Secretariat staff were to arrive in order to prepare the way for such a deployment. We had heard many times that the UN was giving consideration to becoming involved in the Yugoslav crisis, and this was something long advocated by President Izetbegović. While it was to be presumed that the deployment would be to Croatia, the president wanted it to be in Bosnia, to act as a deterrent to the conflict spreading from Croatia to his country. This made good sense to me. Our monitor teams were reporting that tension was gradually rising throughout the country and there seemed no sign that this situation would change. The strength of the JNA was gradually increasing due to its withdrawal from Croatia, and with it the Serbs were becoming more aggressive.

Lord (Peter) Carrington, a former British Foreign Secretary, who had been selected by the EC as Chairman of the International Peace Conference on Yugoslavia in September of 1991, had been making a tour of the republic's capitals in December seeking an agreed solution to the crises. The principles to be followed in the Peace Conference's original statement stated that there should be no unilateral change of borders by force, protection for the rights of all in Yugoslavia and full account to be taken of all legitimate concerns and aspirations. An Arbitration Commission was to rule on major legal issues raised by the conflict. President Izetbegović felt it essential that Bosnia should secure a guarantee of protection. With the likelihood of Croatia gaining its independence, he was running out of options.

As Christmas was not far off, I took a few hours the following day to shop for some family presents. I headed to the Baščaršija market and spent a few hours hunting for gifts. Briefing Lord Carrington might have seemed quite important, but was nothing compared to the task of selecting appropriate things for my wife and four children. During this shopping spree I seemed to be getting considerable attention, with some people pointing in my direction and others looking more than casually at me. It appeared that the TV news coverage of the university forum had placed me on a public platform I had not been exposed to before, and while I was not exactly at ease with it all, it was something I would become accustomed to over the following several months.

During one of our daily briefing sessions I was asked if there were any plans for us to celebrate Christmas. This was something I had not really given any thought to, but having listened to the views of some staff members I thought we probably should. We decided that it would be appropriate to have a traditional Christmas dinner and that as many monitors should be free to attend as was possible. Hugo immediately volunteered to organize the logistics side of the event, and Harry agreed to coordinate the duty schedule to allow for maximum attendance. The hotel manager was consulted on providing a suitable room, which would be decorated appropriately. One of our French monitors promised to obtain some bottles of champagne and indicated that each bottle would have to be opened by 'special means' at the dinner.

In the meantime, the ECMM headquarters in Zagreb planned to hold a policy meeting on 29 December which the regional mission chiefs were requested to attend. It was also to coincide with a changeover of responsibility for the management of the mission from the Netherlands to Portugal, which was due to take over Presidency of the EC from 1 January

1992. This would be an opportunity for the incoming Head of Mission, Ambassador João Salgueiro, to meet all his key staff, and to say farewell to Ambassador Dirk van Houten. I also hoped to ascertain at this meeting whether I would be continuing as the chief in Sarajevo or making way for a replacement.

Christmas Day started just like any other working day. The consolidated reports from the monitor teams had been analysed and forwarded to Zagreb. Replacement monitors, who had just arrived, were briefed, assigned to teams and prepared for deployment, while I was making preparations to travel back the following morning to Banja Luka for another meeting with General Uzalec. We broke at midday and before heading to Christmas dinner I managed to phone home for a short conversation with my family. The dinner was a great success, the maximum available monitors attending, and we managed to make it as enjoyable as it could be under the circumstances. As I was wondering what had become of the promised champagne, our French monitor called for attention and suddenly opened three doors to our rear which led to the snow-covered balcony. Producing a bayonet, he proceeded to resurrect about a dozen bottles from the snow, one of which he placed ceremonially in front of me. Handing me the bayonet, he suggested that I should decapitate the bottle by quickly whipping the blunt side of the bayonet at an angle against its top. Certain that I would make a mess of this procedure, I did as I was told and to my astonishment took the top clean off the bottle with the first swipe. A rousing round of applause broke out, and I felt rather pleased with myself. When the other bottles had been similarly opened, toasts were proposed to the monitor mission, to Bosnia, to our families and to friendship. It was a most pleasant interlude, giving us the chance to relax a little and think of home and family.

The next day, however, it was back to work. I met with General Uzalec in Banja Luka, having initially held a meeting with our monitors stationed there. I was briefed by them on the rising tension in the area caused by an alarming rise in the number of uniformed reservists, almost all of whom were Serb. The monitors' hotel seemed to be flooded with them and they looked and behaved very aggressively. There was also an increase in the number of Serb refugees in the Banja Luka area who had fled from the conflict in Croatia. Many Muslims now felt threatened and many were leaving Banja Luka. The ECMM team in the city reported that on a number of occasions pre-arranged police escorts had failed to turn up, resulting in the cancellation of visits to some municipalities. The subsequent meeting with General Uzalec gave me no cause for optimism. He insisted that he was doing his best to ensure reservists behaved properly, but because of the heightened tension, which he blamed on the decision by Izetbegović to seek recognition, he was powerless to act. I wanted to suggest that it was the arming of the Serbs by the JNA that had increased tension, but without proof of this I thought it better not to.

I flew to Zagreb on 29 December 1991 for the policy meeting and had the chance to meet with the other regional chiefs and Ambassador Salgueiro. In my submission I gave a rather gloomy outlook for Bosnia and predicted that it was likely the Bosnian Serbs would declare their own republic within a short period of time. While I had no information on the number of JNA troops now stationed in Bosnia, it was my view that there was a close relationship between them and the Bosnian Serbs. At a reception afterwards I was introduced to Ambassador Salgueiro. After a short discussion on Bosnia he drew me to one side, asked me whether I would (or not) wish to continue as chief in Sarajevo and told me that he was quite happy for me to remain in post. He warned that Bosnia looked set to explode and that he wanted me to be on the ground to handle things as best as I could. So I would be staying. The next year, 1992, looked set to be a real challenge for all of us – and so it would transpire.

Chapter 6

First Casualties

The New Year dawned as it does for so many – with a slight headache from the previous night's celebration. It had been planned that our monitors would have a free day, where operationally possible, and so a group of us from the HQ decided to visit the ski resort of Jahorina, about 30km south-east of Sarajevo, a popular holiday location. I certainly had no intention of donning skis, as my competence in that regard was close to zero. However, I did look forward to a temporary respite from our demanding role and an opportunity to take in the sights of a place associated with the 1984 Winter Olympics. The snow lay thick on the ground as we drove up through the tree-lined slopes. Jahorina was packed with happy skiers enjoying the winter sunshine, and there was a tangible holiday atmosphere. Laughter filled the air and clothing in every shade of colour adorned the ski slopes. I had brought with me our two interpreters, Darko and Vera, who seemed to be relishing the day. Darko had previously worked with the Olympic committee and was able to give us an account of the huge effort that had been required to stage the events. The carefree atmosphere on these packed ski slopes was, however, in stark contrast to the reality which prevailed in the city below.

On our way back down towards Sarajevo Darko informed me that his parents would be delighted if I would join them for dinner that evening at their home. His father, Dušan, was a Serb, while his mother, Mujesira, was Muslim. Both had qualified as civil engineers and had been partisans during the Second World War. When I told Darko that I would be honoured to attend, he informed me that his father had a large whiskey collection, of which he was very proud, and that it would be expected of me to partake. I told him that I would, despite the fact I hardly ever drink whiskey and never at mealtimes. Darko asked, however, that I do it for his sake, because his family were proud that he was working with me and his father wanted to show his appreciation. I groaned inwardly. Both of Darko's parents were genuine people who were both gracious and hospitable. As soon as the introductions were over, however, Dušan led me to his cellar to select the whiskey. There must have been about a hundred bottles of various brands neatly stacked on two shelves. Knowing very little about whiskey, I decided on a bottle of Scotch for no other reason than I had noticed it was only about a third full and so I reckoned that I would not have to drink too much. However, instead of taking the bottle I had pointed to, he reached behind it and withdrew an unopened one, which was brought to the table and duly broached. It proved a most enjoyable meal, and despite the best efforts of Dušan I managed to escape relatively unscathed from the whiskey deluge. Both Darko's parents expressed their admiration and support for what our mission was attempting to achieve in Bosnia, as well as their pride that their son was helping us in this work. But they were also fearful for Bosnia's future and uncertain about what might lie ahead.

Germany's declaration in mid-December 1991 that it intended to recognize Slovenia and Croatia in January 1992 changed the political landscape in Bosnia. Peter Carrington, recently appointed Chairman of the International Peace Conference on Yugoslavia, had warned of the serious consequences should there be early recognition of the separate republics. He was of the view that such recognition would almost certainly lead Bosnia to seek independence, something which he believed would be wholly unacceptable to the Serb population. In these circumstances there was little surprise that when the Bosnian presidency opted to seek EC recognition, the Bosnian Serbs took their own steps to pre-empt recognition by declaring their own 'Serbian Republic of Bosnia-Herzegovina' on 9 January 1992. The slide to war was quickly gaining momentum.

On 2 January 1992 an agreement on the cessation of hostilities in Croatia, negotiated earlier in Geneva by Cyrus Vance, the UN representative of the Secretary General with Presidents Milošević, Franjo Tudjman and Federal Secretary General Kadijević, was signed in Sarajevo between the JNA and the Croatian Government. It came into force the following day. The agreement was signed by Vance on behalf of the UN, Croatia's Minister for Defence, Gojko Šušak, and General Andrija Rašeta of the JNA. It called for a cessation of hostile military action on land, sea and in the air. The ECMM was to play a leading role in monitoring the implementation of this agreement. Confidence-building measures were also included. The ceasefire line appeared to mirror the areas which had a majority Serb population and which had formally declared themselves as 'The Republic of the Serbian Krajina'. These became known as the UN Protected Areas (UNPAs).

On 5 January 1992 we were busy at work planning the visit to Sarajevo of Ambassador João Salgueiro scheduled for 7 January. The weather had turned bitterly cold, with freezing fog covering the city. I was in my office with Der in the early afternoon working on briefing notes when the door opened and Jean-Loup, my former teammate from Banja Luka came in. He asked me if there was any possibility that I could get him on one of the ECMM helicopters to Zagreb. Two of the helicopters had arrived in Sarajevo as part of a series of shuttle flights and were due to depart the following day for Belgrade before continuing to Zagreb. I could well understand Jean-Loup's desire to avoid a long road journey, so I readily agreed, thanked him for his service and friendship and wished him well.

As an indication of our desire to win the hearts and minds of the three main parties I decided to send ECMM representatives to attend the different religious ceremonies over the Christmas period. The sixth of January marks the Orthodox Christmas, and I arranged to attend the appropriate religious ceremony with two of my colleagues that evening. Early that afternoon, I remember standing on the balcony outside my hotel room and hearing the distinctive sound of rotor blades as two helicopters lifted off from the airport helipad. I had shared a dinner table the previous evening with both crews and had talked with the commander of the mission's helicopter wing, Lieutenant Colonel Enzo Venturini, who, like me, had previously served with UNIFIL. It took us about two hours to drive into the city that evening, such was the density of the freezing fog. By the time we reached the church it was packed to capacity, with hundreds of Serbs assembled outside. We were given some hard looks by many of them and they seemed suspicious of our presence. Having been recognized by one of the officials, however, we were ushered inside and stood amid the throng of worshippers. Many of the Bosnian Serb leadership were present, including Radovan Karadžić and Biljana Plavšić, both of whom noticed our presence and nodded in our direction in what I took to be a sign of appreciation. The ceremony lasted for nearly three hours. At one stage I was quite alarmed to hear numerous shots being fired into the air outside the cathedral, but I was assured it was just part of the New Year celebrations.

It was early afternoon the following day when Der Cogan came bursting into my room. Looking quite shaken, he told me that he had had bad news. The two helicopters, one of which had Jean-Loup aboard, had come under air attack, and an AB 206 Huey had been hit by a missile and had crashed. It appeared that all five occupants were dead, including Jean-Loup. The second helicopter had managed to land without being hit, and its crew were believed to be safe. I was absolutely numbed by this dreadful news and asked Der if there could have been a mistake. Was it definitely an ECMM helicopter? Surely their distinctive EC markings couldn't have been mistaken? Der intimated that he regarded this as a deliberate attack, because the helicopter was in Croatian airspace. I asked him why the helicopters had not reached Zagreb the day before, as planned, and he told me that they had flown to Belgrade, remained there overnight and picked up an additional passenger in the morning before flying to Zagreb. We didn't have the full picture, but it was thought a JNA jet had fired an air-to-air missile from inside Croatia. I stepped out on to the balcony to get some air and to absorb the reality of what I had just heard – and it was hard to take in. It was only the day before that I had stood in the same spot listening to the helicopters as they lifted off. I immediately thought back to Jean-Loup's asking me for a lift and my agreement. How could a simple nod have ended in such tragedy? I shivered with sadness and guilt. If only I had refused his request.

This dramatic news started a flurry of activity aimed at ascertaining the exact details of what had happened. The news organizations (both national and international) were clamouring for details, and amid the uncertainty Der thought it prudent to issue a ban on staff speaking to the media. A local television station, YUTEL, wanted to interview me on the circumstances of the shooting down, but I declined for the moment, telling them that as soon as the factual details were established I would talk to them. Lieutenant Colonel Mangan contacted me from the mission HQ in Zagreb and told me what had happened. Both helicopters had left Belgrade at 10.00am and flown towards Zagreb on the approved route via Hungary. Having refuelled at Kaposvar in Hungary they crossed the border into Croatia at Letenje. About 25km south of Varaždin they were attacked by a JNA MiG aircraft, which had taken off from Bihać in north west Bosnia near the Croatian border. The AB 206 helicopter was shot down and the AB 205, which took evasive action, landed safely. Mangan also informed me that the impending visit by Ambassador Salgueiro was to be deferred. The ambassador had been en route by fixed-wing aircraft from Belgrade, but on landing at Graz in Austria proceeded directly to the site of the crash. Mangan could not confirm the casualty list, but an ECMM team were now at the site.

With so many unanswered questions there was an air of disbelief and anger in our operations office. How could this have happened? Surely the JNA had identified the helicopters with their distinctive white markings and EC logo clearly displayed? Was this a deliberate attack or some rogue pilot acting alone? Why did the attack happen if the helicopters were following the agreed flight path? I told Der that if we could verify the exact casualty list and gain clarification as to who carried out the attack I would agree to be interviewed by YUTEL. When these were established, I did the interview, which I understood was to be for a local television audience only – little did I realize that it would be screened globally over the next 24 hours. This was my first experience of a television interview and I was quite astonished by the reaction it provoked. The ECMM headquarters in Zagreb immediately established a team to compile a summary of information concerning the attack, headed by Lieutenant Colonel Michael Mullooly and two other monitors. The team made recommendations on the establishment of a formal EC board of enquiry and on its terms of reference.

The helicopter attack brought home to us just how dangerous Bosnia was now becoming. The situation was clearly deteriorating, and the conditions of freedom of movement and safety and security which were conditional for the deployment of the ECMM were now under threat. The television footage of the crash scene and the bodies lying on the ground made for grisly viewing. Naturally, it was a very sombre dining room that evening as we sat down to dinner. Jean-Loup had been an extremely popular and gregarious character, and it was difficult to accept that he had been killed on his way home having completed his tour of duty. We held a two-minute silence at table in memory of our five deceased colleagues. The management of the hotel cordoned off that portion of the dining room where we regularly ate to afford us some privacy. At our staff briefing after dinner we decided to suspend all operational activities throughout Bosnia for forty-eight hours, representing a period of mourning for the dead monitors. This decision was supported by the ECMM Head of Mission. It would seem that this was a deliberate and cowardly attack on an unarmed and vulnerable organization, an action which was totally unacceptable. Many messages of sympathy and notes of appreciation came into the office over the next few days.

The operations officer on duty that night, Dirk de Paus, was contacted by the JNA and asked if I would receive a JNA delegation the following morning.The meeting was to be in connection with the helicopter incident, so I agreed. I knew Lieutenant Colonel Dimitrijević, a JNA liaison officer whom I had met a number of times and who spoke good English. He was usually dressed in civilian attire on these occasions, and we got on quite well. On this occasion, however, he was wearing uniform and was accompanied by another officer similarly dressed. He also brought with him a female interpreter who worked for the JNA. She conveyed the JNA's expression of sympathy on the tragic death of members of the ECMM. The JNA, I was told, 'very much regretted this tragic accident'. It was obvious to me that he was delivering a prepared statement. He looked down, not wishing to make direct eye contact, and I had the impression he was embarrassed. When he went on to start giving me an account of what had happened, I interrupted, telling him that while I appreciated the expression of sympathy on the death of my colleagues I did not believe it was a tragic accident, rather that it had been, as far as we were concerned, a deliberate and unprovoked attack. I told him that he could inform his HQ that I was refuting their statement that this was an accident and, furthermore, that our monitor mission would carry out its own investigation to establish the exact circumstances of the attack. I then asked him to leave. He looked directly at me and just nodded. He understood.

A requiem mass was held in the Catholic Cathedral in Sarajevo the following day in memory of our deceased colleagues. Most of our available monitors attended, as did some public officials. Later that evening, I attended a reception hosted by the SDS to which I was previously committed. Members of the government were there, and I received expressions of sympathy from President Izetbegović, Vice President Ganić, Prime Minister Pelivan and Radovan Karadžić, the SDS leader. Operationally, we remained in station over the next two days but confined ourselves to administrative duties. Monitor activities were resumed on 10 January 1992, when clear and explicit guarantees concerning the future safety of the personnel of the monitor mission were given to the ECMM by the JNA. A memorial cross was later erected on the site of the fatal attack.

Aware that the JNA was acting as a separate power beyond the authority of the Bosnian government and responsible only to Belgrade, I needed to satisfy myself as to where the JNA stood vis-à-vis Bosnia. In order to achieve this I planned a visit to some of their major units throughout the republic. My first meeting with General Milutin Kukanjac, the most senior JNA commander in Bosnia and whose HQ was based in Sarajevo, did not go very well. The visit was at my instigation because I wanted to ascertain his views on the ECMM mission. Kukanjac was a heavy-set man with thick jet-black hair and a deep throaty voice. It became apparent very early in the meeting that he knew practically nothing about our mandate or role, though be seemed sufficiently familiar with the mission to vent his annoyance with it. I informed him that I was hoping to visit some JNA units and asked if he had any objections to this. I was at pains to assure him that I was not interested in obtaining any military information whatsoever and that this was not part of our mission. He hesitated before answering that he would give it his consideration. Just before we parted I turned to him and said that by the time of our next meeting I hoped he might be better informed about the ECMM and its role in Bosnia.

As I left Kukanjac's headquarters, Lieutenant Colonel Dimitrijević, the JNA liaison officer who had attended the meeting, approached me and informed me that Kukanjac had been unprepared for the meeting and was caught unawares by what I had said. He added that the JNA leadership in

Bosnia had 'no direction as to how we should treat your mission', though he assured me that he would 'give this his attention' and get back to me. He seemed genuine. I thanked him and told him that it might be helpful if the general would consider providing me with a JNA liaison officer to accompany me when I visited the major units. That was, of course, if he had no objection to my visiting them. We parted with a handshake.

Der had made out a suggested itinerary for the tour of the JNA units which we passed on to Dimitrijević in the hope, though not expectation, that it would meet with the approval of General Kukanjac. Some of the JNA's major units were based in locations where we had monitor teams, so it made sense to select these areas, which also reflected different ethnic majorities. I was pleased when Dimitrijević responded quickly to say that Kukanjac had no objection to my visiting the units and that he would provide a liaison officer to accompany me. I asked Dimitrijević whether that would be him, and he responded that it almost certainly would be. So we commenced our tour on 17 January 1992 with a visit to Bihać in north-west Bosnia. A police escort car led the way, with Der, Darko and I following behind and Dimitrijević taking up the rear in a military staff car. I had asked the police to refrain from their usual practice of blowing the horn or flashing their lights at oncoming traffic, but they seemed not to understand and appeared happy to continue scaring the life out of all those unfortunate enough to meet us on the road. Their constant use of the signal lollipop sticks only added to their arsenal of tactics and to my own embarrassment. We arrived, after a four-hour drive, in Bihać, a largely Muslim town close to the border with Croatia. It played a critical role during the war in Croatia as it was home to a sophisticated underground military airport, which was used as a launch pad for MiG air strikes against both Slovenia and Croatia. This was the same airbase from which the MiG 21 fighter that shot down our helicopter on 7 January 1992 had taken off from. The JNA's X Corps was also based here.

We were met by our Bihać-based ECMM team, comprising Peter Borregaard from Denmark and Alain Olivie of France. After a briefing from them they escorted us to the HQ of the X Corps, where we were introduced to the commanding officer, General Ninković. A man of pleasant demeanour, he made us welcome and, unlike General Kukanjac, appeared to be very familiar with our mission. He had most of his senior staff present, was very open to answering our questions, pledged his support for our mission and promised to give assistance to both of our monitor teams stationed in Bihać. We expressed our concern that as a consequence of the Serbs proclaiming their Republic of Serbian Krajina in 1991, the inhabitants of Bihać were being refused entry into that territory. The fear was that if Bihać was caught between the forces of the RSK on one side and an increasing number of armed Bosnian Serbs on the other, the town was in danger of being trapped in a double siege. When I asked if our teams might be permitted entry into the area of Knin, which came under control of the JNA's IX Corps, he stated he could not grant this as it did not form part of his operational area. I had the feeling the General understood these concerns, but without giving any indication of how this might be avoided. As the meeting concluded I addressed him and thanked him for facilitating this meeting and listening to our concerns. He seemed pleased by this, replying that he was very happy to have met with us and then inviting us to dine with him. There followed a splendid meal, to which all of our monitors were invited. Later that evening, I sought out Dimitrijević to tell him how impressed I was with the manner in which General Ninković had received us and with his knowledge of the role of the ECMM. He gave me a smile and told me that General Kukanjac had taken my comments to heart and had instructed all corps commanders to extend their cooperation to the ECMM. He added that this was a signal that the ECMM was 'officially recognized' by the JNA.

The following morning we proceeded to Banja Luka for a meeting with the V Corps and its new commanding officer, General Vuković. We had also arranged to attend a memorial mass in the Catholic cathedral of Banja Luka that evening to be celebrated by Bishop Komarica in memory of our colleagues killed in the air attack, particularly Jean-Loup, who had met the Bishop on a number of occasions. We stopped off at our team office in the Hotel Bosna and were given an update by two of our team members, Gabrial Kovacs from Czechoslovakia and my former teammate, Pandelis Botonakis. They reported that with a large and continuing influx of Serb refugees from Croatia flooding the city tension was high, but that the arrival of General Vuković seemed to have resulted in an improvement in the conduct of military reservists. This was an issue, he said, that the monitors had raised with the general on their first meeting, and he appeared to have taken measures to address their complaint. I expressed my pleasure that progress had been made and asked if there were any other matters to discuss. He told me that there were a few UN observers also staying at their hotel. I had been made aware of the deployment on 14 January 1992 of fifty UN Military Liaison Officers (UNMLOs) to Yugoslavia as part of the recently negotiated 'Sarajevo Implementation Accord', and I knew that some were to be sent to different areas of Bosnia. Der suggested that it might be a good idea to meet them, so I asked Pandelis to invite them for a meeting after the church service.

We met with General Vuković at his headquarters. While I had Darko and Dimitrijević with me, the general had his own interpreter present, the same young lady who had earlier accompanied Dimitrijević to meet me the morning after the helicopter attack. Vuković was a short, stocky man who looked much younger than his predecessor, General Uzalec. He smoked incessantly, was curt in manner and had little time for small talk, so we broached the usual issues as conveyed to us by the different parties. He listened attentively, said little and, when I made mention of the reservists, immediately interjected to assure me that he had taken action against undisciplined elements, adding that he would not tolerate any misbehaviour. I assured him that I welcomed his efforts in this regard and that monitors had informed me that their behaviour had much improved. He eased up on hearing this and seemed to relax, so I considered that it might be the right moment to explain to him that Muslims were telling us of being intimidated and bullied by Serbs who were putting pressure on them to leave their homes. When I mentioned, moreover, that these Muslims had little faith in the JNA to offer them protection, he merely replied that this was not a matter for the JNA but for the local authorities to deal with. As with General Ninković, we were given plenty of sympathy but not much promise of action on these pressing matters.

The memorial service in the cathedral was a very touching occasion and was very well attended. Bishop Komarica spoke highly of the monitor mission and of the efforts we were making to mediate in what was becoming a very difficult situation. He made special mention of Jean-Loup and his contribution to a 'peace sought by all'. Rade Ćosić and his wife Mary were also in attendance, with Rade interpreting the Bishop's words from the altar. I was caught unprepared when invited by the Bishop to address the congregation, but I did my best to assure those in attendance that the mission would continue to look for ways to accommodate each community and stressed that dialogue, negotiation and compromise were essential to finding acceptable solutions. It was a very emotional moment for me and one I will long remember.

Although fairly exhausted after such a busy day I was anxious to meet with the UN Observer team in the hotel. However, there was no contact from them so I sought out Pandelis, asking him if the UN had received my message. He told me that they had, but that they had declined the invitation on the basis that they were not permitted to discuss anything with monitors. I was puzzled by this and wondered why they would not find it beneficial to meet us. I told Pandelis to let them know that we would, in any event, remain available to give them any assistance or support they might require.

Our final meeting was scheduled for the following day with General Janković, who commanded the 17th Corps in Tuzla, the third largest city in Bosnia. A major industrial centre and famous for its salt lake, it was also the only municipality governed by reformist nationalists, who had won control in the elections of 1990. I was joined for the meeting by Tuzla-based monitors, the Dutchman Johannes van Baal and his Danish colleague, Proben Jensen. General Janković was, frankly, a dour individual and unlike the other commanders I had met seemed none too pleased to meet me. He expressed his objection to the erecting of barricades some days previously by the different ethnic communities, something which had caused much tension in the city. Once again, it was a case of Serbs trusting only the JNA while Muslims depended on local police for their safety. He acknowledged the support of the ECMM team in Tuzla in negotiating joint checkpoints manned by JNA and local police, something which, he stated, was acceptable to both parties.

Before returning to Sarajevo I had a brief chat with Dimitrijević and asked him to convey my thanks to General Kukanjac for facilitating my meetings with the corps commanders. He told me that I would be able to thank him in person, because General Kukanjac had invited me to a meeting with him in two days time. He quickly added that he firmly believed that Kukanjac would be far better prepared for this visit than he had been for our previous one. With that, he shook my hand, smiled and went on his way. On the way back Der and I discussed the events of the previous few days. We speculated that the JNA's attitude to our mission had changed considerably since our first meeting with Kukanjac.

As we prepared to leave Tuzla, Darko told me of the death of the father of Hajrudin Somun, our presidential liaison official, and informed me he was to be buried in his home town of Goražde the following day. I asked whether it would be appropriate for us to attend the funeral. Darko said that while it wouldn't be expected it might still be a suitable gesture. That evening, upon our return to Sarajevo, we discussed the matter and decided we should be represented. I would attend the service with the new deputy chief, Vitor Ferreira, who had recently taken over from Harry Brant. Vitor was an army major from Portugal and had been in the mission area for some time. We agreed that Darko, who we relied on to advise us on the protocol for such occasions, should also attend. When we met with Somun to express our condolences he seemed surprised but pleased to see us. It was very interesting to observe how the funeral procession was conducted. Mr Somun's body was wrapped in a simple shroud and placed on what looked like an open stretcher, which was passed from hand to hand along a corridor of mourners until it arrived at the burial site. His body was then placed in the prepared grave, which was aligned pointing towards Mecca according to religious custom. Not wishing to interfere in any way with this ritual, we kept a respectful distance.

Among the new monitors to arrive that week was a Dutch officer, Johannes van Baal. When he introduced himself to me he mentioned that he was to be the new deputy chief. This was news to me. Apparently, the Deputy Head of Mission had told him in Zagreb that he would be taking up this appointment. I informed him that I had already selected my deputy and that our policy here was that all new monitors must have experience with a team before being considered for a staff appointment. He responded that this seemed fair, and the matter was left at that. I wondered, however, what was really going on.

Our second meeting with General Kukanjac was an altogether different affair from the first. He was well prepared on this occasion and introduced me to his deputy, General Milan Aksentijević. He was very interested to hear my views on the meetings we had had with the corps commanders, on which we had no doubt he had already been adequately briefed by Lieutenant Colonel Dimitrijević. The meeting was cordial and he announced to us that the ECMM in Bosnia was now formally recognized by the JNA. When I pressed him to explain why it seemed that the JNA had no formal communication or regular contact with the presidency of Bosnia he hesitated before saying that this was the choice of the presidency and a matter for the Bosnian government to decide upon. He said that the JNA was in Bosnia to 'protect the citizens of Bosnia on orders from Belgrade'. I wanted to push further by asking him why the JNA was so mistrusted by Muslims but held back. The meeting ended a long and busy week, but despite the frenzied activity I wondered whether we had achieved very much.

Chapter 7

Meeting the Key Players

As our endeavours to secure peace struggled on, the EC agreed to recognize the independence of all Yugoslav republics, albeit under certain conditions. In the case of Bosnia one of the conditions was that it should organize a referendum in which all citizens would participate. I was requested by Ambassador Salgueiro to attend a session of the Bosnian Assembly on 24 January 1992 as his representative. The session was to discuss the holding of a referendum on the future status of the country. Earlier that day, I met with Ejup Ganić, the 'Yugoslav' member of the presidency, who briefed me on the assembly session. I had been aware that members of the Serb SDS had boycotted the parliament in Sarajevo and formed their own assembly on 24 October 1991, thereby ending the tri-ethnic coalition that had governed since the elections the previous year. I was assured, however, that the Serb members of the assembly would be attending this session, the results of which could determine the future of Bosnia. I was sufficiently familiar with the political situation to realize that a motion calling a referendum was likely, and I was told by Ganić to prepare for a long session.

I arrived in the early afternoon with Vitor and Vera, our interpreter from the presidency. Seats had been reserved for us in the middle of the packed assembly auditorium, among the delegates themselves rather than in the public gallery. I had become familiar with some of the leaders and was able to recognize all members of the presidency, who had taken their seats along the front row. The assembly president, the Serb, Momčilo Krajišnik, chaired the proceedings, inviting each leader to address the assembly. The presentations followed along familiar lines. President Izetbegovic addressed the assembly first, as leader of the Muslim SDA party, explaining the wishes of the EC Arbitration Committee on the holding of a referendum, and introduced me as the EC representative, which prompted applause from all sides. He argued that Bosnia had little choice but to hold a referendum. Muslims, he said, did not want to be part of a 'Greater Serbia' and he advocated that a special commission should establish the percentage of Serb-held posts and examine and address their concerns.

Radovan Karadžić of the SDS repeated much of what he had been saying publicly for some time. He admonished the Muslims to take seriously the will of the Serbs to remain in Yugoslavia, and I had no doubt that the stance he adopted (or reiterated) was a clear warning as to the consequences of Bosnia holding a referendum. Conversely, Stjepan Kljuić of the HDZ argued that it was natural to seek sovereignty, as outlined by the EC, and that if agreement could not be reached everybody should resign and new elections held. I wondered, however, whether he had the backing of all Croats in advocating sovereignty. I doubted that his colleague Mate Boban was of a similar view.

There was much argument from Serb delegates regarding the issue of consensus. According to them, no decision could be legally made on holding a referendum unless agreed by all three parties. However, this was countered by Muslim delegates, who asserted that as the Serbs had established their own Serb assembly, the issue of consensus was null and void. As the hours passed there were many recesses to consider individual points. During these periods Vera briefed me on the general tone and content of the main speeches, and she was of the view that both Serbs and Muslims appeared entrenched in their respective positions. However, at about 1.00am it appeared some sort of deal had been reached. A document was circulated to all delegates laying out the form of words of a referendum, but before I could get an explanation from Vera as to what was transpiring there were further exchanges with Karadžić, who complained that what was intended by the Muslim and Croat delegates was not the same as that envisaged by the Serbs; they therefore rejected the document. After a further recess the Assembly President, Momčilo Krajišnik, adjourned the assembly without approval and prior to a vote, whereupon the Serb members withdrew. We repaired to the canteen for a break and a short time later were informed that the assembly would reconvene, this time under the chairmanship of the vice president. With the Serb members now absent, the wording of a referendum was agreed and adopted by the SDA and HDZ with support from five centre and left-wing parties. This was not, I felt, a solution, and I was convinced it would be rejected by the Serbs. I managed to extract myself from the assembly building at 6.30am.

In my subsequent report to Salgueiro I gave the view that the Serbs were never going to support any form of referendum on independence. Their obsessive fear of becoming a minority in an independent state, particularly under Muslim majority rule, was pretty obvious, particularly from their declaration on 9 January 1992 proclaiming in the Holiday Inn hotel (their de facto base) the 'Assembly of the Serb People in Bosnia'. I noted in the report that the legality of the assembly being reconvened after it had been closed by the assembly president might be open to legal argument, as would the action of the same official in concluding the session without a majority in the first place.

In order to ascertain legal opinion on the vexed question of consensus and on whether the assembly president had authority to adjourn the assembly, I asked Hajrudin Somun if he could arrange a meeting for me with members of Sarajevo's judiciary. He responded quickly, saying that a hastily arranged meeting was to take place the same afternoon in one of the court offices. When I arrived with him there were about six judges in the room and another person standing to one side. After introductions I thanked them for facilitating the meeting. The person who had stood alone now came forward and explained he was the deputy minister of justice and he wished to inform me that there could be no discussion with the group on the issue of consensus. I was completely thrown by this and tried to gather my thoughts. The judges facing me seemed uncomfortable and embarrassed. I addressed the minister, saying that I was merely trying to get a legal opinion on what was a very important matter. However, he simply repeated that the issue was not open for discussion, and I had little choice but to comply with his request as long as he remained in the room. He offered me coffee and then invited each judge to introduce themself to me. Conversation was both general and cordial. After a short time the minister stood to leave, offering his apologies and saying he had a meeting to attend. As soon as he was gone the judges looked relieved and some even smiled. I turned to Somun and asked him what I should do. He told me to carry on as planned. The minister, he told me, was Serb and had probably been informed of the intended theme of our discussion.

'He wanted you to know that judges are not as impartial as you might think', he said. 'You will understand shortly.'

I took a chance and addressing the judges asked if any of them would object to discussing the matter of consensus. When no one replied, I asked if I might have a legal opinion on the subject. One of them, a woman, finally spoke, telling me that she was sorry for the way I had been treated by the minister but that I must understand that any legal opinion on this subject would depend on which of them responded to me. She told me that she, as a Serb, believed that the vote in parliament to hold a referendum on independence was illegal, whereas her colleagues, who were Muslim or Croat, would say that the vote was legal. It dawned on me that what she was saying meant that legal opinion in Bosnia could not be definitive because it was always influenced by ethnic considerations. It meant, in effect, that there was no commonly agreed law; Bosnia would appear to have reached a point where people could only interpret the law through the lens of ethnic affiliation. Would it, therefore, be long before morality was to follow suit? I found this rather unsettling and thought that if this were to be the criterion by which the legal profession gave judgement, there seemed little hope for the future.

On leaving the meeting Somun turned to me and said, 'Now you can understand just how difficult and intractable events here in Bosnia are becoming.'

My subsequent report back to ECMM HQ emphasized the need to obtain a definitive ruling on this issue.

On 28 January 1992, I had my first official meeting with Radovan Karadžić. It was held in the office of Biljana Plavšić, a professor of biology at Sarajevo University and one of the Serb members of the collective presidency. The other Serb member of the presidency, Nikola Koljević, a professor of communications at Sarajevo University, also attended. The meeting was held at my request, because I wanted to meet each party leader in order to listen to their views on Bosnia's future and take the opportunity to explain to them what it was that our mission was trying to achieve. Karadžić was a tall, heavy-set man with long, streaky grey hair which he frequently pushed back from his forehead with his hands. He opened the conversation with a compliment, quickly followed by a note of caution: he was pleased to meet me and thanked me for my arranging the meeting, then said that he hoped that I was not being influenced by the untruths told by the 'other parties'. He told me he had seen me at the parliamentary debate on the referendum, so I must be aware of how Izetbegović and his allies had manipulated the vote, I must know that this had been illegal and he hoped I would report this to my superiors in the EC. I thought of tackling him on the issue of the Serbs having created their own assembly, but decided to hold off for now. I viewed the meeting as a public relations exercise with the hope of establishing access to, and exercising some influence over, the Bosnian Serb leadership, something which might be required over the next few months. To ensure he understood my reason for calling the meeting, I explained that I would be meeting the leaders of each of the political parties over the following days. He assured me he was available at any time for discussions. Both Koljević and Plavšić were silent throughout the meeting, obviously content to let Karadžić dictate the conversation. From my experience in dealing with the leadership of the SDS I could see that he clearly called the shots.

A few days later, I met with Stjepan Kljuić, one of the Croat members of the presidency and a founding member of the HDZ. A native of Sarajevo, he was a strong supporter of Bosnia's independence. However, his view was in stark contrast to that of many Croats who favoured President Tudjman's vision of expanding Croatia's territory to take in as much of Bosnia as possible. This was in line with what Milošević and he had agreed at Karadjordjevo in early 1991. Kljuić was a mild-mannered man who enjoyed smoking a pipe and had a penchant for wearing dickey bows. I asked him for his views on the referendum debate. He told me that he feared for the republic's future and that the Serbs would not accept living in Bosnia as a minority if the country was granted independence. He said that the Bosnian Serbs would look to Belgrade and the JNA for assistance. Upon hearing this I asked him if the JNA was not supposed to represent all citizens, not just Serbs. In theory, he replied, it should, but the reality was quite different. I did not feel it was the right time to question him about his views on the recently established 'Herceg-Bosna' or his deputy leader Mate Boban's rather different views on the future status of the Bosnian Croats. I had a high regard for Kljuić but suspected his leadership might well be challenged by the more radical wing of the party.

On 5 February 1992 I received a call from the presidency asking if I could meet with the Chairman of the International Peace Conference on Yugoslavia the following day. At this point I had little knowledge of this peace conference beyond the fact that its Chairman was the former British Foreign Secretary and former NATO Secretary General, Lord (Peter) Carrington. I readily agreed to meet with him, arrived at the presidency the following day with Der and was asked to wait until Carrington had concluded his meeting with Izetbegović. The waiting area was fairly full of officials and the usual media, so I remained in the lobby downstairs. Carrington soon appeared and asked for 'the Irishman Colm Doyle'. We met at the bottom of the stairs, where he was accompanied by Ambassador Henry Wijnaendts of Holland, who had been directly involved in the establishment of the ECMM and now had the role of coordinator in the International Peace Conference. When I introduced myself to Carrington he shook me warmly by the hand and asked if I would accompany him in his car to the airport. I nodded to Der and indicated that he should follow us in our own staff car.

Our car had hardly moved off before Carrington leaned round and said that he had spent the entire day listening to Serbs, Croats and Muslims, all of them telling him what they wanted him to hear. Each side, he said, contradicted the other, and he suspected that they were all being economical with the truth.

'I'm told that you know everything that's going on here', he said. 'So tell me, Doyle, what do you think?'

I wasn't expecting this sudden request and realized I should have had some briefing document prepared. Nevertheless, I quickly gave him my impressions of what I felt was happening based on my own perception and the reports I was receiving on a daily basis from our ECMM teams. He listened without comment, occasionally exchanging looks with Henry Wijnaendts. I had just concluded giving my views when we arrived at the airport. Before he got out of the car he leaned across and told me that he had learned more from me in the previous fifteen minutes than he had from listening all day to Bosnian politicians. He asked me if I would be willing to update the peace conference delegations when they came to Sarajevo over the next few months and requested that I meet with Ambassador José Cutileiro, who would be leading the talks on Bosnia. I agreed, although I realized that I would need to have approval from the ECMM headquarters back in Zagreb. We shook hands again, he thanked me and within minutes he was on his way back to London aboard a private jet. I gave Der the good news that he would have to arrange updated briefings in advance of any conference delegation arriving to Sarajevo. This job, challenging as it was, was becoming more interesting every day.

During the second week of February 1992 I made another visit to Mostar, Trebinje and Neum. The ECMM headquarters in Zagreb had informed me that the new HoM would be visiting Bosnia within a few weeks and that I should make the appropriate arrangements for him to meet with the respective political and military leaderships. I was anxious to bring myself up to date on developments in the Neum region, where we had concerns about the suspected advance of Croatia's influence. As was usual on these trips, I took Der with me, and also Hajrudin Somun from the liaison office. Someone had arranged for us to have a police escort, and just before our departure I noticed Lieutenant Colonel Dimitrijević of the JNA join our convoy. The meetings in both Mostar and Trebinje followed the usual patterns: courtesy visits to the mayors followed by meetings with the party representatives and then a short meeting with the JNA leadership. Positions had not changed, with each side accusing the other of harassment, threats and intimidation. The JNA claimed they were losing the confidence of the population, particularly Muslims and Croats, which was hardly a surprise to us. What was increasingly evident was how entrenched each side had become, and despite our best efforts to persuade them of the dire consequences should compromise not be reached, there seemed to be no turning back. I was becoming very frustrated.

In Neum I was met by a Croat delegation which included Milenko Brkić, the Bosnian Minister of Religious Affairs and acting head of the HDZ since the removal of Stjepan Kljuić. Also in attendance was Mate Boban, who was in the process of taking over the party leadership. I was left in no doubt as to the political aspirations of Boban, which centred on allegiance to Croatia's Tudjman and future integration into a 'Greater Croatia'. Whether Brkić held a similar view I could not determine, but I was surprised to see him in attendance. On our way back towards Mostar our convoy stopped at a crossroads with a signpost indicating a village called Ravno, about 1km away. I had heard rumours of this village having been destroyed and wondered why we had stopped. Der opened the car door saying he would check it out. There seemed to be an argument brewing between Somun, Minister Brkić and the JNA liaison officer. Brkić and Somun were both demanding that we be allowed to visit Ravno, but Dimitrijević was having none of it. He claimed that this visit was not sanctioned and that Ravno was out of bounds, and he insisted that the convoy continue to Mostar. I walked up front to hear for myself. A second JNA jeep had suddenly arrived containing armed soldiers brandishing their weapons. I drew Somun, Brkić and Dimitrijević aside and tried to calm them down. Dimitrijević was furious and accused both Brkić and Somun of exploiting the situation. I could understand his position and calmly pointed out to him that if he insisted, I would not demand to visit the village. I reminded him, however, that the JNA had promised to allow our monitors freedom of movement throughout Bosnia, and that should include Ravno. I told him that if he preferred I could contact General Kukanjac. He paused for a moment, turned on his heel and shouted instructions to the JNA troops. After a few moments of confusion he turned back towards me and in a calm voice informed me that we would be allowed to drive into the village, but that I should not speak with any inhabitants and should only stop in the village square.

The village of Ravno was one of the first to be attacked by the JNA in November 1991. It was a predominately Croat village with a population of about 200 and was almost completely destroyed. Its fate was decided by its location, which was directly on the route taken by the JNA in its attack on Dubrovnik. As we drove slowly and carefully through what remained of the settlement there was not a civilian in sight. Dimitrijević need not have worried about speaking to the inhabitants – there was no one there to speak to, just gutted houses, some still smouldering. It was obvious that those still standing had been torched from the inside. A few soldiers lingered along the streets staring at our slow procession. We drew up behind the lead JNA jeep, which stopped in the square. Opposite us was a Catholic church with its doors and windows blown open. I stepped out of the car and walked through the church door. It was eerily quiet except for the sound of splintering glass underfoot. I could smell the smoke, and a quick look around told its own story of what had happened here. Most of the church had been burned from the inside out, as I had suspected. It seemed such a cowardly act – as if burning this church would somehow erase the faith of its congregation. There seemed little doubt that the destruction had been caused by the JNA, the army supposedly representing all citizens, and the solemn expression on the face of Dimitrijević told its own story. There was really nothing to say, so I got back in the car and we headed away from this dreadful scene.

Back in Mostar I had a quiet word with Somun. I expressed my disappointment at the manner in which I felt I had been used to get access to Ravno. While I realized we were the first 'outsiders' to gain entry to the village, I let it be known that the manner in which permission was obtained was not acceptable and that my position, and that of the ECMM, must not be exploited in such a manner again. I hoped he understood the message. I wondered whether his action was a genuine effort to help me or if he had some other objective in mind. Later that evening, I spoke with Dimitrijević, and when I thanked him for allowing me visit Ravno I think he realized I was not very pleased at the manner in which the permission had come about. Der predicted that the JNA would bring the issue up at our next liaison meeting, which he would be attending, and I had no reason to disagree with him.

The following week I met with Ambassador Cutileiro and Henry Darwin, both representing Carrington's Peace Conference. Cutileiro had special responsibility for Bosnia, while Darwin, a great-grandson of the naturalist Charles Darwin, was a career diplomat and lawyer specializing in international law. While Cutileiro was a short, slightly stocky man, who dressed impeccably, Darwin was very tall and thin and always seemed to be wearing suits whose sleeves were too short. Both had come to Sarajevo for negotiations with party leaders but were anxious to speak with me about the referendum debate and its likely outcome. Cutileiro told me that Lord Carrington would like me to ascertain from both President Izetbegović and Radovan Karadžić what each of them thought might happen after the referendum results were announced. If I could do this within the next two weeks, he said, it would be most helpful. When I agreed to this request, he went on to ask that I should be available in case anything came up at the discussions which might need to be clarified. I briefed them both on my impressions following the assembly debate on the holding of a referendum, adding that I believed the Serbs were totally opposed to any referendum and that without their agreement life might become very difficult in Bosnia.

The talks were to take place at the official presidential residence, the Villa Konak near the city centre. These were to be the first round of talks on the Bosnian constitutional arrangements under Cutileiro's chairmanship. Although I was not directly involved in the talks I was invited to join the delegation the following evening for dinner at a beautiful restaurant in the old city. I had my driver drop me close to the entrance of the old quarter and made my way towards the restaurant. When I arrived I was surprised to see President Izetbegović chatting with Cutileiro and Henry Darwin, and even more surprised that both Karadžić and Boban were also present. I had thought these party leaders could not stand each other, yet all seemed friendly – though I doubted that this would have been the case had the media been present. Security was pretty tight and onlookers were being kept well back. During dinner Cutileiro gave me some detail on the plan for the referendum, informing me that the Conference for Security and Cooperation in Europe (CSCE) would be sending a delegation to observe its conduct. President Izetbegović had a few encouraging words for me, expressing his support for the work of our mission and informing me that the citizens of Sarajevo were well pleased with what we were trying to achieve.

At one stage during the meal Karadžić, who was sitting next to me, was engaging in some amusing banter in Serbo-Croat with the Croat leader Boban. He then turned towards me and said he would explain in English.

'While I was serving a term in prison', he said, 'I came across an acquaintance of mine and asked him what sentence he had received. He answered "ten years"'.

'What were you guilty of?' Karadžić asked.

'Nothing' he replied.

'You must have done something,' said Karadžić. 'You can only be sentenced to eight years if you've done nothing'.

I wasn't sure whether to laugh or just shrug. Instead, I took the chance while he was in such a jovial mood to ask him what he thought might happen in the event of Bosnia being recognized as independent.

He turned very serious and simply said, 'There will be much violence.'

In a further development that week I was informed that Ambassador João Salgueiro was planning to visit Bosnia and would appreciate an opportunity to meet with the president, party leaders and the commander of the JNA. I passed this information on to the presidency, asking for their cooperation in facilitating such a visit. In the schedule that came back from the presidency I noticed that the Serb representative scheduled to meet the ambassador was Momčilo Krajišnik, the speaker of parliament (I assumed that Karadžić was unavailable), even though he and his fellow Serbs had abandoned that institution since the referendum debate. I welcomed this as it would give the Ambassador the opportunity to listen at first hand to the concerns of the Serbs about the referendum.

I was on hand at the airport to welcome Salgueiro and his delegation, which included his Military Adviser, Colonel Don Ethell of Canada, the head of the Irish Delegation, Sean Farrell from the Department of Foreign Affairs and the mission spokesman, Mr de Silva. Salgueiro was a small man, immaculately dressed and fluent in English. He had the habit of frequently fiddling with his tie to make sure it fitted correctly, but he did not smile very much. Following a quick briefing from the monitor team I went through the schedule of visits with him. He questioned me on the forthcoming referendum and asked for my view of the likely outcome. While I was in no position to predict the result, I did indicate that there was a strong possibility of civil unrest should the vote be in favour of independence. I also told him of my concern for the security of our mission and informed him that we were drawing up plans for an evacuation should the situation deteriorate badly. He was certainly surprised at my mentioning this, but I reassured him that in military terms such precautions were normal.

President Izetbegović made the ambassador welcome and gave the usual assurances that the ECMM was playing an important role in Bosnia. He expressed the hope that the mission would be made available to oversee the referendum process and give assistance where necessary to the election monitors that were to be supplied by the CSCE. Having in mind the earlier request of Cutileiro, I asked the president how he thought the Serbs might react if the vote for independence was carried. They would not be very happy, he said, but they would soon come to accept it. He added that he did not believe there would be any violence, and I immediately recalled what Karadžić had said to me when I asked him the same question. I gave Salgueiro a dubious look but held my tongue. Momčilo Krajišnik, however, was more forthright when asked the same question; he stated that Serbs would never accept the results of the referendum and that the ambassador must be aware that the vote to hold it was illegal and contrary to the principle of consensus. Serbs, he said, could not and would not be forced into accepting something they were totally opposed to.

General Kukanjac's changed attitude to the ECMM was evident in the manner in which he received the ambassador and his delegation – he had lined up his senior commanders to shake hands with Salgueiro. As I was the one to carry out the introductions I stood beside him, and each officer saluted before shaking hands with the ambassador; I, in turn, was similarly saluted by each of them. I was quite amused by this and privately wondered what their reaction might be if they knew that in my other life I was simply an Irish Army Commandant. However, I was happy to play the part, and with introductions over, Kukjanac was anxious to let Salgueiro know that the JNA now enjoyed a very good relationship with the ECMM. Salgueiro seemed pleased, but then asked what the role of the JNA would be in the event of this referendum resulting in independence. Kukanjac paused before answering that his army was 'here to protect all the citizens of Bosnia' and that they had no intention of interfering in the referendum process. He cautioned, however, that the JNA would defend themselves if attacked and, ominously, that the 'the future of Bosnia may be decided by this referendum'. Following the meeting Ambassador Salgueiro asked me for my views on what Kukanjac had said. I told him that I thought the JNA would stand back during the referendum, but it would depend on what instructions they might be given from Belgrade. What happened after the vote, I added, might largely depend on what the Serbs do – that was the big question. I cautioned that I did not see the Serbs accepting the referendum result, and as such the ECMM would need to be prepared for any eventuality.

When Salgueiro departed the following day his spokesman, de Silva, stayed on. He told me he wanted to get a feel for what was happening in Sarajevo and asked if he could stick close to me for a few days. I wondered if he was on some kind of assignment but was happy enough to accommodate him. It was not long before he was given a flavour of Bosnian politics. Once again it was Der who supplied the information – apparently the Minister for Information wanted to meet me on an urgent matter and requested that I call his office. The minister in question was Velibor Ostojić, a Serb originally from Foča, whom I had not previously met. Requests for meetings with members of the government usually came through Somun's liaison office at the presidency and not directly from ministers themselves. Somewhat intrigued, I agreed to the meeting and decided to take de Silva and Darko with me.

Ostojić, a hard-line Serb, lost no time on getting to the point. He told me that as Minister for Information he believed that his department should have full responsibility for, and control over, state media, including Sarajevo television. He asked for my support. I was dumbfounded and looked across at de Silva, who appeared equally shocked. I was well aware that the Serbs had little influence in the state television service, which was dominated by Muslims and under the control of the Interior Minister, Alija Delimustafić (a Muslim). With the overall situation in Bosnia rapidly deteriorating, it was obvious that control of the airwaves was becoming increasingly important. I wondered if this move was an attempt by the Serbs to increase their influence. But if Ostojić thought he could rope me into interfering in the internal affairs of Bosnia, he was mistaken. I made it clear to him that the ECMM had no intention of taking sides on the issue of who should have responsibility for Bosnia's media. Such matters were, I told him, for the government of Bosnia to decide, and we had no mandate to become involved. Moreover, I added, I strongly objected to his demanding my organization's support for such an idea. He listened, paused and then changed course. He asked me if I knew that in the previous week he had been attacked outside his apartment. I told him I did not. He went on to say that he believed the attackers were from the Interior Ministry. I asked him if he had reported the incident to the police, but he said he had not – on the basis that they were 'all Muslims'. I informed him that I would ask the Ministry for their side of the story, but I knew there was nothing to be gained by listening to him any further and stood up, nodding to both de Silva and Darko that we should leave. A few days later, when I spoke with Avdo Hebib, the assistant Minister of the Interior about Ostojić's allegation of being assaulted, he just smiled and asked whether I was aware that Ostojić was alleged to have been having an affair with someone's wife.

'That's why he was beaten up', he claimed.

Chapter 8

Blockade

The process of preparing for the referendum to be held on Saturday, 29 February and Sunday, 1 March 1992 gathered pace. All eligible voters were to be asked to declare yes or no to the following question:

> Are you for a sovereign and independent Bosnia and Herzegovina, a state of equal citizens, the peoples of Bosnia and Herzegovina – Muslims, Serbs, Croats, and members of other nations – living in it?

To implement the assembly's decision a 15-member organizing committee was formed under the prime minister, with representation from members of the government, presidency, assembly and electoral commission. The SDS, led by Radovan Karadžić, opposed the referendum, declared it illegal and called on the republic's Serb population to boycott it. This hardly came as a surprise to us given what had occurred in previous parliamentary debates. One view expressed to me about the boycott was that Karadžić feared if Serbs entered the voting booths there would be no control over how they voted – but by boycotting the process the SDS could observe which Serbs did vote and then intimidate or punish them. I was concerned about what might happen in Serb-inhabited areas, despite Karadžić calling on SDS members not to disrupt the referendum proceedings. I directed our teams to observe and report on developments without interfering. We would then provide advice to the election monitors as requested, but that aside, we would have no direct role in the process.

In the light of the leading role being played by the EC in the international response to the Yugoslav crisis, Portugal, which at that time held the EC presidency, coordinated the efforts of the referendum observer teams to ensure that the republic was covered as thoroughly as possible. Ambassador Moriera de Andrade was selected for this task, with representatives from fourteen countries, mostly members of the CSCE, acting as observers. I met with the ambassador and the Referendum Coordinating Committee (RCC) on 27 February 1992, and they seemed to be happy that preparations were proceeding satisfactorily. I had the impression that the government was very keen to ensure that every step was being taken in accordance with set procedures.

Throughout the previous few days both the police and, in some cases, the JNA had been very much in evidence, especially at bridge crossings and road intersections, often with sandbags stacked for protection in case of violence. Tension was on the increase, with a number of violent incidents taking place throughout Bosnia. Roadblocks, set up primarily by armed Serbs, were becoming quite frequent though not, at this stage, widespread. One of our teams reported a fatal shooting near Travnik when a driver attempted to go through a Serb roadblock. With tension rising Der and I discussed the steps we might have to take if the situation became critical, to the point of having to evacuate. Together with the operations cell he had drawn up an evacuation plan, which included pulling in all our regional teams and moving directly to the airport. We had given our views to HQ in Zagreb, suggesting that a suitable aircraft be readily available to airlift all personnel out should the need arise.

I attended a press conference with the Referendum Observer Group (ROG) and Ambassador Andrade on 28 February 1992. The international media were there in large numbers, all looking for answers to the usual questions: will the JNA move in if trouble breaks out? Will Serbs attempt to intimidate voters? Where is trouble expected? What percentage of the population will turn out? I decided to attend in civilian clothing rather than our standard 'whites', to ensure impartiality, even though I was not obliged to do so. Following the press conference I joined the ambassador for lunch in the parliament building's restaurant. Our conversation was general in nature and we both purposely avoided discussing the referendum. Privately, however, I suspect that he, like me, was thinking of little else.

On 'referendum weekend' the voting proceeded, for the most part, smoothly. In addition to the foreign observers, representatives from Bosnian political parties were permitted to monitor the voting and the count. The SDS, having boycotted the process, stayed away. Most polling stations reported that voters generally did take advantage of the opportunity to vote secretly, and voter registration lists caused relatively few difficulties. There was no evidence, as far as I was aware, of anyone outside the polling stations watching to see if any Serbs were disobeying the boycott. Our teams had no approaches of an inappropriate nature made to them by any official observers. However, that all wasn't entirely well was evident from the many roadblocks set up by armed Serbs which had increased in number across the city. Another cause for alarm were incidents of shootings by Serb irregulars. In addition, we received reports from our monitor teams of undisciplined military reservists harassing and even attacking villages on the outskirts of the city.

The polling stations closed on Sunday, 1 March at 7.00 pm and the counting began immediately. Once completed, the polling committees forwarded their results to the regional headquarters and from there to the Election Commission in Sarajevo. I attended the post-election press conference that evening and Ambassador Andrade asked me to sit close to him. I could only surmise that he wished the ECMM to be associated with what was to be considered to have been a successful electoral process. The referendum had been conducted in a manner which permitted the citizens of Bosnia to vote freely and in secret, whether they were for or against a sovereign and independent Bosnia. While the Serbs had boycotted the process, nearly two thirds of eligible voters participated and almost all voted for the republic's independence; this being the case, the result of the referendum was a clear endorsement of the will of most Bosnians. But as I was heading back to my hotel later that night I had no inkling that events were already in train that would change Bosnia's destiny.

Early the following morning, as I entered the hotel dining room alone, a waiter called me over to the window, pointed outside and asked if I noticed anything different. I responded that all looked rather quiet to me. He told me that this was because barricades had been erected all over the city and no traffic was moving. I immediately rushed upstairs to the operations office, where the staff officers were busy on the phones taking down information. Der and Vitor Ferreira informed me that they were receiving reports of armed Serbs establishing checkpoints over much of the city. Shots had been fired and all the main roads into the city had been blocked with buses and trucks. Two ECMM monitors had been trapped in the city overnight. I asked them if they knew anything more, and they told me that there had been a shooting at a Serb wedding in Baščaršija in which the father of the bridegroom was shot dead and the Orthodox priest wounded. It was a lot to take in. I asked Vitor if he knew where the two ECMM monitors were now, and he told me that they were safely on their way back, having been allowed through the checkpoint on the main road near the Hotel Bristol. Much relieved, I asked him to check on all our regional teams to see if these barricades were just confined to Sarajevo.

I contacted Somun at the presidency and asked him for an update. He informed me that Vice President Ganić was chairing a meeting of the *križni stab* (crisis committee) to consider demands which had been made by the Serbs. He asked if I would make my way there to discuss how best to defuse the situation. I gave this some consideration and decided to delay going until I had the opportunity to get a clearer picture of the situation. I convened a meeting with my own operational staff and we tried to figure out exactly what was going on. The first question was to establish why the barricades had been erected. Was it because of the shooting at the wedding, as the Serbs were claiming, or because of the referendum, which seemed more likely? If the shooting was the cause, then how had it been possible to erect these barricades so quickly and in such strategic positions that they effectively cut off the entire city? We concluded that the action must have required detailed planning and could hardly have been a merely reflexive response to a random act of violence. Accordingly, the Serbs would appear to have made the first move against the government of Bosnia, and I was now convinced that Karadžić's warning about the threat of violence should Bosnia be recognized was genuine. I had always feared that it was, though I had hoped otherwise.

I decided I should attempt to make my way to the city centre and see at first hand what was going on. In the meantime, I instructed Vitor to restrict all movement of ECMM personnel for twenty-four hours. Having informed Somun that I would meet Vice President Ganić at the Holiday Inn hotel, I headed into the city with Der, instructing the driver to go slowly, keep the headlights switched on and ensure the EC flag was flying uncovered. As we approached the city I felt very nervous. No one else spoke. The closer we got to the city centre, the less traffic and fewer pedestrians we met. Even the trams, it appeared, were not running. As we neared the crossroads close to the Bristol hotel we were confronted by a roadblock. I ordered the driver to stop about 40m short of it, and as we came to a halt a sudden burst of rifle fire came from a high building to our left, directed over our vehicle, followed by what may have been return fire. Whether we were the target or not, I had no idea who had fired but, given the white vehicle, the EC logo and the flag, they must have known we were ECMM personnel. Anyway, if the intention was to scare us it had the desired effect. I was on the point of ordering the driver to turn back when another vehicle passed us, with a large Red Cross flag draped across its roof. As it proceeded to drive through the checkpoint its passenger stuck a hand out of the window and gestured to us to follow him. I nodded to our driver and we moved forward. No sooner had we passed through than firing started again with some intensity. It was merely the first of a series of unsettling moments.

On reaching the Holiday Inn I found the lobby packed with officials, election observers, police and media. It was a chaotic scene. I located Ejup Ganić huddled with Ambassador Andrade and other officials, and upon seeing me they took me aside to inform me that the situation was very dangerous and that the Serbs had given the government a list of demands on which they sought agreement before they would lift the barricades. I asked what their demands were and was told that they required all activities regarding international recognition to be halted with immediate effect. I asked if I could be given a copy of these demands, and they agreed. I also asked if I could meet Karadžić, but was told that he was not in Sarajevo but in Belgrade. The SDS's crisis committee was, however, in the hotel, accompanied by armed guards. I asked if the government had responded in any way to the demands and was told that they had conveyed to the Serbs their willingness to negotiate, but only after the international observers were given free passage to the airport, where an aircraft was waiting to evacuate them. They asked if I could provide assistance in the negotiations. I sought clarification first on the role of the JNA, to which Ganić responded that he was unsure. I turned to Der and asked him for his view. His assessment was that, given the seriousness of the situation, we would have to assist with the evacuation, and that the ECMM should lead the convoy. I agreed but felt we should attempt to make contact with the Serb side and the JNA, so that the barricades could be lifted to allow safe passage to the airport.

As Der headed in the direction of the office of the hotel manager, Danilo Dursun, to find out on which floor the SDS crisis committee was located, Lieutenant Colonel Dimitrijević, who had just arrived in the hotel, made his way over to where I was standing. I briefed him quickly on the situation. He was keen to stress that the JNA had not been involved in any way with events overnight. I told him that I fully accepted this but that I could use the help of the JNA to escort the international observers to the airport and would need to move before darkness fell. He immediately promised to provide transport for the election observers and agreed to accompany the convoy to the airport. I knew that, under the circumstances, we were going to need all the help we could get.

In order to determine the level of resolve of those Serbs manning the barricades, I decided to chance approaching one of them in the hope that we might open some dialogue which might lead to the roadblocks being dismantled. Der arrived back to tell me that we would have to negotiate directly with the Serbs in order to get the barricades lifted. This led me to believe that Karadžić was not on hand to make this decision personally, so I turned to Ambassador Andrade and asked if he would accompany me to the barricades to talk with those in control. With his agreement, I then looked for a Serb to join us. To my surprise, Ostojić suddenly appeared at my shoulder and offered to accompany us. He joined us in our approach toward the main barricade, which was located just beyond the parliament building across the bridge at Skenderija. I wanted to ensure that we were fully visible to those manning the barricade so as to avoid any surprises or mistakes. There was no vehicular traffic moving, which was not surprising given the tangible tension that had descended upon Sarajevo. We drove very slowly towards the bridge and I had our driver stop the car in the middle of the road, close to the bridge on the north side of the Miljacka River. Though there was no traffic, we could see many people crouched behind windows and doors, peering anxiously at the scene. It was an anxiety I wholly shared.

With Der alongside me and Ambassador Andrade and Minister Ostojić walking behind, I moved out on to the bridge and proceeded slowly and carefully across it. I could now clearly see those manning the barricade, all armed with weapons pointing in our direction. As I made my way closer to them, my attention was drawn to a figure crouched low and moving in the same direction parallel to me at the side of the bridge. I immediately recognized Martin Bell, the BBC war correspondent. What in God's name was he up to? He caught my eye and seemed to indicate that I should carry on and ignore him. I just hoped he was not going to get us killed. We moved forward again, ever so slowly, and as we neared the far side of the bridge a figure armed and wearing some type of headgear raised his hand for us to stop. We complied. He must have recognized me because he suddenly addressed me by name and called me forward. With Ostojić on hand to translate, I explained to him that while I understood the concerns of the Serbs, blockading the city was serving no useful purpose. I then informed him that the demands of the Serbs were being considered by the government and suggested that, as a gesture of goodwill, he might lift the barricade. This, I told him, would go a long way towards easing the tension. His reply, however, was quick and brusque. He told me that while he respected the efforts of the ECMM, the barricades could only be dismantled on the personal order of Radovan Karadžić. I expected nothing more, so I thanked him for listening and we moved back to the other side of the bridge. A quick glance back over my shoulder revealed Martin Bell interviewing the same Serb, hoping, no doubt, to get an exclusive for the BBC.

We headed back to the Holiday Inn again, where preparations were ongoing to gather the international election observers together and transport them to the airport. It was all pretty chaotic, but Dimitrijević had returned with two JNA buses, which were now parked outside the hotel. Nobody seemed to know the exact number of international observers that had been provided to oversee the referendum, or indeed how many were supposed to be staying at the Holiday Inn. I was told that some of them even had family members, including children, with them. In addition, it had been decided that other foreigners who wished to leave Sarajevo were to be permitted to travel on the buses. One of the observers, Thomas Hutson, a US Embassy official based in Belgrade, said he would try to get me the official number of election monitors and went off to attempt to garner that information.

Darkness was now falling, and with it came added concern at having to go through the city at night. Der was only too aware of this and urged me to move as quickly as possible. I told him that we should give it another thirty minutes, then we would move regardless. Thirty minutes later, as the convoy was about to leave, Tomas Hutson came running out of the hotel, telling me he could not find any more observers and that hopefully everybody was aboard. Dimitrijević then arrived in his staff car and we briefly talked about how, in the event of being stopped, we should deal with armed elements manning the checkpoints. We agreed that he and I would negotiate with them jointly, in the hope they would see reason and allow the international observers through unimpeded. I had no idea whether the checkpoints had been alerted to expect our arrival, and if Dimitrijević knew he was certainly keeping this to himself. When I asked how many checkpoints there were between the hotel and airport, I was told six or seven. I was very apprehensive and could see the worried look on Der's face. We both knew we were heading into the unknown, and in the dark, too, something neither of us would normally have attempted.

We moved off at a slow pace. As I was depending on Dimitrijević to take the best route to the airport, my mind was focused on how to negotiate our way through the checkpoints, calculating the possible scenarios and risks. We did not have to wait long before we were stopped. As Dimitrijević got out of his staff car I followed suit and asked him to explain to everyone that the buses were under the protection of the JNA and EC monitors and request that we should be allowed pass through. Dimitrijević translated and after a few more minutes of discussion there was a shaking of hands and we were permitted to proceed. A further two checkpoints were similarly negotiated, although it was becoming increasingly obvious that some of those we encountered were under the influence of alcohol. This worried me, but we had little choice but to press on. The next checkpoint was different – as we approached, shots were suddenly fired, directed over our vehicles but close enough to cause alarm and provoke some screams from the first bus. We all stopped, and as Dimitrijević began to speak to the checkpoint personnel, I stepped aboard the first bus to see if anybody had been injured. Fortunately, nobody had been hit, but a few people were crying and understandably terrified. As I went forward to join Dimitrijević I passed one of the Serbs who was pointing a rifle in my direction. When I glanced over at him he calmly drew a finger across his throat and leered at me. He was obviously not sober which alarmed me all the more.

It took almost thirty minutes to negotiate our passage through this checkpoint, and we still had a further two to come. Near the final checkpoint more shots were fired, which I assumed were the result of drunken militants firing randomly rather than directed at us. I knew this checkpoint would be close to the airport, which was located at Butmir, a mainly Muslim-inhabited area. Despite more random shooting we made it through after the usual negotiations, and to the great relief of all the airport complex came into view. The aircraft was all fuelled up and ready to go. We waited until the plane was airborne, and then I went to thank Dimitrijević. He cautioned me to be wary on our return to the city, because the checkpoints were manned by individuals who had been drinking heavily. He told me to stay close behind him.

We followed him closely through the first few checkpoints without incident and broke off to return to our base at the Hotel Bosna in Ilidža. Although I was exhausted after the day's events I had a feeling, given what we had accomplished, of quiet satisfaction and huge relief. Der agreed that we had taken a gamble in attempting to evacuate the international election observers at night and under dangerous conditions, but it had worked. We learned later that as we were negotiating our way through the checkpoints a candlelit peace march involving an estimated 1,000 citizens led to the lifting of some of the barricades, although one marcher was killed and two others injured when shot by a barricade guard.

An envelope had been handed into the hotel addressed to me and containing the demands of the Serbs that I had requested from Ganić earlier. It also included a hastily prepared statement from the presidency in response to these demands which was due to be published in the following morning's daily paper, *Oslobodjenje*. Apart from the reference to international recognition, the demands called for a review of the Ministry of Interior's organization, no doubt prompted by Ostojić, the immediate arrest of those responsible for the killing at the Serb wedding and a division of Sarajevo TV into ethnic channels. In response, the presidency agreed to arrest the persons responsible for the killing of the Serb and also confirmed that the referendum results 'would not prejudice the structure of BH currently under discussion by the EC'; and on the question of Sarajevo TV, the Serb demand would be considered. I spent a late hour preparing a report to the ECMM Head of Mission with my comments attached.

The following morning, as a result of the lifting of some barricades, the city appeared to be returning to some degree of normality. However, later that same morning, we began to receive reports that Muslims were now erecting defensive barricades. It would seem there were widespread rumours that 'Chetniks' were heading towards Sarajevo under the leadership of Željko Raznjatović, aka 'Arkan', the commander of the feared Serb paramilitary unit known as the 'Tigers'. While we were unable to substantiate this, it did not surprise us greatly, given the sense of fear and suspicion that now prevailed throughout the city. In the afternoon a meeting was held through the offices of Sarajevo TV between the presidency, the SDS and the JNA at which agreement was reached to mount joint military and police patrols, the police to comprise both Serbs and Muslims. This arrangement seemed to calm Muslim fears and eased tension within the city. However, our team reports from the regions indicated heightened tension throughout Bosnia. It was becoming more difficult for these teams to move freely, something which was essential in obtaining an independent view of the ever-changing political landscape. I had an uneasy feeling that with international recognition now almost certain the consequences for Bosnia would be both fearful and bloody.

At our normal daily briefing the following morning we discussed the implications of Bosnia's sovereignty being recognized. We were concerned about what the Serbs might do in the event of formal recognition and what the consequences might be for the ECMM. It was decided that an evacuation plan would be put in place so that all our personnel could be withdrawn at short notice should the circumstances demand it. Der Cogan and his operations team were tasked to prepare for this eventuality, with emphasis on withdrawal routes for our teams and the availability of C-130 aircraft to evacuate through the airport. I then recommended to ECMM headquarters in Zagreb that we should be given notice about when recognition might be confirmed.

The UN had maintained a small peacekeeping presence in the former Yugoslavia since January 1992. The United Nations Military Liaison Officers Yugoslavia (UNMLOY) had been established with representatives in both Belgrade and Zagreb. It consisted of about fifty unarmed military officers, some of them Irish, and was commanded by an Australian, Colonel John Wilson. These were the forerunners of a UN force which was in the process of being established, to be named the United Nations Protection Force (UNPROFOR). One of the problems in establishing any UN peacekeeping force is the time it takes between it being sanctioned by a United Nations Security Council resolution and getting 'boots on the ground'. UNPROFOR was no different. As an interim measure, military personnel were provided from existing missions and sent to Yugoslavia as liaison officers. They maintained close liaison with the leadership of the warring factions in both Serbia and Croatia, paving the way for UNPROFOR's arrival.

While my offer to meet those who were deployed to Banja Luka had been turned down, I still hoped to meet with Colonel John Wilson to see if we could be of assistance to his mission. I knew John quite well, having served with him in Lebanon during my tour of duty there with UNTSO in 1984. Among the small group of United Nations observers deployed to Sarajevo was Commandant Eddie O' Brien, whom I knew well. He had been in my junior class in the Cadet School, so I took the chance of inviting him to my hotel for a chat. Over coffee we discussed the ongoing situation and spoke about the impending deployment of UNPROFOR. I told him that the ECMM were ready to help in any way that we could. He seemed genuinely pleased to hear this and promised to pass on my offer to his boss, Colonel Wilson. However, I somehow got the impression that the UN was happier to 'do its own thing' and keep its distance from the monitor mission, which I found both strange and unsettling.

A week after the referendum, I was summoned late in the evening by the duty officer to take a phone call from the JNA. It was Dimitrijević, who rather alarmingly warned me of a possible terrorist attack on our hotel. I asked him where the threat had come from, but he could offer little in the way of clarification. He did say, however, that those who might attempt the attack could possibly be wearing JNA uniforms. I quickly got hold of Vitor and asked him to check downstairs to see if our security detail was in place. This detail was provided for on a daily basis by the Ministry of the Interior and comprised about half a dozen uniformed and armed police. I also asked Der to alert all our regional teams. Vitor returned quickly to tell me that there was no one downstairs and that it seemed as if the police had all been pulled out. I had a bad feeling about the situation so immediately told the duty officer to contact the Deputy Interior Minister, Avdo Hebib, who was responsible for our security. Luckily he was still in his office, and when I gave him the information I had received from Dimitrijević he assured me that we were quite safe. I asked him where our security detail was. He seemed to have been caught off guard, but after a moment's silence came back with a promise to investigate. I pushed him into promising that a security detail be sent to the hotel immediately and that he would meet me the following morning. While the police security was restored later that evening, I never got to find out what exactly happened and whether the threat was real or just an attempt at unsettling our routine. It was a reality check, however, and a lesson that we should not take anything for granted here in Bosnia.

Following these troubling events, my first meeting with the newly arrived headquarters staff of UNPROFOR took place on 16 March. It was a few days before I was to depart for home and I wanted to give as much support as I could to the Force Commander, Lieutenant General Satish Nambiar of India, and his Deputy, Major General Phillipe Morillon of France. Together with the Force Chief of Staff, Canadian Brigadier General Lewis MacKenzie and the Head of Civil Affairs, Cedric Thornberry from Ireland, we all attended a reception hosted by the Bosnian government to welcome the UN force. The initial HQ was to be located in the Holiday Inn hotel.

There were many dignitaries present, including government ministers, to wish UNPROFOR well. I took the chance to invite Cedric Thornberry to a St Patrick's Day celebration, which we had planned for the following evening. He was pleased to accept.

On St Patrick's Day morning I went to meet with Borisa Starović, who had asked to see me before I left Bosnia. I had admired him very much from the time he had facilitated my holding of a student forum at the university, and I wanted to thank him for his support and friendship. We met in his small office and over a cup of coffee he spoke to me of his wishes for Sarajevo. He lamented the state of affairs across Bosnia and told me of the history of the city of Sarajevo, before presenting me with a book about the city which contained many old photographs from his grandfather's time. He wanted me to have it, he said, so that I might understand more about 'the history of this unusual place'. I left Borisa's office feeling the better for having met and listened to him.

The Guinness tasted good that evening. A dozen bottles of 'Paddy' adorned the table, green napkins had been acquired and all one hundred people at the function, even the Muslims, Croats and Serbs, swore they had Irish connections. Johannes van Baal, the Dutch monitor who on reporting for duty had tried to persuade me he should be my deputy, had managed to type the words of all the songs on my only CD, the Furey Brothers. He placed a typed copy on each table, obviously hoping that all would be converted, as he had been, to their music. I asked him why he had told me that he was to be my deputy when he had first reported. He responded that the Dutch deputy chief of mission in Zagreb had suggested that he try to persuade me to accept this, as it was known that the Irish duo of Doyle and Cogan were running the show in Bosnia. The deputy chief wanted, he said, 'to break up the Irish Mafia'. I asked him how he felt about this and he said, with a wide grin on his face, that he was 'damn proud to be working with the Irish Mafia'.

While 17 March is an important day in Ireland's calendar, this day in 1992 became a critical one for Bosnia as well. While we were celebrating our national day in Sarajevo, party leaders were preparing to sign an agreement in Lisbon which proposed ethnic power-sharing on all administrative levels and the devolution of central government. All Bosnian districts would be classified as Muslim, Serb or Croat under this plan, even those areas where no ethnic majority was evident. The agreement was signed by all three leaders on 18 March, but it was to be short-lived – ten days after signing it President Izetbegović withdrew his support.

My last few days in Sarajevo were busy with farewell visits to government officials and members of the presidency and with media interviews. I spent a good part of this time briefing my successor, Major Antonio dos Santos of Portugal, and arranging meetings for him with the party leaders and government ministers. I was happy that Vitor was staying on as deputy chief which was a big advantage for dos Santos. Continuity of leadership was, of course, important, and I knew that Vitor had a good handle on the situation. Der and I were scheduled to depart on 22 March 1992 but we had an important engagement to fulfil before we left. Both of us were invited to Darko's wedding on the day before we were due to leave. His fiancée, Sanja Lazić, worked as a lawyer in Sarajevo and, like Darko, her father was Serb and her mother, Muslim. I felt privileged to have been invited to the ceremony. The reception was held in the JNA Club and it was wonderful to be able to relax among their families and friends and to put aside Bosnia's troubles for a short time. Darko's father Dušan came over to my table and, greeting me profusely, positioned another bottle of whiskey in front of me with a smile. As Darko's colleagues from the presidential liaison team, Harjudin, Vera and Nijaz, were among the guests, I had the chance to thank them for all their help and guidance. I also thanked Lieutenant Colonel Dimitrijević of the JNA for assisting me on many visits and hoped he would soon be home in Belgrade. I decided to leave the reception earlier than most and I slipped away from these happy people with mixed emotions. I was grateful for their hospitality, friendship and undaunted spirit and I hoped they would all enjoy a bright and peaceful future – but part of me feared that this would not materialize.

My initial arrival in Yugoslavia had been in the back of a truck, but I was dammed if I was leaving the same way, so I had contacted Ambassador Salgueiro a few days before my departure and persuaded him that I should depart by a more comfortable mode of transport. Having said goodbye to

(*Above*) Colm Doyle, about to board an ECMM helicopter on his first day of duty, 4 October 1991.

(*Below and overleaf*) The mined and blocked bridge linking Bosanski Brod in Bosnia and Slavonski Brod in Croatia which my team and I crossed to mediate on 21 October 1991.

2226

(*Above*) Communication dishes on the balcony of our operations office.

(*Below*) My first day as Bosnian Head of Mission, with my staff in Sarajevo, 26 November 1991.

(*Above*) Introducing President Alija Izetbegović to Antonio dos Santos at a reception for the incoming UNPROFOR on 20 March 1992. On my right is Ejup Ganić, Vice President.

(*Below*) Meeting with Lord Carrington in his office at Christie's, London, 7 April 1992, the day I was appointed as his Personal Representative for Bosnia.

(*Above*) The Peace Conference negotiating team at our hotel in Lisbon, 22 May 1992. From left to right: Jola Vollebregt, secretary, Colm Doyle, Ambassador Jose Cutileiro, Henry Darwin, Tadeu Soares.

(*Below*) Lord Carrington, having boarded an UNPROFOR armoured car, is escorted from Sarajevo airport to the Presidency on 3 July 1992. I took the photograph from another armoured car.

(*Above*) Testifying at the Karadžić trial in the Hague in 2010.

(*Left*) Being questioned by the media at a press conference in Belgrade after I was evacuated from Sarajevo by helicopter, 12 May 1992.

(*Below*) Outside the War Crimes Tribunal building in the Hague during my evidence at the Karadžić trial, 27 May 2010.

mission colleagues, Der and I headed to the airport, where an aircraft was waiting on the tarmac. We settled on board, opened a couple of beers and drank a toast to Bosnia and the ECMM. I felt very fortunate that I had had someone like Der by my side over the previous few months. He was never shy about giving his opinion or recommendation, which was what I needed. However, once I made a decision he always accepted it without question and would implement it faithfully. His support was total. As we flew out of Sarajevo I looked over the red-tiled rooftops which merged quickly with the surrounding mountains and forests. I began to shake off the chains of command and responsibility and I silently toasted the peoples of Bosnia. I couldn't help but wonder what fate lay in store for them but I thought I would never return to this place. I never imagined then that I would come back so soon.

At the HQ in Zagreb we briefed the HoM, and the delegation heads gave our assessment of the current situation. We predicted a difficult period for Bosnia and a testing time for the ECMM. I was asked about the presence of UNPROFOR and pointed out that it did not have a mandate for Bosnia; though its presence there might act as a deterrent, I considered this would be minimal. I went on to say that each side seemed bent on following its own course: the Serbs under Karadžić followed the Belgrade agenda and most of the Croats under Boban took their orders from Tudjman. Muslims were caught in the middle. Later that evening over dinner with the ambassador, Der and I were able to give him details of our efforts to evacuate the referendum observers which he was very keen to learn about. He told us that our actions had generated some very positive comments from the EC, before adding that he had received a phone call from Ambassador Cutileiro earlier in the day. Apparently, he wanted to talk with me in the evening. He didn't elaborate, so I was left wondering what this might be about. I was pacing my room when the phone rang. It was Cutileiro wishing to thank me for the 'invaluable service' I had given to Lord Carrington's Peace Conference and for the manner in which I had led the ECMM in Bosnia over the previous few months. He had only just heard that I was finishing my tour of duty and wished to express his own appreciation for the work I had done. I was very flattered that he had taken the time to contact me, and I thanked him for his remarks. I got the impression, however, that he wanted to say something further, but he hesitated and, after wishing me well, hung up.

I was woken the following morning by someone banging at my door. I opened it to find Ambassador Salgueiro's personal assistant asking me to get dressed quickly and come to Salgueiro's office. I had no idea what this was about but hastily made tracks. He met me as I entered and, holding his hand over the phone's mouthpiece, whispered to me that I should be very careful how I answered the request I was about to hear. Completely baffled, I grasped the phone, with no idea whom I would be addressing. It was José Cutileiro. He apologised for contacting me so early in the morning but said that Lord Carrington had instructed him to ask if I would be interested in joining the peace conference as his personal representative for Bosnia. He acknowledged that this might come as quite a surprise – indeed, I was completely flabbergasted by this sudden and unexpected development. After a pause I told him that I would have to inform the military authorities at home. Because I was a serving officer of the Irish Defence Forces, the assignment, I told him, would have to be approved by them. Moreover, I would have to talk to my wife. He said he understood completely, before adding that the EC would arrange the secondment and all additional details; but they did need to know if I was willing to take up the offer. The post's duration, I was told, would be about two months, but it might last longer, depending on developments. Lord Carrington had asked that I respond immediately. I told him that my immediate reaction was to say yes. Expressing his delight, Cutileiro informed me that Lord Carrington would phone me in a few days and probably request that we all meet in London.

As soon as I got back to my room I phoned Grainne to let her know. I could sense her unease at the prospect of my being away from home for a further period. I felt guilty, but the adrenalin rush pushed family considerations aside. My association with Bosnia, which I thought just a day ago was coming to an end, was about to be extended, and as I flew home the following day my thoughts were concentrated on what the future might hold rather than on what the past had brought. I wondered if I had made the right decision.

Chapter 9

From Soldier to Diplomat

It was at the EC Foreign Ministers' meeting in Brussels on 27 August 1991 that the decision was made to convene an International Conference on Yugoslavia. The objective of the conference was to bring about a peaceful solution to the Yugoslav crisis, and it would bring together the Yugoslav federal presidency, government and the presidents of the Yugoslav republics on the one hand, and the president of the European Council, the European Commission and representatives of member states on the other. Lord (Peter) Carrington, a former British Foreign Secretary who had also served as Secretary General of NATO, was appointed chairman. The mandate given to the conference was based on three conditions: there should be a genuine cease-fire; none of the republics would be recognized as independent except as part of an overall settlement agreed by all republics; and there should be no change of boundaries except by consent and by peaceful means.

From the outset the conference was faced with exceptional challenges. It commenced its work without any cease-fire, partly because there was an expectation that the establishment of the conference in itself would be conducive to halting the conflict. However, it did not have this desired result, thereby complicating its task. The nature of the conference changed as a consequence of the EC's invitation to the republics to apply for recognition. Carrington had suddenly lost his only weapon and thereafter had no real leverage which he could bring to bear. However, he persisted, constantly shuttling between capitals trying to persuade leaders to see reason and agree on compromise. The 18 March agreement on Bosnia was one such compromise, but like so many others it failed to see the light of day.

To be invited by Lord Carrington to join this peace effort was something I had never envisaged. That a middle-ranking Irish officer was about to be projected into the cauldron of Balkan politics seemed highly unlikely, but it was all because this distinguished British diplomat thought I could make a contribution. I could scarcely believe it, yet I knew it was something I could not turn down. While I should have been thanking my family for tolerating my absence over the previous six months, I found myself waiting for Carrington's phone call. A week after I arrived home, the call came from London through Paul Sizeland, Carrington's conference cabinet secretary, who asked me to hold for his boss. Thereafter, arrangements were made for me to fly to London the following day.

The Berkshire Hotel in Oxford Street was a far cry from the Hotel Bosna in Sarajevo, and although its opulence was impressive, I had little appetite for it. I had knots in my stomach, and as I walked along Oxford Street, clutching my briefcase, I wondered if I had made a mistake in agreeing to work for Lord Carrington. I thought I could be out of my depth and that it might have been wiser to settle for a return to military service. I had not told my superiors in the Defence Forces that I was flying to London for these talks, preferring instead to hold off informing them until after this meeting. These thoughts were racing through my mind as I approached Lord Carrington's office, which was located at the head office of Christie's, the famous international auction house on King Street of which he was chairman. I was met at the entrance by a suitably uniformed concierge, who led me up an impressive circular staircase.

As I walked into his office Lord Carrington rose to greet me warmly, and I immediately felt at ease. With him were two of his advisers on Bosnia, Ambassador José Cutileiro, the Portuguese diplomat, and Henry Darwin, recently retired from the FCO, both of whom also welcomed me. Also present was a photographer from the *Independent* newspaper who took some pictures of Lord Carrington and me sitting together. Once the photo session was completed he got straight to the point, telling me that he was very pleased I was willing to assist and that I should know that I had made a big impression among the different ethnic parties in Bosnia who all held me 'in high regard'. He went on to explain the role he had in mind for me. In essence, I was to act as Carrington's personal representative for Bosnia and be based in Sarajevo. He stressed that my knowledge of the leaders of the government and political parties would be of great benefit to the conference. I was tasked with keeping in touch with political leaders, impressing on them the need to avoid conflict and carrying forward the reconciliation of different opinions. I would be required to report on developments regularly.

Conscious that the Defence Forces had no idea that I was attending this meeting, I politely asked that a request for my secondment be sent to the Irish government. Lord Carrington assured me that this would be done by the Portuguese in their capacity as holders of the EC presidency. José Cutileiro then informed me that I should submit my reports through him and added that he would be the main channel of communication with the conference. He also mentioned that I should maintain contact with the headquarters of both the ECMM and UNPROFOR. A general discussion followed on the situation in Bosnia, which had been given recognition the previous day by the EC and from where an escalation in fighting was already being reported. It was requested that I be ready to return to Sarajevo by the end of that week.

When I stood to leave, Lord Carrington shook my hand, wished me well and impressed upon me that I would be 'representing Europe'. He also cautioned that because I was well known in Bosnia there might be some people there who would wish to see me harmed. He fully accepted, he said, that as a soldier I could take good care of myself, but he warned me that in this new diplomatic role I should take no unnecessary risks. He added that the ECMM would be instructed to supply me with whatever support I might require and the presidency would provide me with suitable accommodation. I was told that there would be 'many rounds of negotiations and peace talks' convened over the coming months.

After the meeting ended, José Cutileiro and Henry Darwin accompanied me downstairs. I told them that I would require written verification of my appointment before the Irish government could sanction my return to Bosnia and said that I believed it would be much better for me to be accommodated in the same hotel as the ECMM in Sarajevo. Cutileiro promised to attend to the matter of my secondment by way of a letter to David Andrews, the Irish Minister for Foreign Affairs, straight away, but I wasn't convinced that everything would go smoothly within the few short days remaining. Anyway, I was informed that a flight to Sarajevo would be arranged for me in the coming days and that I should first fly to Paris and await further instructions.

Before I returned home, Henry invited me to lunch at his club, which turned out to be the rather posh Athenaeum in Pall Mall. Its membership includes cabinet ministers, peers and senior civil servants, and Henry was very proud of being a member. He told me that his great-grandfather, the celebrated naturalist Charles Darwin, had also been a member back in the 1830s. Sipping a drink in the luxurious surroundings of the smoking room, Henry gave me an account of his career, which had been spent in the legal branch of the FCO; having retired in 1989, he was invited to provide advice to Lord Carrington in his capacity as chairman of the peace conference. He told me he was also chairman of the working group on 'succession issues'. He seemed to enjoy the challenges this presented and appeared determined to find solutions to the many legal problems with which he was confronted. After a very pleasant lunch I took a taxi back to the airport. I had enjoyed meeting these three eminent people, and I hoped their confidence in me would not prove misplaced.

Three days later, I caught an early flight to Charles de Gaulle airport. Cutileiro had phoned previously to inform me that I needed to be there by 11.00am and that I should take a taxi to another airport, Le Bourget, a short distance away. I was rather curious to know what this might mean but, time being short, I just followed directions. I quickly learned that in order to get a taxi to take me to Le Bourget I should not inform the driver where I wanted to go until after my luggage was in the boot and I was sitting inside the vehicle. The first three taxis refused to take me when I gave them my destination – it seemed they only wanted passengers who were headed for the city. When the fourth taxi came alongside, I threw my case in the boot and only informed the driver of my destination after I was sitting inside. He wasn't very pleased but had little choice but to take me there. When I arrived I was met by an official who brought me into a waiting room, offered coffee and told me that Cutileiro and his party would be there soon. After about twenty minutes Cutileiro arrived, accompanied by Henry Darwin, Jola Vollebregt, the senior conference administrator and Tadeu Soares, the executive secretary. Cutileiro wasted no time in letting us know that because of the deterioration of conditions in Sarajevo (following the country's recognition by the EC on 6 April and the subsequent outbreak of armed conflict), it was essential to broker a cease-fire. He emphasized that it was important that I attend talks with the party leaders and said I should provide him with the benefit of my knowledge.

Then we walked on to the tarmac and boarded a private Lear jet for our flight to Sarajevo. Flying on a private plane was not common practice for me. In fact, this was to be my first experience of such travel, and although I was quite excited by the prospect, the reality was rather disappointing. The aircraft was very small, cramped and noisy. Ambassador Cutileiro, who was quite short in stature, fitted easily into his seat, and while I myself had no great difficulty in doing likewise, poor Henry Darwin, who was over six feet tall, could only sit with his legs dangling out at an angle. The steward had literally to hop over them. The noise level was such that conversation was kept to a minimum. In any event, most of my thoughts were centred on what might lie before us.

Although it was only just over two weeks since I had left Bosnia, everything had changed. Of course, knowing what had taken place since my departure, I shouldn't have been surprised, but the reality was, nevertheless, quite shocking. Within two days of the EC's recognition of Bosnia as an independent state, armed conflict had taken hold. The JNA had quickly moved to take control of key locations and installations, including Sarajevo airport. Armed Serbs overwhelmed the poorly equipped government troops and took over large tracts of territory, beginning with attacks on Muslim villages in eastern Bosnia. These forces comprised mainly Serb military, paramilitary and police, with suspected support from the JNA. They attacked towns and villages in a systematic and standard fashion: houses and apartments were ransacked or burned; civilians were rounded up and in many cases killed; men were separated from their families and forcibly removed to prison camps; many women were abused or raped; there was forced migration of whole communities, mainly Muslim. The term 'ethnic cleansing' was become increasingly commonplace.

While we had flown out of Paris in brilliant sunshine, our aircraft touched down in a wet, cold and gloomy Sarajevo. The conditions seemed to match the atmosphere. We were met by a cluster of reporters and photographers. I stood back to let the ambassador do the talking, but a few of them directed questions at me. In the main they were interested in why I had returned to Sarajevo so soon, how long I would be staying and what my view was of the situation there. I was saved from the onslaught of questioning by my successor at the ECMM, Major Antonio dos Santos, who grabbed me by the arm and led me to his vehicle. He was accompanied by the Presidential Head of Protocol, Mile Akmadžić, who was on hand to escort our delegation to the familiar surroundings of the Hotel Serbia in Ilidža, where the negotiations were scheduled to take place. I nodded to the ambassador, indicating that I would travel with dos Santos, and we moved off without further delay.

Dos Santos then briefed me on the situation, explaining that during the previous few days Serb policemen had attacked police stations in the city as well as the Ministry of the Interior training school, and the Bosnian presidency had subsequently declared a state of emergency. This resulted in a show of defiance from a large gathering of peace demonstrators who rallied in protest. As the throng approached the parliament, two young women were killed on the Vrbanja Bridge. The parliament was then occupied overnight by demonstrators, though the majority of them continued their protests outside. The following day, unidentified gunmen, suspected of being Serb snipers located in the nearby Holiday Inn hotel now occupied by Radovan Karadžić's SDS 'crisis committee', opened fire on the marchers killing six people. While the Bosnian government had hoped the international community would deploy a peacekeeping force following recognition, it did not appear in time to prevent war breaking out. UNPROFOR was, after all, still in its embryonic stage.

It was very obvious, as we headed out of the airport, that the JNA now controlled the entire complex. Military checkpoints had been erected and armoured vehicles were clearly visible. Dos Santos informed me that the only flights in and out, apart from ours, belonged to the JNA, who were evacuating military families only, though there were queues of people desperately trying to get out of the city. As we drove through the rain towards Ilidža I could see how things had changed. There were signs of random checkpoints having been set up, though none were manned, there was an absence of moving traffic in the area and few people were to be seen. Antonio informed me that the city had now pretty well shut down. Most roads leading to the different 'ethnic areas' were blockaded, with access under the control of paramilitaries, most of whom had little or no military training. It was a tremendous change from when I had left the city a few weeks previously, and I had an uneasy feeling about what we were seeing. I wondered if there was any realistic hope of progress.

Our arrival at the Hotel Serbia was greeted by another assembly of cameras and reporters, all clamouring to interview Cutileiro. He informed the gathering that our delegation was about to commence negotiations with each of the political parties with the aim of achieving a cease-fire. As I stood at the back, Martin Bell of the BBC approached me. He asked me directly whether I was aware that some 20,000 refugees, mostly Muslims, had been forced from their homes in eastern Bosnia and were en route, largely on foot, to Tuzla. I was completely taken aback by this sudden question, particularly as he must have been aware that I had only just arrived back in the city. It was, however, evident that he wanted me to do something about it. I asked him if he had any evidence and he said that he had it all on camera. So I agreed to raise it with Karadžić during our discussions and said I would respond to him thereafter. I think he was a bit surprised that I agreed to do this so readily, but it seemed the logical thing to do. I was aware how much these leaders were willing to lie to suit their own particular purpose, my first six months in Bosnia having taught me that. Letting Karadžić know that there was television evidence of such a large group of refugees might give him pause for thought.

Throughout that afternoon discussions were held separately with the leaderships of the three parties. This was a delicate logistical challenge, bearing in mind that they were not on speaking terms and did not wish to be seen together. We had to be careful in deciding which delegation we should meet with first and in what order the others should follow – the last thing we needed was for any of them to feel insulted, and Jola Vollebregt's diplomatic skills were fully tested in this regard. I attended these meetings as an observer rather than a participant. Cutileiro chaired the discussions, constantly urging the leaders to show flexibility and compromise, his core objective being to reach agreement on a cease-fire, after which negotiations could follow. After each group left the room we held a short review of what we felt was achieved and considered what approach we might take with the next party. I was flattered to receive a welcome back from each party leader, with a promise from each of cooperation in my latest position as Lord Carrington's personal representative. I had told Cutileiro of Martin Bell's question to me earlier, and he suggested I take it up with Karadžić during the discussions.

I had the opportunity to do so soon afterwards. Upon hearing the allegations, Karadžić questioned the authenticity of the footage (which he had not seen). When I told him that the BBC had filmed a large refugee convoy on the move from north-east Bosnia, his response was that he didn't trust the BBC. He added that there was no proof that the people filmed by the BBC were Muslims. His response was as I expected. It was remarkable how every allegation of an atrocity by one side was somehow twisted to appear a heroic act of defence. I was to become immune to such rhetoric over the next few months, particularly from the Serb leadership. Anyway, as we concluded negotiations for the day, we happened again upon Karadžić and his delegation giving a press interview in the hotel lobby. Martin Bell was asking him for his reaction to the evidence of the fleeing refugees, but he was getting little satisfaction, just the usual brazen denials.

Cutileiro and his party were being accommodated at the presidential residence at the Konak near the city centre, and we arranged to meet there the following morning. Having opted to stay at the Hotel Serbia, I registered and requested a room in the wing furthest away from the ECMM's office. I had no sooner taken possession of the room when my former deputy Vitor Ferreira and a few other former colleagues arrived to welcome me back. They all seemed genuinely pleased to see me and wanted to wish me well. When I had a chance I took Vitor aside and told him that I wanted him to know that I was there in a different capacity and that I no longer had any connection to the ECMM. I added that I hoped dos Santos did not feel in any way threatened by my presence. Vitor told me that dos Santos hadn't said anything but that he would let me know if he did.

I was anxious to learn from the monitors what changes they had noticed in the republic since my departure in March. It became clear to them that the major change had only occurred since 7 April, when both the EC and the US gave recognition to Bosnia. Each ethnic community then began acting irrationally, out of fear of the others. Rumours quickly spread, many of them false, of impending attacks or of atrocities being committed in nearby towns and villages, and this applied throughout Bosnia. These rumours would lose nothing in the telling and were widely believed, causing a polarization of ethnic groups in villages and towns. In some cases it was likely that false rumours of atrocities themselves became the spark which ignited violence elsewhere, and so conflict began. From there it was a short step to the creation of front lines, followed by escalation into full-scale war. They gave me the example of Derventa in northern Bosnia, where the Serb element in the municipal leadership had moved to a nearby village. They accused Muslims and Croats of forcing them out, while, conversely, the Muslims and Croats accused the Serbs of desertion. Shortly thereafter, Serb forces began shelling the town. They told me that my former colleague Pandelis Botonakis had attempted to mediate by crossing the fluid front line between the town and the village but had been stopped by sniper fire, which prevented any safe passage. Movement of monitors was becoming increasingly dangerous.

Recognition had certainly not endeared the ECMM to the Serbs. As the security situation deteriorated throughout April, monitors operating near front lines were being subjected to increasing hostility from Serbs in the form of obstruction and eventually threats. There were incidents of shooting very close to monitors. A Bihać-based monitor team came under small arms fire, and when the monitors left their car to take cover, an artillery shell impacted directly in front of the vehicle, destroying it. It was very useful to hear this sobering news from expert witnesses, most of them military officers, about what exactly was happening on the ground. However, nobody at this stage had any idea as to what was happening in the more inaccessible parts of eastern Bosnia.

Early the following morning, I made my way to Konak, where further discussions were to be continued. I was able to brief Cutileiro and the others on what I had learned from the monitors the previous night so that they would be better prepared in their negotiations. The talks then resumed and followed the familiar pattern: one side blaming the other, citing incidents of killings and expulsions yet not giving any indication of how they might offer solutions or the means of obtaining a cease-fire. Ejup Ganić, the vice president, wanted to make an appeal through us to the international community to provide weapons to the Muslims 'to defend themselves'. He was showing signs of desperation. While each side gave their commitment to support the peace conference, Cutileiro impressed on all the need for an immediate cessation of hostilities. He wished them to know that he would be working on preparing a framework for a cease-fire agreement which he expected to be supported by all sides, and he further stated that the ECMM would be expected to verify compliance with it.

There was an unexpected development during the afternoon when Cutileiro learned that the UN had made arrangements to meet with the party leaders at UN headquarters in the city. It seemed that the Deputy Force Commander, the Frenchman, Major General Philippe Morillon, had initiated the process. He had the reputation of being outspoken, impulsive and tough. The ambassador was not best pleased, asking why it was that the UN should be taking on the role of peacemaker when they had absolutely no mandate to do so in Bosnia. However, we were informed some time later that they were offering their 'good offices' for a meeting which would be chaired by the EC. The meeting was scheduled for the following morning. That evening, our delegation worked on the wording of a possible cease-fire agreement, in the hope that the three sides might agree to its implementation the following day. I stayed overnight with the delegation at the Konak.

I was somewhat concerned when we headed for UNHQ the following morning. UNPROFOR had moved from the Holiday Inn to the PTT building on the western side of the city – a large three-storey building originally used by the national telephone company. Given Cutileiro's reaction the previous evening, I wondered if I might have to intervene as a peacekeeper myself between the UN and EC. The force commander, Lieutenant General Satish Nambiar, was an experienced field commander. He was a direct contrast to Morillon in style, being quietly-spoken, diplomatic and, in short, a gentleman. Following introductions, Cutileiro expressed his concern to

Nambiar that the UN should have initiated a meeting without reference to him. I could see Morrillon was seething, and at the first opportunity he demanded that Cutileiro be more respectful of his commander. A hush fell over the room which was eventually broken by Cutileiro, who in diplomatic language explained that there had obviously been a misunderstanding and he would be pleased to have the meeting.

A discussion then followed regarding the wisdom of putting all parties in the same room at the same time. Cutileiro expressed the view that it would be inappropriate to give Karadžić, as leader of the breakaway Bosnian Serbs, a seat at the table, while President Izetbegović represented a legitimate recognized government. The two could not be equated. He did, however, agree to the suggestion that the JNA commander, General Kukanjac, should be present to represent Serb interests. General Nambiar recognized the rationale of Cutileiro's argument and agreed to the holding of bilateral discussions with each of the parties. I certainly agreed with the ambassador in this regard, having held such discussions on numerous occasions when leading the ECMM.

Small subsidiary meetings then followed with each ethnic party, much along the lines of those held earlier. The UN took a back seat, leaving Cutileiro in the chair. He succeeded in brokering a cease-fire, much to the relief of all concerned. It was signed at the UNHQ and was to come into effect at midnight. The parties had signed a commitment to declare an immediate and total cease-fire on all the territory of Bosnia and to cease all activity that might provoke fear and instability; all threatening artillery would be removed under the control of the ECMM and all irregular forces would be disbanded. The agreement also made reference to the three main parties having equal access to television. The parties reaffirmed their opposition to any territorial gain by force and agreed on the right of return for refugees. However, I had the feeling that no matter how many cease-fires were negotiated, the party leaders had scant intention of honouring them.

The issue of access to television was one of the subjects raised by the Bosnian Serbs during negotiations. They claimed that Sarajevo TV, predominately controlled by Muslims, was being harshly critical of Serbs in what they perceived as a propaganda campaign against them. It was agreed with Cutileiro that in order to allay these concerns I would chair a meeting with the board of Sarajevo TV, with a view to giving Serbs more access to airtime. This issue would not be referred to within the cease-fire agreement document. However, I had been very aware of how much a bone of contention access to television was for the Serbs back in March, when it was listed as one of their demands in return for the lifting of barricades after the referendum results were announced.

Sometime later, Cutileiro chaired a press conference back at Hotel Serbia giving details of the cease-fire conditions. He also mentioned that as Lord Carrington's representative I would convene regular meetings with a working group comprising representatives of each party and the JNA to discuss issues of concern. After he and his colleagues departed for the airport I managed to get through to Grainne on the phone to let her know how I was getting on and give her my initial impressions. My calls to her were always a welcome respite from the tense situations which seemed to engulf us all, and a kind of reality check to boot. She reassured me that all was fine at home, and told me to take care. I was briefly comforted, until firing resumed at about 3.00am, the shelling apparently directed around Baščaršija. So much for any hope that this latest cease-fire would hold. The comments I noted in my diary that night were mostly questions: why am I here? Have I put myself ahead of my family?

Chapter 10

Downward Spiral

It was during that first week in April 1992 that serious fighting occurred in Bosnia. The town of Bosanski Brod in north-east Bosnia is divided from its Croatian twin Slavonski Brod by the river Sava. It was from here that the JNA had earlier launched attacks to defend the besieged barracks in Slavonski Brod during the Croatian war. Now the Serbs moved to ensure control of the town with the help of the JNA. The Muslim defenders had limited arms and ammunition and their resistance was short-lived. Thousands of refugees fled. Next to be targeted were the towns of Bijeljina and Zvornik, two strategically important places close to the Serbian border. They represented a part of Bosnian territory that Serb nationalists considered rightfully theirs for no other reason than that they linked parts of northern and eastern Bosnia to Serbia proper. Though his units had previously been active in Croatia, it was the brutal attack on these towns that gave Željko Ražnjatović, aka 'Arkan', commander of a feared Serb paramilitary unit known as *Tigrovi* (the Tigers), such a fearsome reputation. Their modus operandi was as follows: while the JNA cordoned off the towns Arkan and his 'Tigers' took up sniper positions, hunted down Muslim leaders, many of whom were members of the SDA, and carried out summary executions. He was ably assisted by another extreme Serb radical paramilitary leader, Vojislav Šešelj, born in Sarajevo, who commanded a group called *Beli orlovi* (the White Eagles) and who later acknowledged that the operation had been planned in Belgrade. The clean-up following these operations had been taking place while we were negotiating in Sarajevo. Later television footage would show Arkan being kissed by Biljana Plavšić, one of the Serb members of Bosnia's presidency in Bijeljina after carrying out the 'operations' in the town. In the coming weeks equally horrifying events took place in towns such as Višegrad and Foča. In the late spring and summer of 1992 the Bosnian Serbs and irregulars from Serbia would leave a dreadful trail of death and destruction behind them.

That the JNA appeared to be openly supporting the Serbs was a disturbing, if not surprising, development. The JNA was a formidable fighting force, among the largest and best equipped in Europe. Bosnia, protected by its high mountains and situated in the interior of the federation, had been a principal armoury for Yugoslavia. While the Bosnians took for granted its important defence role, they had never imagined that the very army that was there to defend them could become aggressors. We hoped, and many Bosnians believed, that they would remain impartial, particularly given General Kukanjac's declaration that the JNA would not take sides. It was, however, long suspected that Milošević had given instructions, as far back as January 1992, to have Bosnian Serbs serving in the JNA throughout Yugoslavia transferred to units in Bosnia, thereby effectively turning part of the JNA into a de facto Bosnian Serb army loyal to Belgrade and sympathetic to Karadžić's SDS. By the time that the Federal Republic of Yugoslavia (consisting only of Serbia and Montenegro) was created on 27 April 1992, the renegade Republika Srpska would inherit a professional army, complete with weapons and equipment and consisting of about 90,000 well trained and disciplined men already in Bosnia.

The morning after the cease-fire signing I followed up on the issue of Sarajevo Television by arranging to meet with the management board in the afternoon. The ECMM provided me with one of their vehicles to make the short journey to the television station in the Alipašino Most area. Any movement on the open streets was now dangerous, so I felt more secure in a car which flew a clearly visible EC flag. My invitation to the Serbs to have a representative present at the meeting was declined – they maintained that it was now too dangerous to travel to the television building, which was located in an area under Muslim control. While I could understand their security concerns I was frustrated at their refusal to attend, given that this subject was a major issue for them. In any event, the meeting itself was to prove fruitless. While the board expressed their willingness to give a proportionate amount of airtime to Serbs, it soon became apparent that this was not what the Serbs wanted. According to the board, the Serbs were actually demanding a physical proportion of the television station facilities, including offices, studios and equipment. This had never been the intention during the cease-fire negotiations. At the meeting's end I returned to my hotel frustrated and annoyed. I later met with Serb representatives and informed them that what they were demanding had never been under consideration and was not an option. How could they expect to be given a proportion of the television building and facilities when they were unwilling to even attend a meeting there?

Over the next few days I had meetings with the leaders of Muslim SDA and Croat HDZ. I had to keep in mind that I was now representing Lord Carrington and not the ECMM, though the thrust of the discussions was much the same as before. It was also important to me that the ECMM did not feel that I was threatening their role or undermining them in any way, as continued cooperation with them was of the utmost importance. With this in mind, I assured Major dos Santos that I would keep his office fully informed as to the general content of these meetings. We were, after all, seeking the same solutions.

General Nambiar, UNPROFOR's Force Commander, invited me to lunch at his headquarters as a follow-up to the earlier discussions with Cutileiro, a meeting also attended by the UN Head of Civil Affairs, Cedric Thornberry. While Bosnia was the General's first UN mission, Thornberry was an old UN hand. Originally from Northern Ireland, he was one of the founders of the Northern Ireland Civil Rights Association in 1968. His UN service included periods in Cambodia, Namibia, Cyprus and the Middle East. It did not take him long to express the view that the early recognition of Bosnia by the EC was madness. Failing to take into account the Bosnian Serbs' determination to forcibly resist such a move was, he believed, a mistake. While I could well appreciate this view, the soldier in me wanted to respond, but as I was new to this role I had to keep quiet. I developed the distinct impression that if UNPROFOR were handling the crisis their way of moving things forward would be very different to that of the EC. It was obvious to me from listening to Thornberry that there was no love lost between UNPROFOR and Ambassador Cutileiro, but whether that included General Nambiar I could not ascertain. Whatever the reality, the last thing I needed, in a complex and evolving situation, was a rift between the UN and EC.

After the meeting I decided to take a tram back to Ilidža rather than wait for a car from the ECMM. There were very few trams operating in the city now as many had been targeted by Serb heavy weapons and sniper fire. Just as I was leaving the PTT building, where the headquarters of UNPROFOR was located, a tram was arriving. As I boarded, I could see it was only half full. I took my seat and was waiting for it to move off when I became aware of the attention of those on board. Suddenly, one passenger began to clap, and general applause followed. One passenger who spoke some English turned to me and told me that I was 'very brave to share our danger by travelling in the tram'. He went on to say that he was proud of what we were trying to do for the Bosnian people and that he hoped we would succeed. I had no idea from which ethnic background the passengers came but I felt overwhelmed, and at the same time sad, that these people were in such a dangerous situation, one that was unlikely to improve any time soon. Within a few hours of taking that tram ride the terminal, located about 1km from UNPROFOR in the direction of downtown, was virtually destroyed by mortar fire, and the trams did not operate for many years thereafter. There seemed little doubt that whoever was trying to shut down the city, whether or not it was Bosnian Serbs with or without JNA assistance, they were succeeding.

I re-established contact with the presidential liaison team to the ECMM and met with Hajrudin Somun, Darko Ivić and Vera Ljubović in their office in the presidency building. They seemed pleased to see me. Hajrudin explained that the presidency thought it very sensible of Lord Carrington to appoint me as his envoy, as I was very familiar with the situation and trusted by all sides. He cautioned, however, that the situation had changed dramatically since my departure and said that they all feared for the future. They all told me that although I was no longer representing the ECMM, they would continue to help in any way they could. I told him that I was grateful for the offer of help, especially given that it would be useful for me to have access to President Izetbegović and other members of the presidency from time to time. In fact, I wasn't sure how my sudden arrival back in Sarajevo would be received by officials and I was pleasantly surprised by Somun's reaction. I had felt a bit isolated since returning, realizing that I would be mainly working on my own; so receiving assurances from both the ECMM and Somun's team lifted my spirits and gave me confidence.

As I passed through the hotel lounge I saw Martin Bell sitting by himself. I made my way over to him and he invited me to join him for coffee. I asked him why he stayed local, unlike the other media representatives who couldn't wait to rush off each day. He smiled and said that while he agreed the situation would deteriorate and the conflict intensify, it would start in Sarajevo, and not too far from here – 'Mark my words', he said. I suspected he might be right, although part of me wanted to believe that our mediation efforts would prove otherwise. I mentioned to him that as I was now representing Lord Carrington I needed to take care about exposing myself to unnecessary risk. However, this might make it more difficult for me to find out exactly what was happening throughout Bosnia. I therefore asked Martin if I might be allowed to see his daily reports so that I could be better informed about developments. He gave me a slightly dubious look and asked how he might benefit from such an arrangement, but I hinted that I might just be willing to let him know in advance if anything of interest was about to happen.

That afternoon, I took a call from the duty officer at UNPROFOR who asked me if I would be available to come by 4.00 pm. I was told that Cyrus Vance would like to meet me and that he was expected to be leaving for the airport at 4.15 pm. He requested that I accompany him in his car. I was aware that the former US Secretary of State under President Jimmy Carter was the UN Secretary General's Special Envoy to Croatia and that he was visiting Sarajevo to meet with UNPROFOR, but I had little idea why he wanted to meet me. Although the UN force had no mandate in Bosnia, its headquarters was based in the city, and I presumed Vance needed to be updated on its deployment in Croatia in support of his peace plan for the country. There had been much discussion as to why a peacekeeping force for Croatia should have its headquarters in Bosnia. This was, of course, no concern of mine, so I told the duty officer I would be available.

On my way to the PTT building a convoy of UNPROFOR staff cars, including the force commander's, passed me heading towards the airport. I thought perhaps I had got the time wrong and that Vance had already left. He was, however, still in the PTT building, finishing a cup of coffee as I arrived. I was ushered into the room and introduced to him. He smiled as he shook my hand and said that he had met with Peter Carrington early that morning in London who had told him to see me before he left Sarajevo. He asked if I would join him in the car that would be taking him to the airport, so we headed off for the short drive accompanied by a UN escort. He told me that he was due to meet with President Milošević in Belgrade that evening and asked what he should say to him. Not expecting for a moment that a senior diplomat would ask my opinion on matters like this, I thought for a moment, then told him that it might be worth raising the matter of evidence emerging of wholesale cleansing of towns in eastern Bosnia by Serbs, including paramilitaries from Serbia and, allegedly, the JNA. I also mentioned the name of Arkan, who, I assumed, would be known to Milošević. I added that he might want to mention that the ECMM was aware of this and that the peace conference would demand Milošević's guarantee that there was no flow of weapons or paramilitaries going to the Bosnian Serbs from Serbia. I hoped I didn't sound arrogant, but he simply nodded and thanked me.

We arrived at the airport to be met by a UN honour guard and a line of UNPROFOR's senior commanders. Before getting out of the car Vance turned and shook my hand. I waited in the car while he attended to the formalities and headed for his aircraft, then turning to the driver asked if he might drop me off at my hotel. When I arrived back I noticed that many of the hotel staff, people I had become acquainted with over the previous six months, were now gone. I sought out one of the managers who spoke some English and asked him what had happened – where, I asked, had they gone? He looked uncomfortable and told me that they had 'moved elsewhere'. I pressed him on this, asking whether they had left because they were non-Serbs, and he said that they had simply left Ilidža voluntarily and moved to the city centre. I knew what this meant. Ethnic cleansing was happening here, too, and right in front of us. I soon learned that all staff who were non-Serb had been fired from their jobs, ordered to pack a bag, collect their families and leave Ilidža. I knew there had been a small Muslim majority in this suburb, but now it was controlled by Serb forces. Moreover, I was aware that Ilidža was strategically important to the Serbs, as control of it would prevent Muslim fighters linking up with nearby Visoko, where they had supplies of weapons and ammunition. I felt a rising anger inside and a feeling of frustration and failure that neither the ECMM nor I could do anything to stop this appalling state of affairs.

I was already in a bad mood as I headed to my room. En route, I bumped into Vitor. After I told him what I had learned about the fate of the staff he informed me that Karadžić had moved his entire crisis committee into the hotel. I paused for thought before asking whether we could object, on the basis that the ECMM was based there. Major dos Santos had already lodged an objection, but the presidency said they could not do anything about it. We would just have to bear with it and keep close tabs on them. We had also heard that both Serb members of the presidency, Koljević and Plavšić, had resigned. The ECMM, the SDS crisis committee and almost the entire international media were now all sharing the same accommodation. Could it get any worse, I wondered? I had my answer within a few short days.

The Bosnian government was initially hopeful that the JNA would be won over to its side, but this hope was short-lived, and relations deteriorated quickly thereafter. An effort had been made to bring the two sides together at an earlier meeting in Skopje, Macedonia. When this failed to resolve the impasse, President Izetbegović demanded that the JNA withdraw from Bosnia or else transform itself into a Bosnian army. As soon as it became clear to him, however, that the JNA was siding with the Serbs, he set about establishing his own army to protect the newly declared state. He appealed to citizens of all ethnicities to come to the defence of the republic by issuing a call-up to the reserves known as the Territorial Defence Force (TO). The resulting 'army' comprised trained reservists, police and even some Serbs. Sefer Halilović, a Muslim originally from the Sandžak region, was appointed commander, with a Serb, Jovan Divjak, as his deputy. Another valued contribution came in the form of the special police, which comprised about 200 well trained and disciplined men commanded by a Croat, Dragan Vikić. Other militia units that would gain prominence over the next few years included the 'Green Berets' and the 'Patriotic League'. However, at this early stage, the fledgling Bosnian army was little more than a name, and the mobilization ordered by Izetbegović infuriated the Bosnian Serb leaders, who interpreted the president's action as a declaration of war.

In this febrile context many Serbs began leaving the city and relocating to the mountain resort of Pale, about 20km from Sarajevo. Much of the Bosnian Serb leadership was also resident there. On the evening of 19 April I took a phone call from Sarajevo TV. They told me that they had just been warned by the Serbs in Pale that they had thirty minutes to stop transmitting or their building would be shelled. They appealed to me to contact Karadžić and get him to ensure such an attack did not occur.

I immediately got word to one of Karadžić's crisis committee members, repeating what I had been told and warning of the consequences if the shelling took place. He promised that Karadžić would be informed immediately and that he would get back to me. He called me about ten minutes later with a message from Karadžić assuring me that no such attack would take place. I passed on the message to the television station but suggested that the staff should take no chances. Within about twenty minutes one of the ECMM members came rushing up to tell me that the television station had been shelled and that at least two staff had been killed. I turned on the television to see immediate coverage of the attack and the consequent damage. I headed down to the hotel lobby and, recognizing one of Karadžić's henchmen, literally grabbed his shoulder. Through an ECMM interpreter I told him to let Karadžić know that I was about to condemn the attack on Sarajevo TV and would be holding him accountable for it. As soon as he had left I made my way to the ECMM office to get the latest details. Dos Santos was able to tell me that one of his monitor team had seen the top of the building being struck. As we were discussing the attack Vitor arrived to tell me that both Karadžić and Koljević were outside in the corridor and wanted to see me. Both looked uncomfortable. Karadžić spoke first, stating that he knew nothing of the attack. I was quick to respond, telling him that as far as I was concerned he was fully responsible for the deaths and that I intended to make a public statement to that effect. He denied responsibility but I insisted he was accountable. I was not going to give him a chance to say anything more and so walked away. I knew he was taken aback by my harangue but I didn't care. I subsequently condemned the attack in an interview with the BBC, in which I accused the Bosnian Serbs of responsibility for the unprovoked shelling of the TV station.

There is no doubt that the Serbs were obsessive, even paranoid, about Sarajevo TV. As long as the Muslims controlled the national television station, Karadžić and his people had little chance of influencing most of the population. In this battle over control of television, relay installations were a target. The ECMM was able to establish that, within a short period of time (from when I had chaired the television discussions) Serbs had taken action to redress the balance. Seven of the nine television transmitters scattered throughout the republic were seized by Serbs, who then managed to reorient the transmitter aerials towards Belgrade and relayed programmes from there. These seizures meant that by the spring of 1992 Sarajevo TV could reach only a relatively small part of Bosnia. The private television station YUTEL, which also occupied the main television building, was to cease broadcasting within a few weeks when its transmissions were also interfered with, thus confining coverage to the city of Sarajevo alone.

The following morning I had arranged to meet Professor Zoran Pajić, who lectured in international law at Sarajevo University. I had become friendly with him after he invited me to address his students during my period as head of the ECMM. I was a bit nervous driving towards the city, parts of which were being periodically shelled, particularly around Baščaršija. We met at a colleague's house and he introduced me to a group of his friends. He told me he was pleased to see me back, though he wished it could be in better times. As expected, the conversation centred round the political situation. He spoke in a calm and reasoned manner and expressed the view that Sarajevo could not escape being torn apart. Sadly, I shared his pessimism. As long as the main political parties were drawn along ethnic and religious lines this outcome would be inevitable, and the hardliners on each side were bent on pursuing their own nationalist agenda. He even told me that some of his Serb colleagues at the university had already left their posts. I asked if that included Borisa Starović. The news I then received hit me hard. I was told that somebody had attempted to kill Borisa earlier in the month; he had been shot in the head and was in a critical condition in hospital. I was horrified to hear this dreadful news about someone I had so admired ever since he facilitated my meeting with his medical students. I asked Zoran what had happened and he told me that while he did not have all the facts, it appeared that Borisa had been shot by another Serb after he had refused to leave the city and join other Serbs in Pale. It seemed unbelievable that someone would want to deliberately target prominent citizens to justify their misguided ideology. That it should have happened to Starović was tragic.

As I prepared to leave, Zoran asked me to accompany him to his home. He wanted to show me something. I followed him from the city centre and soon arrived at his apartment block, outside which a number of people had gathered. I could immediately see two craters in the middle of the road directly in front of the building. The roadway was also covered in glass, and on looking up I could clearly see that many of the windows were shattered. It was evident that the damage had been caused by mortar bombs, and I had no doubt as to where they had come from. He told me that this shelling had happened the previous evening. Some of the bystanders recognized me and came over. They did not speak, but the look on their faces said more than words could. It was Easter Sunday, and having found out which hospital Borisa Starović was being treated at, I went to visit him. He was propped up in bed, his head heavily bandaged. He looked haggard and gaunt, the polar opposite of his usual exuberant self, but managed a weak smile when our eyes met. His voice was hoarse. He lamented the fate of Sarajevo and told me again that all he ever wanted was to make good doctors.

Back at the hotel, I was briefed by Antonio dos Santos and his operational staff on the latest developments. ECMM teams were encountering greater difficulties in carrying out their assigned tasks, and while monitors were doing their best to calm the increasingly agitated warring parties, they were having little or no success. Shooting incidents very close to monitors were on the increase. Indeed, a monitor team attempting to get through to Foča, one of the towns cleansed of Muslims by Serb paramilitaries, was stopped as it approached the outskirts by the JNA, who refused to allow them through. When they asked why they were being denied free passage they were told that it was for their own safety, which could not be guaranteed. The team, however, believed that it was to prevent them from witnessing ethnic cleansing taking place in the town and its environs.

As I was walking down the corridor with Vitor following the briefing I met Nikola Koljević, Karadžić's deputy and, until he resigned, one of the Serb members of the collective Presidency. Koljević always spoke in a soft manner and was considered a moderate. However, I could never take to him and had no trust in anything he said. I decided to take him to task and asked him if the ECMM had been refused entry to Foča by the JNA. If they had been, I reminded him, it was in direct contravention of the agreement that all sides had signed up to. I also told him that we believed there had been ethnic cleansing going on in Foča and that unless the mission was given access to the area I intended to inform the EC about it. Koljević assured me that there must have been a misunderstanding. He suggested that it would be ideal if he could accompany the monitor team so that he, too, could access the area. I knew he was bluffing, so I told him that this would be fine and that we would like to leave immediately. At this point he looked decidedly uncomfortable and responded that he would have to discuss the request with Karadžić first. He informed me that this could not be done at once. Of course, I was not in the least surprised when the ECMM was informed the following morning that due to security issues it would be impossible to guarantee the safety of a monitor team visiting Foča.

As each day passed it seemed more probable that Bosnia would break out in ethnic violence, not only within Sarajevo but throughout the republic. I was being kept busy meeting representatives from the different parties, but little in the way of progress was being achieved. I had meetings with President Izetbegović on 20 and 21 April 1992, and at both of these he mentioned the urgent need for some kind of military intervention. He was well aware that although the UN had its UNPROFOR headquarters in the city all its units were deployed in Croatia and, furthermore, that it had no mandate in Bosnia. During our discussion he acknowledged that the appeal to all Bosnians to mobilize had only further alienated the Serbs. His deputy, Ejup Ganić, was more animated, even to the point of asking me if I could somehow arrange for the Muslims to acquire weapons from arsenals of the JNA. Such discussions only served to convince me that conflict was coming, despite our efforts to prevent it. It seemed to be a case of when rather than if.

Vitor now came to see me. He informed me that there was a lady on the phone who wanted to speak with me, and only me, urgently. The lady told Vitor her name was Mrs Čerkez and gave him her phone number. I had to try the number a few times before I finally succeeded in getting an answer. She told me she was Muslim and as an English teacher gave lessons to clients in her own home, many of whom were officers of the JNA. Apparently, she had come into possession of some documents from a briefcase which had been inadvertently left in her house by a JNA officer. She was not prepared to give me any further information but admitted that she was very scared and was very anxious that I should have the documents, because I was the only person she trusted. She asked if I would meet her at the Princip Bridge. She sounded desperate and wanted an assurance that I would be there. The exchange left me reeling slightly, and all sorts of questions were running through my mind. Was this some kind of trick? Who exactly was she? Why did she contact me? Without thinking too much, I blurted out that I would try to meet her, or that somebody from the ECMM wearing uniform would be there in my place.

I tried to assess rationally what this was all about and decided to confide in Vitor. He agreed that it sounded rather odd but said he would send monitor Jeremy Brade and another of the guys in uniform to meet her. I told him to instruct them to pick up the documents and tell her they would be passed on to me immediately, explaining that I had been unexpectedly delayed. I knew Jeremy well from my previous tour; he was an ex-British Gurkha officer and I had found him to be very professional. Normally I would have been happy to meet this woman myself, but given my new role I considered it prudent to keep my distance. It was unfortunate that there was considerable shelling towards the city centre that day, and when both monitors arrived at the agreed location there was no sign of Mrs Čerkez. Having waited for thirty minutes with no sign of her, they returned to base. As it transpired, I was called to another meeting with President Izetbegović and only heard of developments later that evening. With events moving so quickly I had hardly time, in any event, to dwell on the incident. Vitor came back to let me know that repeated efforts to contact Mrs Čerkez by phone had failed.

Chapter 11

Carrington Comes to Town

On 21 April 1992 Ambassador Cutileiro phoned to let me know that he, Lord Carrington and the Portuguese Foreign Minister, João Pinheiro, would be travelling to Sarajevo in two days' time. Apparently, Lord Carrington wanted to meet the party leaders in order to emphasize the need to confirm the cease-fire agreement of 12 April. Carrington had also requested a meeting with UNPROFOR's commanders and, if possible, General Kukanjac. I was asked to make the necessary arrangements. I responded that it might be prudent to let Carrington know that the security situation was pretty dangerous and there could be no guarantee of his personal safety. Cutileiro replied that Carrington would be on a tight schedule and would, in any event, only be in Sarajevo for a few hours. He then asked me if I had a location in mind which might offer the best chance of safety. I expressed my doubt that the Serbs would be willing to meet in the city, given the security situation, and so recommended that the talks be held in the airport complex (though it might prove problematic to persuade President Izetbegović to travel there). Nevertheless, I agreed to begin working on organizing the meeting.

Word spread fast that Carrington was due to visit. I had a meeting with Antonio dos Santos, Vitor Ferreira and Jeremy Brade to discuss the details and the complex logistics. They were ready to provide me with any assistance I required. Jeremy would go to the airport the following morning and pick out suitable areas for reception, conference and catering. However, our preparation for this important visit was interrupted by some heavy artillery fire directed at the vicinity of Baščaršija, where over 100 shells fell. We also learned that many snipers were positioned in high buildings throughout the city, with anybody and everybody now a potential target. It was becoming impossible to determine who controlled the different roadblocks, as their positions were frequently moved. Abandoned trucks and buses were everywhere. Between snipers and roadblocks, taking a drive through the city was certainly not for the fainthearted. I was hoping the tension would ease before Carrington's arrival, though I had my doubts.

That afternoon, I had a visit from a French official claiming he was working for the French Minister of Health, Bernard Kouchner, and requesting me to facilitate a meeting between Kouchner and Lord Carrington. He told me that his minister would be arriving at Sarajevo airport the same day as Carrington. I had not been aware of this visit, nor, as far as I knew, had the presidency. Although the official pressed me to agree, he was not able to tell me the purpose of the meeting, and I found this surprising; nobody had heard anything about it, nor had any information come through my own channels. Maybe it was being deliberately kept from me, but I now faced an obvious dilemma and was at a loss to know what to do. On the one hand I had no wish to be the cause of a diplomatic or political incident, but on the other I had the responsibility of providing the best schedule for these important discussions regardless of diplomatic niceties. I knew Kouchner to be the founder of the organization Médecins sans Frontières (Doctors without Borders). However, being aware of how short Lord Carrington's visit was to be and of the need for maximum security, I decided to refuse the request, only hoping the decision would not come back to haunt me later. The French official was, of course, not best pleased.

My watch showed exactly 6.00am as I was woken by the sound of fierce anti-tank and machine gun fire just outside my bedroom window. The noise was deafening and I was under the bed in a flash, my ears ringing from the barrage of gunfire. My room was located on the second floor and overlooked one side of the hotel. After some time I crawled out of my shelter and crept to the window on all fours. Peering out slowly and carefully I could see a halftrack armoured car directly below me with its machine gun blazing away at an unseen target toward the trees in the distance. There was a lot of incoming rifle and machine gunfire, with some rounds impacting on the halftrack and some on the building itself. It was obvious the area was under attack, and since Ilidža had been cleared of Muslims, it was Serb defenders who were taking the hammering. There must have been about eighty personnel in front of the building, some in police uniforms but most wearing civilian clothes. All were armed and returning fire. I assumed, correctly as it turned out, that the attackers were from the nearby Muslim areas of Hrasnica and Butmir. The detonations and the sound of machine guns and small arms were deafening.

Taking a chance, I quickly threw on some clothes and ran downstairs at a crouch and across the lobby, before taking the stairs on the other side of the hotel to the offices of the ECMM. From there I had a good view of the battle scene below and across the hotel grounds. It soon became evident that this was a full-scale assault on the suburb, with the Serb police defending themselves and where possible responding with fire. A two-storey building directly opposite us, in use as an old people's hospital with the name 'Herzegovina' on it, was taking many hits. Many armed Serb police were crouching along its nearside wall taking cover. As I looked around the office I could see Vitor frantically trying to get someone on the phone. He told me that many of the city's phones were out and that both the central post office and phone exchange had been destroyed. I urged him to attempt to make contact with the presidency and inform them that we knew this was an attack by Muslims on a Serb suburb and urge them to stop this action immediately.

Looking out again I saw a television cameraman edging his way to a corner of the hospital building trying to shoot footage. He suddenly dropped the camera and staggered back clutching his arm. He was dragged by one of the Serbs fighters through the doorway of the hospital with blood pouring from a hand wound. Hit by shrapnel, he was later evacuated. I hurried downstairs again and found most of the media crouched in the dining room taking cover behind chairs; there were also many armed Serb police there. As I moved towards the main window overlooking the large front lawn I could see someone shouldering an anti-tank weapon across the pathway at the corner of the hospital. He fired, and the force of the back-blast from the weapon blew in the large hotel window directly in front of us. This caused a minor panic as everyone hit the floor trying to avoid the splintering glass. I noticed Martin Bell, who looked across and commented above the noise, 'I told you it would start here.'

The gun battle went on for what seemed like a long time. At no point did I see any attacker, but the firing was intense, both incoming and outgoing. We could see there were casualties but it was too dangerous to venture outside. The hotel staff must have received instructions from the management to clear the front of the hotel following the shattering of the dining room window, because they began moving furniture and fittings away from that side of the hotel. From that day on we dined in a makeshift room at the rear of the building.

Throughout that morning I made several attempts to contact both Muslim and Serb representatives to see if I could get them together to agree a cease-fire. I also needed both sides to realize that the impending visit of Lord Carrington was dependent on some sort of cease-fire holding and that I needed assurances on this. Many Serb representatives were still using the hotel as their base and I managed to make contact with them and agreed a meeting for the afternoon. Vitor had succeeded in getting through to the presidency, and through Hajrudin Somun we managed to arrange for an SDA representative to attend. This would be at a lower level than I hoped for, but I was well aware that neither side would agree to a meeting if I demanded to see Izetbegović and Karadžić.

Around midday, with intensive fighting still going on outside, I was cornered by Martin Bell and asked if I would be willing to do an interview for BBC News. I wasn't particularly keen on this, but thought that at least viewers would get an accurate account of what was happening so agreed. Characteristically, Martin suggested we conduct the interview outside. I wasn't convinced, but took a chance on his judgement. Martin and his crew moved out through the hotel's side entrance and I followed. After a few minutes deciding between us where the safest place to position ourselves was, we commenced the interview. The main focus was on the outbreak of fighting and whether this might affect Carrington's plan to visit the city the following day. I had no way of knowing and simply said that I would be advising his office of the situation later that day. I could barely hear Martin's questions such was the ferocity of the shooting. I had never imagined that I would be doing television interviews while bullets were flying in all directions, and I was very relieved to get back inside.

The shooting eased somewhat in the early afternoon and I made contact with Ambassador Cutileiro. He was aware that we were having an eventful day and was equally aware of the escalation in fighting, having been watching the live television coverage which was dominating the news. I brought him up to date with the situation and outlined to him the arrangements I had made for a meeting with both sides. He asked me if it would be safe enough for Carrington to begin his visit, and I told him that only if the fighting eased might it still be possible, though I was in negotiations with the warring parties and would have a clearer picture later. He seemed satisfied with this and said he would brief Carrington on developments. I went looking for Antonio and Vitor to discuss arrangements for the meeting with Serbs and Muslims and what might need to be done for the airport meeting the following day. They assured me of the ECMM's support 'in every way'.

We managed to get both sides round the table later that afternoon. The shooting had subsided, and although a tense atmosphere still existed, a degree of normality had returned. I kept the meeting pretty short. This was not the time to force discussion of a cease-fire; I simply wanted to impress upon them the importance of Carrington's visit and why it was essential that each party leader have the chance to put their points to him and his delegation. I tried to get the message across that if fighting were to occur on the following day it would be interpreted as a clear signal that the respective leaders had no interest in peace talks or had no control over those whom they purported to represent. I was not prepared to listen to any arguments as to why fighting had broken out that morning. Each side would doubtless have the opportunity to raise this during discussions with the visiting delegation. After they left I didn't feel any better, suspecting that the meeting represented only a suspension of hostilities and worse was yet to come. Moreover, I was increasingly coming to the view that Bosnia's party leaders were losing touch with both reality and reason.

At about 5.00 pm we saw a convoy of UN vehicles draw up at the rear of the hospital block opposite the hotel. By late afternoon shooting had stopped and most of the Serb fighters were taking stock. The UN had agreed to move some of the hospital residents away from the area, but I had no idea where they were being taken. There was also a considerable JNA presence in the immediate vicinity. A tank commander interviewed in the aftermath of the fighting admitted that the JNA had returned fire that day, and I presumed this to mean that they had fired on the Muslim attackers. Anyway, as I stepped out on to the balcony of the ECMM offices I could see Martin Bell and his BBC crew interviewing a member of the Serb military police. He told Martin that his brother and two cousins had been among those killed. The once beautifully manicured hotel lawn was showing deep ruts left by the Serb halftracks, which had been criss-crossing the lawns during the fierce fighting. Discarded equipment and some burned-out vehicles lay abandoned below, and a distinct smell of cordite still hung in the air. The bodies of fourteen fighters recovered from the immediate scene were being removed, a grim reminder of what had happened that morning. I did not hear how many casualties the Muslims had suffered.

Following the meeting I was besieged by the media, a new experience for me and one I wasn't entirely comfortable with. At my meeting in London with Lord Carrington I had asked him how I should deal with the media in such circumstances. His response had been that it would be my call. That evening I was contacted by RTE and then the BBC World Service. From then on, interviews became almost part of my daily routine. I managed a few phone calls back to Ireland, including one to Grainne. The family had seen some of my interviews, particularly the one from outside the hotel which had been repeated on other newscasts. There was nothing she could say other than to advise me to stay safe and not take unnecessary risks.

Jeremy Brade got back to let me know that the airport had been unaffected by the fighting. He had met the manager, Mile Jovičić, and informed him of the impending visit. Mile was doing a splendid job of trying to keep the airport open, particularly since many of his staff had left because of the deteriorating conditions. Flights in and out were uncertain and the situation at the airport was unpredictable. The JNA now had control over the building, and most of the flights were military. Jovičić had shown Jeremy three locations which he thought might be suitable to hold discussions in, but he discarded the first two for security reasons, Jovičić's own office and the VIP lounge in the new terminal building. Jermey was recommending the third option, the restaurant on the second floor of the old terminal;

it was sheltered on three sides, with the fourth side facing the apron, the runway and the village of Butmir, and he considered it safe. Curtains would be drawn over the windows on that side. I was happy to leave those details in Jeremy's capable hands since I had quite enough on my plate as it was.

I phoned Ambassador Cutileiro later that evening and after I had brought him up to date he informed me that Lord Carrington would travel to Sarajevo the following morning. Accompanying him would be the EC President of the Council of Ministers, João Pinheiro. I decided to make no mention of Minister Kouchner, even though I was still concerned about the consequences of refusing him permission to meet Carrington. It had been a long and very trying day. I had experienced many different emotions, from apprehension to fear, with a rush of adrenalin thrown in. It was the first time I had seen fighting at close hand. I bumped into Vitor in the lobby, which was now a lot quieter than earlier in the day. He persuaded me to share a beer with him and a few of my former colleagues up in my old office, where he pointed to the beer fridge that I had installed in the corner of the room when I had first been appointed chief. Anyway, we did our best to empty it that night, and I think we deserved it. As I fell into a fitful sleep I could hear sporadic gunfire and the distant sound of shelling – a sound that would become all too familiar.

In the morning I had a rather spartan breakfast in a makeshift dining room at the rear of the hotel before preparing to head to the airport to await Lord Carrington's arrival. There had been no notable escalation of shelling during the night and I had my fingers crossed that Jeremy had the necessary arrangements in place. I met Ambassador Salgueiro in the lobby and together we were driven the few kilometres to the airport. After a meeting with Jeremy and his monitor group which was attended by the airport manager we discussed the order in which the meetings would take place. I suggested to Mile Jovičić that he should be on hand to greet each delegation as they arrived in the visitors' room, but said that Salgueiro and I would receive Lord Carrington as he disembarked from his aircraft. I pointed out to Mile the importance of ensuring that the SDA delegation, which was being led by President Izetbegović, should avoid encountering the Serbs, who were being represented by Karadžić and Koljević. While the SDA leadership were travelling from the city with an armed police escort, the Serbs were scheduled to arrive by helicopter from Pale. Jovičić assured me that all was in hand.

Jeremy informed me that the only Croat representative attending would be Franjo Boraš, who was already at the airport. Ambassador Salgueiro then interjected, asking to know the order in which the meetings would be held. I told him that the delegation would meet the Croats first, followed by the Muslims and then the Serbs. This would be followed by meetings with General Kukanjac and, finally, with senior UNPROFOR staff. As I headed upstairs to the visitors' room I saw the president's convoy arrive and Mile standing by to meet him. Entering the room, I saw Franjo Boraš and welcomed him. He seemed on edge, which I could understand; he probably felt a bit isolated, being the only Croat representative, and even I was not sure of his status within the HDZ. The Croats had recently undergone leadership changes, and Milenko Brkić, who I had been informed was the newly appointed leader, was not in attendance.

Soon afterwards President Izetbegovic entered accompanied by Ambassador Salgueiro and Hajrudin Somun. He greeted me before he sat down and was offered coffee. I then slipped outside to find out the arrival time of Carrington's plane, and Mile Jovičić informed me it would be delayed by thirty minutes. Just then I was informed that Kouchner's plane would be landing shortly before Carrington's. In the midst of all the arrangements I had completely forgotten about Kouchner. It didn't get any easier when Somun, who had come out from the visitors' room, came over to inform me that Izetbegović wished to meet Carrington's plane when it landed. Though I had suspected he might wish to do so, this was something I wanted to avoid. The last thing I needed was the Serbs thinking that Izetbegović, as leader of the SDA, was being considered superior to them or, indeed, to the Croats. I needed to make the position quite clear and unambiguous: that Lord Carrington was coming to meet each party's representatives and that it was only in his capacity as leader of the SDA, not as Bosnia's president, that Izetbegović would be meeting him. To have it otherwise, I told him, might well be treated as an insult by the Serbs and Croats, and we could not give the Serbs even the slightest excuse to disengage from these talks.

I asked Somun to explain to Izetbegović that the aircraft would be met by the ECMM, Ambassador Salgueiro and me, and by us alone. Of course, I could see Somun was not very pleased with this, but he went back inside and informed the president of my decision.

Jeremy Brade soon appeared to inform me that Bernard Kouchner's aircraft was about to land. I asked him if he could arrange for the plane to be guided to the other terminal, as I did not want Kouchner in the room when Lord Carrington arrived. In any event, within a few minutes I caught sight of Kouchner striding resolutely towards us with some of his officials, and before I knew it, he appeared in the room and with a grand gesture headed over to the president; after shaking his hand he sat down beside him. Among his aides I recognized the French official who had approached me two days earlier. I was furious. If this was a deliberate attempt at an ambush, I seem to have been the victim. I slipped over to the French official and gestured to him to follow me outside. I was seething with anger and told him that while I meant no disrespect to his minister, he had exactly ten minutes to remove him from this room. I warned him that if this was not done I would have Carrington's plane diverted and Kouchner would be the cause of these talks being abandoned. I gave him no opportunity to reply and turned away. I have no idea what transpired in the room, but after a few minutes the minister emerged from the room, gave me a less than friendly look and, hurrying to a car drawn up alongside the apron, climbed in and was driven away, much to my relief.

Within a few minutes of Kouchner's departure Carrington's aircraft landed. As he emerged, closely followed by Pinheiro and Cutileiro, Ambassador Salgueiro and I moved forward to meet him. Following introductions we moved across the tarmac, heading towards where the media were assembled. Carrington asked me about the chances of a cease-fire. I cautioned that we might have 'gone beyond' cease-fires. He acknowledged that I might be right, but said that we had to persist. He then informed me that the party leaders were being summoned for peace talks in Lisbon the following week and that my help would be required in facilitating this. While he was then answering some questions from the assembled media, Mile Jovičić informed me that both Karadžić and Koljević had just arrived by helicopter.

The first meeting was with Franjo Boraš of the HDZ. With the Bosnian Croat leadership in a state of flux, it fell to Boraš to represent the party, a role he seemed to be uncomfortable with. He was outnumbered, sitting opposite Carrington and his delegation of four including myself, and he seemed nervous and ill at ease. What had been happening in Sarajevo over the previous few days was mostly about Serbs and Muslims, with the Croats playing a minor role. I felt that Boraš was quite happy to agree that the cease-fire of 12 April should be reaffirmed. The interests and concerns of the Croat leadership lay, however, not in Sarajevo but in Western Herzegovina, the base of the leader of the Bosnian Croats, Mate Boban, who enjoyed the backing of Croatia's President Tudjman and the powerful 'Herzegovinan Lobby' in Zagreb.

The Muslim delegation under President Izetbegović was eager to please Carrington by readily agreeing to reaffirm the cease-fire. However, as Izetbegović was convinced that the JNA was now working in tandem with Karadžić's SDS, his appeal to Carrington and the international community was for military intervention. He argued that as Bosnia was now an internationally recognized state, it should be protected from its enemies, namely the Bosnian Serbs, who were, of course, also Bosnian citizens. Carrington argued equally strongly that Muslims had no choice but to negotiate with Serbs and that there was no possibility of any intervention. Towards the end of the discussions I slipped out of the room to meet up with Mile Jovičić, telling him to have Karadžić and Koljević ready in five minutes. I was well aware that both of them had been waiting under heavy guard in the empty government hangar. At their meeting with Carrington they concentrated on the 'unprovoked' Muslim attack on the Serb community in Ilidža. I had already made Carrington aware of the earlier cleansing of Muslims there by the Serbs, but he was focused entirely on achieving assurances from Karadžić that he would sign the affirmation of the cease-fire of 12 April 1992. He also added that the conference concerning Bosnia's future would continue in Lisbon on 27 April.

During a coffee break in the meetings Carrington moved over to the window facing the airport apron. He was holding a copy of *Time* magazine in his hand and nodded to me to join him. The cover of *Time* showed a photograph of Slobodan Milosević under the heading 'Butcher of the Balkans'. He held it up to me and asked what I thought. I told him that it seemed an appropriate headline. At that juncture I decided to mention the incident with Kouchner to him. I had been concerned about it and needed to clear the air. However, after I had given him the basics he just smiled and told me that we had far more important issues to address. I was relieved, and before we resumed I told Jovičić and Jeremy Brade that the renewed cease-fire document was being prepared and would require the signatures of Boraš, Karadžić and Izetbegović.

The first meetings had been reasonably calm, but General Kukanjac was not a happy man when his turn came to meet Carrington. Accompanied by his interpreter, he was in an angry mood following what he described as a Muslim *Zelene beretke* (Green Berets) attack on his command headquarters. I was fast learning that when describing attacks by one side on the other exaggeration was regularly employed. In this case, Kukanjac informed Carrington that the Green Berets had also fired at his headquarters 'from everywhere, using self-propelled rockets, mortars and grenade launchers', and he warned that he would not stand idly by while citizens attacked the JNA. (I suspected that this might have been his justification for the JNA to return fire the previous night.) Carrington, however, calmly assured him that all three sides had agreed to reaffirm the cease-fire agreement and that I would be present to witness each party signing the document being prepared.

The final meeting was with Generals Morillon and MacKenzie of UNPROFOR. Until now the peacekeeping force had concentrated on Croatia rather than Bosnia, where they had no mandate. Yet they were facing difficulties within the city. Their movement was restricted by increased shelling by the Serbs, who controlled the surrounding high ground, and by an increasing number of barricades within the city itself. Many of their senior staff were accommodated at the Delegates Club, a government facility close to the presidency building. The route from there to their HQ at the PTT building was becoming a hazardous and challenging trip. The force commander, General Nambiar, who had been on his way back from Croatia to attend the meeting, had been unable to land at the airport due to shelling nearby and had been diverted to Belgrade. Both put forward the view that Izetbegović was seeking some form of intervention and was no longer interested in a cease-fire, something we had already realized ourselves. When informed by Lord Carrington that the president was agreeing to reaffirm the cease-fire, they were not surprised, but Morillon simply responded by expressing scepticism.

At the end of the meetings we reviewed the day's proceedings. I had the distinct impression that although each side had given their assurances of complying with this renewed cease-fire, its observance would be short-lived. The Serbs wanted their own entity and would never agree to live in an independent Bosnian state as a minority under Muslim rule. As for the Muslims, it was their belief that a secure future could only come after military intervention. The Serb-dominated JNA were facing the option of siding with the Serbs or withdrawing altogether from Bosnia. In these circumstances, what benefit was there in a cease-fire that was unlikely to hold beyond a few hours? I hardly had time to dwell further on this issue, however, as Carrington announced he had to leave. He was scheduled to meet President Milošević with Pinheiro and Cutileiro later that day in Belgrade. I was informed that I would have to ensure that the document was signed. Karadžić was still at the airport so I could have him sign it, and I expected that it would not be too problematic to get Boraš to return. I would, however, have to work harder to persuade Izetbegović to do so.

I needed to contact the presidency to find out when Izetbegovic would be available to return to the airport for the signing. It was also important that Karadžić and Koljević be kept in a location where they were unlikely to come face to face with him. Such was the distrust between the two sides that this had become a priority. Carrington was depending on me to get the agreement signed, and I had no intention of failing to deliver. I checked with the airport manager, who told me that they were talking with General Kukanjac in his office. Turning to Jeremy Brade, I asked him to inform Karadžić that all sides were agreeing to sign the cease-fire document

The Serb delegation were still in the airport, though while 'committing' to the latest agreement I heard that both Karadžić and Koljević were eager to learn from General Kukanjac as to when General Ratko Mladić would be moving to Sarajevo. This appeared to be the main topic of conversation between them as they waited in the airport manager's office. I had heard of Mladić, who at this time was based in Croatia, and it was rumoured that he was close to Karadžić; his moving to Sarajevo could only be a bad omen. Jeremy then informed me that Karadžić had agreed to sign the document. I received this news with relief and decided to have a word with Karadžić myself, telling him that I would be informing Lord Carrington of the Serb support in this matter. He responded by stating that he did not believe Izetbegović would sign. However, I countered by suggesting that the president could not afford not to sign, though I said this more in hope than expectation. As we spoke, it occurred to me that Karadžić had been wearing a heavy coat throughout the day and had made no effort to take it off, despite the day being bright and mild. I suspected he was wearing body armour underneath it.

I made contact with the presidency and spoke with Somun to inform him that Karadžić had agreed to the document and would be signing it shortly. I stressed that I required reassurance that the president was also willing to return to the airport to sign. Though he told me that Izetbegović was in a meeting, I urged him to make sure the president was aware of this, emphasizing that the more time passed the more suspicious the Serbs would become. He assured me that he would deal with it and inform me when the time came, but I had an uneasy feeling about this.

I informed Karadžić of these developments. He was still convinced that Izetbegović would not sign. However, I was relieved that the Serb delegation made no move to leave the building and seemed content to sit and wait. As time passed, I paced up and down the terminal corridor willing the phone to ring. Then Jovičić came in to tell me that the presidency was still in session and that a request that the signing be put back until 6.00 pm had been received. I was now concerned that it would be dark by then, with an increased risk of shelling, something that was becoming the daily norm. It was time to take the initiative, so I made contact with Somun, who informed me that Izetbegović's meeting was still ongoing. I asked to speak to the president on the phone, and when told this was not possible I asked Somun to convey to the president that if he did not come to the airport I was prepared to issue a statement to the media informing them that the Muslims, unlike the Serbs, were unwilling to sign. I told Somun that if I did not hear from them I would assume Izetbegović was not coming. I hoped I would not seem to be being too pushy, but I had the feeling he was suitably alarmed. He assured me he would contact me as soon as possible.

Shortly after the deadline Somun made contact and informed me that Izetbegović would be at the airport within thirty minutes and would be accompanied by Boraš. I breathed a sigh of relief and made contact with Martin Bell, who had been waiting patiently with his crew. I told him to ensure that his camera crew set up in the restaurant hall, where we had a table ready for the signing. The UNPROFOR escort arrived and I believed I could finally feel more confident of a result. However, just when I thought everything was falling into place, the sound of gunfire erupted, most of it coming in our direction from the nearest residential complex south of the airport and then from nearby Butmir. It gradually increased in intensity. The UNPROFOR troops hit the ground and took shelter behind armoured vehicles. I had entered the building to get the documents for signing when bullets struck the window ahead of me. I made my way cautiously to where Karadžić was waiting and found him pretty upset. He immediately pointed the finger of blame at Izetbegović, raging that the president would use the shelling as an excuse not to come to the airport. I responded that this was all the more reason why he must sign the agreement and that I had already been informed that Izetbegović was en route. I told Karadžić that if Izetbegović did not sign, the Serbs would have gained the upper hand and be seen as the ones who supported Carrington's initiative. I knew I was taking a chance in saying this but hoped he would understand my reasoning. We managed to reach the restaurant hall, where Martin Bell was already waiting. Karadžić, still wearing his long coat, sat at the table and signed. I read out the wording, mainly to have it recorded on camera, and reminded him of his responsibility. The agreement was succinct. It read:

> The three Parties, SDA, SDS, and HDZ have agreed to respect fully and unconditionally the Cease-fire Agreement reached on 12 April 1992. On this basis the three parties further agree to

> resume talks on the future constitutional arrangements for Bosnia Herzegovina, under the auspices of the EC Conference in Lisbon on Monday, 27 April 1992.

As soon as it was done, Karadžić headed for the hangar where the Serb delegation's helicopter was waiting. Jeremy Brade later told me that both Karadžić and Koljević left the building at a crouch, sheltering behind a JNA tank. Karadžić ran straight but could not bend too low, due, I presume, to the flak jacket under his winter coat. Koljević, however, zigzagged across the apron, dodging the bullets coming from the Butmir side. Once they made it to the helicopter, it wasn't long before it rose and flew low over the nearby houses in the direction of Lukavica, the JNA military barracks, and safety, a short distance away. The helicopter had hardly taken off before Izetbegović arrived under heavy escort. Both he and Boraš proceeded to sign in the same manner as Karadžić. The BBC crew was again on hand to record it and managed to get a quick interview with Izetbegović.

I finally had the document with the signatures on it, and by now all shooting had stopped. The president did not delay, quickly returning to his vehicle and being whisked away under escort. When I was informed that his convoy had headed towards the nearby residential buildings, close to where the shooting had been fiercest, I had an uneasy feeling. What if the outbreak of shooting was deliberately aimed at frustrating the signing? Why was the gunfire emanating from Muslim-occupied locations? Why did it stop just when the president arrived? I had a bad feeling about the entire episode and it made me realize that nothing in Bosnia was what it seemed. The question now was how long this latest agreement would survive. That said, as I made my way back to Ilidža I felt pretty good. I had achieved what Carrington had asked of me, shooting had stopped (at least for now) and perhaps things might actually improve. Back inside the hotel there were media requests waiting for me, but I ignored these for the moment and went to see Antonio dos Santos, thanking him for the support he and his team had given me. I was suddenly very tired and decided it would be an early night, but first I had to contact Carrington's office with an update. I had just finished speaking on the phone when all hell broke loose. The peace was shattered by fierce gunfire and shelling around the hotel which had us all diving for cover. I looked at my watch. It was 9.00 pm. As Martin Bell was later to record in his BBC report, 'In Bosnia when a cease-fire is signed, it's time to duck for cover.' Looking out from the balcony of the ECMM office we could see the night sky being lit up by flashes from weapons (including tank fire from the JNA), shells exploding and fires taking hold. I felt an overwhelming sense of anger, frustration, disappointment and failure. It was then that I understood that these leaders, all of them, while quite willing to put their names to any cease-fire agreement, had not the slightest intention of adhering to it. After an hour or so, and with no let-up in the barrage, I made it back to my room and crawled into bed. I fell into a fitful sleep to the continuing accompaniment of gunfire and shelling.

The situation had eased off around 7.00 am the following morning, and soon after I set about calling a meeting with party representatives for 3.00 pm. These meetings were to become a daily occurrence. I did some local and international media interviews during the morning, trying to get the message across of the need to honour agreements signed, but I doubt if they had any effect. I had to continue regardless and I was also aware that Carrington was planning on holding talks in Lisbon and that there would be a need to persuade the SDS, SDA and HDZ to attend. The negotiations were scheduled for the following weekend, and I knew that it could be difficult arranging travel, given the intensity of fighting in and around the airport. With the city slowly being squeezed shut by the gradual Serb encirclement, this next task represented a significant challenge.

I chaired the meeting in the afternoon which was attended by representatives of the three main parties and the JNA. Apart from Lieutenant Colonel Dimitrijević, I had not met any of them previously and thus had no idea of their seniority. However, none of them could have doubted the extent of my anger when I spoke of the breakdown of the cease-fire. While the Croat representative had nothing to say, the Serb and Muslim officials were at each other's throat with allegations and counter-allegations of breaching the cease-fire. The best I could do was to warn them that the forthcoming peace talks in Lisbon depended on there being some semblance of calm over the following few days. Granted, it wasn't much of a carrot, but it was all I had to offer. When the meeting adjourned I had a short talk with Dimitrijević, and we agreed that while the situation did not look good we would endeavour to keep our lines of communication open.

That evening, I had the chance to phone through to Grainne. She had watched some of the interviews, and while the publicity seemed flattering she advised me to 'keep the head and do what you can.' Later, I sat for a while with Martin Bell and we discussed the situation. He had little doubt that the conflict would intensify. I found him keenly aware of what was going on. He was bright, had great vision and a passion for what he was doing. I enjoyed his company, although not always when it came to selecting positions for my interviews. Two days beforehand, as we stood on his balcony having a glass of wine while preparing for an interview, some shots were fired in our direction and I spilled the wine diving back through the doorway. We talked about the likelihood of this or any subsequent cease-fire holding. In spite of my feelings of frustration and anger at the cease-fire breaking down, I knew that we had little choice but to persist with efforts to improve the situation. As long as we could persuade the parties to come to the negotiating table and at least discuss ways and means of containing the conflict, then that was what we should do. If a cease-fire did not work, or was broken, we would simply have to try again – the citizens of Sarajevo were owed that. At 1.15am, however, the shelling started all over again.

Chapter 12

On the Brink

I was busily occupied over the following few days attending meetings with Stjepan Kljuić, the board of Sarajevo Television and General Kukanjac. Kljuić, who was a founding member of the HDZ and a member of the Bosnian presidency, advocated that Croats should support the elected government of Alija Izetbegović; in this he differed from the other Croat presidency member, Franjo Boraš, who leant more towards the leadership in Zagreb. When I met Kljuić I was unsure of his exact status but had no wish to raise it as an issue. However, in referring to the forthcoming talks in Lisbon I asked if he would be representing the Croats. He told me that a decision had not yet been made and that it might be Milenko Brkić who would travel as the Croat representative. This was a clear indication to me that, as I suspected, Kljuić had been, or was about to be, sidelined in favour of Brkić, who was obviously on the right wing of the HDZ. This was not a good sign, as it indicated to me that the HDZ leadership was very much under President Tudjman's influence.

Meeting again with the board of Sarajevo Television yielded no good results either. There was still an impasse over giving airtime to the Serbs, not that it was relevant any more. Given that the Serbs were reluctant even to drive to the television station, positioned as it was in the Muslim-dominated area of Alipašino Polje, there was little pressure coming from their side. In any case, now that most of the relay transmitters were directed towards Belgrade, Serbs had less to complain about. In the meantime, General Kukanjac was becoming a very anxious and embittered commander. While he may have given the impression that his army was maintaining a neutral stance, information coming into the monitor mission from North-East Bosnia indicated that elements of the JNA were supporting the ethnic cleansing orchestrated by Serb paramilitaries. As the most senior military officer in Bosnia, Kukanjac still held command authority with loyalty to

Belgrade. He may well have been ignorant of Milošević's intentions, but as an old Yugo-centric officer he was generally hostile to Serb nationalism. I had picked up from a conversation overheard between Karadžić, Koljević and General Kukanjac at the airport that all were anxious to know when General Ratko Mladić might be coming to Sarajevo to take command. I suspected then that Kukanjac might not have known what role he was expected to play, and it was a difficult position that he found himself in.

I found myself wondering if holding meetings or trying to negotiate cease-fires had any point. One part of me felt anger and frustration that all sides, and in particular the Serbs, were simply playing along so as to be seen to cooperate, while actually following their own agenda, which had little to do with negotiation or mediation. Moreover, each side lied in an attempt to portray itself as the victim. I knew there was little alternative, but I was coming to realize that despite our best efforts, events were being orchestrated with scant regard to the potentially awful consequences.

On the morning of Monday, 27 April 1992 I took a phone call from a Mrs Banjac, who pleaded with me to intercede on behalf of her husband, Jasenko. She explained to me that he had worked for the national telecommunications company and lived in Ilidža. During a period of shelling he, along with others, had taken cover in a basement and while there managed to connect a telephone line so as to be able to maintain phone contact. She went on to explain that Serbs had found the connection and taken her husband away. She believed he was now a prisoner and detained in the area of Vraca, an area of Sarajevo held by the Serbs. She understood that he was being tortured and appealed for my help in finding him and securing his release. I promised her I would do my best, and at our daily inter-party meeting that afternoon I brought up the question of Banjac and demanded of the Serb representative that I be given the full details of his arrest. I told him that I wanted the matter brought directly to Karadžić's attention and that I expected a response within two days. Before I left the meeting I asked Lieutenant Colonel Dimitrijević if he would follow up on my request about Banjac with whatever sources he might have. He promised to do his best.

That afternoon, Cutileiro made contact and asked me for an update. I think he sensed my increasing frustration at the lack of any noticeable progress and wanted to reassure me that my efforts were very much appreciated by Carrington. He went on to explain that the talks scheduled for Lisbon were dependent on the three sides being represented at the highest level. I told him that the Serb delegation was already on its way to Lisbon but that my understanding was that Izetbegović's delegation might be reluctant to travel, given the worsening situation. I then spoke with Somun at the presidency, requesting a meeting with Izetbegović. I was pleased when he readily agreed, having wondered if my rather abrupt demand of a few days ago that the president return to the airport to sign the cease-fire had caused a strain in our relationship. Within the hour I was sitting with him and his deputy, Ejup Ganić. Izetbegović's daughter, Sabina, who was his interpreter, was also in the room. I had given some thought to how I should approach the discussion and opened with a question about when Carrington could expect him in Lisbon for the peace talks. He seemed somewhat surprised, as if he didn't know. He asked how, under the circumstances, it would be possible to travel there. Having no idea whether he was aware of the impending talks or if he had any wish to participate, I pressed on, telling him that Karadžić and Koljevićwere already on their way there to represent the Serbs and that if he did not attend he would be handing the Serbs the moral high ground, which, I argued, they would ruthlessly exploit. Izetbegović then asked how he should get to the airport, before adding that the government's only aircraft had been illegally taken by the Serbs and flown to Belgrade. He also stated that he felt he should remain in Sarajevo during this critical time. I attempted to be measured in my response, explaining that while I understood his position, the talks were of the highest importance and reluctance to attend might send out the wrong message. I asked him whether, if I could secure an aircraft and provide his delegation with a UN escort to the airport, he would be willing to attend. He then turned to Ganić and spoke with him for a few minutes before informing me that he would travel, but only for one day.

With this achieved, I now sought out the HDZ representative, Milenko Brkić, to confirm whether he, too, would go to Lisbon. On my way out of the presidency I stuck my head into the office of the Croat membership of the collective presidency and was fortunate enough to catch Brkić there. When I explained in similar terms to him the need for representation at the Lisbon peace talks, he assured me he would be available to travel in the same aircraft. I thought this was working out just fine and hoped Cutileiro would be able to do the rest, so I wasted no time in contacting him, briefing him on the meetings and explaining that both the SDA and HDZ delegations had committed to attending the Lisbon talks. But despite this commitment, I told him, we had logistical problems to address before the flight from Sarajevo to Lisbon could go ahead – we needed a plane to take them there and a UN escort to transport them to the airport. Cutileiro said that he would organize the plane and asked if I would discuss the escort with UNPROFOR. I then phoned the presidency and briefed Somun on the plan, recommending that the president be ready to go to the airport from the presidency building from lunchtime the following day. I was informed that Izetbegović would also be travelling with his daughter Sabina, his personal bodyguard, Nurudin Imamović, and Zlatko Lagumdžija. I knew Lagumdžija, a Muslim who was the leader of the non-nationalist Social Democratic Party (SDP) in the government and also a deputy prime minister. I presumed he was in the delegation so that Izetbegović could demonstrate that his views were not necessarily those of Muslim nationalists alone of but secular Muslims as well. This would refute the allegation by the Serbs that Izetbegović was aiming to turn Bosnia into a Muslim state.

The following morning, Tuesday, 28 April, I made contact with UNPROFOR and General MacKenzie, who agreed to have a UN escort at the presidency building to collect the delegation at 2.00 pm. While waiting to hear back from Cutileiro, I made a visit to the Mayor of Sarajevo, Professor Muhamed Kreševljaković, a former lecturer at Sarajevo University, who wanted to meet with me about the city's food supply. He was very alarmed at the escalation of the conflict. Moreover, as mayor, he was conscious of the rapidly diminishing food supplies in the city and the problems of bringing in more. He informed me that he was preparing an appeal to the President of the EC Commission, Jacques Delors, and that he wanted to highlight the plight of his citizens, the urgent need for assistance in the form of food and medical supplies, and the importance of lifting roadblocks. I fully agreed with his assessment of the situation and his view that the city could be facing a humanitarian nightmare. I promised him I would arrange delivery of his appeal to the EC.

Cutileiro got back to me later that morning, confirming that an aircraft had been arranged from Paris to collect the president and his delegation for the flight to Lisbon. It should arrive in the afternoon by about 4.00 pm after a short refuelling stop in Graz, Austria. He gave me details of the company providing the aircraft which I needed to pass on to Mile Jovičić, the director of Sarajevo Airport. Jovičić had already heard that the president was due to fly to Lisbon and was keen to know more about the arrangements. I told him that an aircraft from the Darta company was scheduled to pick up the delegation later that afternoon and that the president would be brought to the airport under UN escort. I then asked him under whose jurisdiction the air traffic control over Sarajevo lay and he told me it was with Belgrade, cautioning that they would be aware of the flight and might refuse it permission to land. I was not very happy to hear this, fearing that Belgrade might interfere with our plans, but there was little I could do but wait and hope.

I had to arrange transport for myself and once again asked the ECMM to help me. I was told that Antonio dos Santos was on home leave and Vitor was acting chief. Vitor arranged for a car to come and take me to the presidency building for 2.00 pm. I was hoping I had left nothing to chance and that things would go smoothly, but I should have realized that in Bosnia nothing ever went according to plan. When Vitor and I arrived at the presidency, Somun took us into Izetbegović's office. I briefly outlined to his delegation the plan for moving him to the airport and expressed the hope that all would go well. The president seemed satisfied and told me he was looking forward to a successful outcome of the discussions. I was not thinking beyond the departure of his aircraft, so I made a quick call to the airport director, who told me that the authorities in Graz had faxed him requesting confirmation that Sarajevo airport was safe to receive the aircraft. He assured me that he had replied informing them that the airport was safe and his staff were ready to receive the flight. He had also told them that all incoming flights would be landing at their own operational risk. Vitor came over to tell me that the UN escort were assembled on the roadway at the rear entrance to the presidency.

We waited. The president seemed quite relaxed, enjoying coffee with his officials while I was pacing just outside his office. At 4.00 pm I began to become worried that Belgrade might have done something to prevent the aircraft landing. Izetbegović asked me how long it would be before they could move to the airport and I could only say that we could not do so until such time as we had confirmation that the aircraft had landed. He smiled and shrugged his shoulders. I liked Izetbegović. He was always courteous and I believed him to be a man of integrity. I contacted Vitor, enquiring as to the status of the plane, and was told that there had been a delay in Graz. The plane had not yet taken off but it was only a thirty-minute flight. He assured me that the centre for approval of flights in Belgrade had given the all clear for landing in Sarajevo. It was after 7.00 pm before I was able to enter the president's office and inform him that the flight had left Graz and was en route to Sarajevo. I took a chançe that the plane might have landed by the time we reached the airport, for I worried that delaying any longer increased the chances of the convoy being attacked en route. I led the group downstairs and out through the rear of the presidency. The president's car was waiting between two UN armoured vehicles, with my car to the front. I took Darko Ivić along, and there were also some Ministry of the Interior police vehicles to the front and rear of the convoy. We moved off, and as soon as we were mobile I contacted Vitor again. There was still no word on the aircraft.

We arrived at the airport around 8.00 pm without incident. There was no traffic and no pedestrians were on the road. An uneasy calm seemed to have descended on the city which I found rather unsettling. We were met by Jovičić and Vitor, and some JNA liaison officers attached to the airport staff were also present. Jovičić had placed his office at the president's disposal and soon it was filling with people. They were all deep in conversation which helped to pass the time. Izetbegović seemed quite calm and not frustrated by the waiting, although I assumed he would want to know why the aircraft had not yet landed after I had told him that it had departed Graz. Jovičić then explained to the group that the control tower reported the plane had yet to take off from Graz. I apologised to Izetbegović, but he was gracious in his response, assuring me that he appreciated my endeavours to get them safely to Lisbon.

At some time around 10.00 pm I realized there would be no aircraft coming to Sarajevo. Despite all the assurances given, we were still stuck in an office at the airport, with the president of Bosnia virtually a prisoner.

Moreover, we faced the prospect of escorting him back through hostile territory to the centre of the city. I felt foolish, embarrassed and frustrated, but I had requested that the UN escort remain at the airport, just in case. Having apologised once more to Izetbegović and his delegation, we headed back towards the city having failed to accomplish the mission. Fortunately, we made it back without incident, and it was agreed that we would start all over again the following morning. I knew I would be making many phone calls before the night was over. Back at the hotel, I called the aircraft hire company in Paris, the airport authorities in Graz, Cutileiro's office in Lisbon and even the Air Traffic Regional Headquarters in Belgrade. I managed to establish from the aircraft hire company that the original flight had been cancelled and another one was scheduled for 10.00am the following day. When I asked why the aircraft had not flown to Sarajevo as scheduled, I was offered the excuse that the Austrian authorities at Graz had hesitated in giving approval and that when it was finally given the pilot was unwilling to fly.

Early the following morning, I went through much the same routine as I had the previous day, though this time it would work out pretty well. When I arrived at the presidency I met Darko, who informed me that the Croat leader Milenko Brkić had decided not to travel. Izetbegović and his party were, however, ready to move, under UN escort. The convoy arrived at the airport without incident. A French Falcon jet was already on the apron, having arrived from Graz at 10.00am. We drove straight up to the aircraft and within minutes the president, his daughter, his personal bodyguard and Zlatko Lagumdzia were airborne. I thanked the UN escort, arranged to let them know when they would be required again on the president's return and breathed a sigh of relief as I watched the aircraft climb into the clouds. As I headed back with Darko he casually remarked that he hoped 'the return journey is as smooth as his departure'. I replied that we needed to ensure that a UN escort was in place for the president's return. I wasted no time in letting Cutileiro know that Izetbegović's delegation was on its way. When I mentioned to him that the Croats had pulled out he did not seem too perturbed. He told me that he would like me to pay a visit to Pale, now the new location of the SDS headquarters of the 'Serbian Republic of Bosnia'. It seemed the negotiators in Lisbon were trying to persuade the Serbs to withdraw some of their heavy weapons from positions overlooking Sarajevo as a goodwill gesture, and it would be beneficial if I could provide some confirmation that this was taking place.

At our commission meeting that afternoon I raised the issue of the city's food supplies and issued an appeal that there should be no restrictions at checkpoints on deliveries of food. During this meeting Lieutenant Colonel Dimitrijević was able to confirm to me that Jasenko Banjac was indeed a prisoner of the Serbs and being held at Vraca; he informed me that my demand had been passed on to the Serbs and it was expected that he would be released very soon. I thanked him for the message and decided not to ask him as to how he had garnered this information. It was one piece of good news in an increasingly bleak context. That evening, fighting broke out again in various parts of the city and the almost daily shelling intensified. Whether this was due to the absence of the president or not, I had no idea, but it seemed that any excuse was sufficient to start the onslaught. I sought out Jeremy Brade to brief him on what Cutileiro wanted from my visit to Pale and suggested that he be available to accompany me. I suspected that the Serbs would use their usual stalling tactics, but I was determined to be allowed to examine the repositioning of their weaponry so I could verify whether they had indeed complied with what had been demanded of them in Lisbon.

In order to get to Pale, however, I needed to inform the Serbs of my intention, and I succeeded in contacting Biljana Plavšić, one of the former Serb members of the collective Bosnian presidency. She had not, as yet, moved to Pale, as she was concerned about her elderly mother, who still lived with her in a high-rise apartment building in the city. I had met her on a few occasions when attending meetings with members of the collective presidency. An outspoken nationalist, Plavšić had shown her true colours when in the full glare of television she greeted the brutal and dangerous Serbian paramilitary leader, Arkan, with a kiss after he had 'cleansed' Bijeljina a few weeks previously. We agreed to meet at the edge of the city at 2.00 pm from where we would be escorted to Pale. I asked her that there should be no publicity surrounding my visit. I didn't, after all, want to give the impression to the Lisbon peace conference that my visit to Pale was somehow giving legitimacy to the newly declared Republika Sprska (Serb

Republic). However, I suspected that my visit might be exploited somehow, and I had no confidence that Plavšić would keep her promise.

That same morning, 30 April 1992, the deputy prime minister, Rusmir Mahmutčehajić, asked to meet me. After arranging with Plavšić to meet that afternoon, I made my way to the deputy prime minister's office. Mahmutčehajić was Muslim, a noted academic and leading intellectual. He was a strong advocate of a multi-cultural and politically diverse Bosnia founded on mutual respect between the different ethnic groupings. A man in his mid-forties, I noticed he had very poor eyesight. After introductions he invited me to sit and, opening his desk drawer, he extracted two sheets of typed paper which he offered to me. He went on to explain that this was the transcript of a telephone conversation between one of the Serb delegates in Lisbon, Nikola Koljević, and an associate, Mladjo Karišić, who was based somewhere in the Serb-held outskirts of Sarajevo. The transcript recorded Koljević telling Karišić that I was to be shown Serb artillery positions from which weapons had been withdrawn, as agreed at the Lisbon talks. Koljević added that 'Doyle cannot be fooled because he is a military man.' Immediately, I wondered how Mahmutčehajić had come into possession of the document, and I asked him if there was anything else in the transcript that was relevant and that I should be aware of. He answered that the official in Sarajevo was admitting to Koljević that the army had been engaged in shelling the previous night. I paused for a second before asking if by 'the army' he (and they) meant the JNA. He replied that they did. I told him it would be useful to have a copy of the document and he assured me this could be done.

I then set out in an ECMM car with Jeremy Brade for my rendezvous with Biljana Plavšić. I had briefed Jeremy on what I wanted to achieve from my visit, having given him the gist of my conversation with Cutileiro. Plavšić was waiting when we arrived at the rendezvous point, where we were met by a Serb driving a brand new unregistered VW. The ECMM had mentioned to me a few days previously that Serbs had ransacked a vacated Volkswagen assembly plant in Vogošća, stealing hundreds of new cars. During my time as ECMM chief we had visited the factory, after which we were invited to a function by the German management team and their families. They were, at that time, becoming concerned about the deteriorating security situation in

Sarajevo and had asked us to advise them about when they should consider leaving. When we believed the situation had got to a stage where foreign citizens were seriously at risk, we had indeed advised the Germans to leave, which they promptly did, leaving everything behind them. Now all these new cars were in the hands of Serbs.

We had scarcely travelled a mile in the VW before we were forced to move off the road in order to give way to a convoy of M-84 tanks heading in the same direction. Here was the first evidence of large elements of the JNA moving to Pale, and in the process reappearing as the Army of Republika Srpska (VRS). When I asked Plavšić if she could explain the reason behind this sudden convoy I was given the silent treatment. Such was the volume of military traffic on this newly constructed route to Pale that we could make no further progress, so I informed her that I was returning to Sarajevo. She seemed almost relieved. I told her I would attempt the trip the following day, and she agreed to accompany me again. I later contacted Cutileiro and gave him the details of my unsuccessful attempts to reach Pale.

Friday, 1 May 1992 started well. It was my forty-fifth birthday, and although I hadn't told anybody I was surprised by the BBC television crew, who invited me to their office. When I arrived I was greeted by a smiling Martin Bell, who produced a birthday cake prepared by the hotel staff. I had no idea how they had found out, but it was an enjoyable hour's break from the reality of the situation in which we found ourselves. Bell was aware that there had been large convoys of JNA military hardware moving in the direction of Pale. As I was leaving the hotel I briefed Jeremy Brade, who was to accompany me, letting him know that I was determined to check whether the Serbs had pulled back their heavy weapons. I needed to verify this to Cutileiro as soon as we returned from Pale.

As arranged, Plavšić was waiting in a car at the agreed meeting point. I got into the car with her while my own vehicle, with Jeremy Brade as passenger, followed closely behind. During our drive towards Pale I casually mentioned that it was my birthday, though I wished it had come in 'better times'.

She immediately told me, 'We'll have to do something about that.'

I thought no more of it, and as we progressed along the route, now clear of military traffic, she offered her opinion as to why Serbs should be entitled to a greater percentage of Bosnian territory. It was her contention that Serbs lived on some 64 per cent of the territory of Bosnia and as such had a right to 'own' that amount. When I asked her how she came up with that exact figure she tried to explain that Muslims were 'mostly urban dwellers', while Serbs were more rural.

Serbs, she said, were 'of the land and, therefore, not only deserve but are entitled to more territory'. She went on to say that before the Muslims had increased in number, Serbs had occupied the territory and that was why they were entitled to a bigger share. She then told me that it was important for Bosnian Serbs to be able to join with their fellow Serbs in Serbia, which was why the eastern portion of Bosnia was so very important for them. I decided to take her on and asked whether this provided sufficient justification for the clearing of Muslims from the towns and villages along the eastern border with Serbia.

She gave me a cold look and calmly responded, 'If it takes the lives of three million people to solve this conflict then let's get on with it.'

I was stunned into silence by her belligerent tone.

It was obvious that we were expected in Pale. We were ushered into a room and after the usual welcoming rituals I was introduced to a line of Serb officials recently appointed to the government of Republika Srpska. I knew that I was about to be subjected to a long lecture on the Serb view of Bosnia's crisis, but while accepting that this was part of what I had to endure, my primary task lay elsewhere, so I interrupted, directing my attention to Plavšić. I impressed upon her that I was in Pale to see for myself evidence that the artillery and tanks overlooking Sarajevo had been withdrawn far enough so as no longer to pose a danger to the city. I requested that Jeremy Brade be taken to these positions now so that we could verify what had been agreed in Lisbon. Plavšić agreed to arrange for Jeremy to be taken there immediately, and he left in the company of an official who spoke English.

For the next two hours I listened to the Serb view of how unfairly they were being treated by the international community, why it was important for them to have their own entity and why they could not and would not live in a country dominated by Muslims.

As one female member explained, 'We Serbs will only feel safe if we have all-round protection. We are on our own and we can trust nobody, particularly Muslims.'

Of course, I had heard all of this before, and while I understood some of their concerns, they seemed to have an almost obsessive mistrust of Muslims. I asked why they were continuing to shell Sarajevo, and the response was as I expected – that Serbs were only trying to protect their ethnic kin still in the city. I was finally rescued by the return of Jeremy, but although I was anxious to listen to his report I was unable to leave right away. I was on the point of thanking our hosts when the door was suddenly opened and amid a flurry of activity, including the sudden appearance of cameras, a large birthday cake was wheeled in, with Plavšić proudly announcing that Mr Doyle was pleased to be celebrating his birthday in the fledgling new state of Republika Srpska. I had to grit my teeth, and I left with the distinct feeling that I had been stitched up.

I asked Jeremy for his assessment of the Serb positions as we drove back towards the city. His conclusion was even bleaker than I had expected – as far as he was concerned, they had made absolutely no effort to move any of their heavy weapons back. He saw no fresh track-marks or empty tank placements, and most of the tanks and artillery that he saw were still well within range of the city. On the basis of this information I contacted Cutileiro to inform him of our findings. He told me the talks would be immediately suspended. It later transpired that Karadžić had given an interview to Belgrade Television expressing his satisfaction at the progress being made in Lisbon, claiming that the Serbs were to get more than half the territory of Bosnia and that the exact borders were to be negotiated later. However, Sarajevo Television reported that nothing had been signed because the Muslim delegation had first demanded a withdrawal of the heavy weapons overlooking Sarajevo and that the Serbs should cease the shelling of the city. My report to Cutileiro was to change all that.

It seemed utter madness to me that, given the importance of the talks, the Serbs in Pale were willing to ignore the demands from Lisbon. As a military officer I knew it would have been a very simple matter for the Serbs to pull back the weapons, if only for a short period, to show us that they were complying with the agreement. They surely should have realized that failure to act on this matter would cause the suspension of the talks. To me this was a total disregard for the endeavours of those attending the peace talks. It was all the more strange knowing that Koljević had, according to the phone transcript, instructed the Serbs to ensure I could see evidence of weapon withdrawals. With the talks now cancelled, I would have to make arrangements to be on hand for Izetbegović's return to Sarajevo.

Back at the hotel, I was brought up to date by members of the ECMM on the developing situation within the country. Within the city and in particular around the hotel, the monitors had had numerous lucky escapes amid fierce fighting. The operations room had, for example, been hit by shrapnel on more than one occasion. Under these circumstances it was impossible to guarantee the safety of monitors. The Mission's teams in both Bihać and Banja Luka were ordered to withdraw to Croatia on 29 April 1992, and teams from Tuzla and Doboj were pulled back to Sarajevo. Vitor also mentioned to me that he had been contacted by UNPROFOR HQ and asked to inform me that the Under-Secretary General for Special Political Affairs, Marrick Goulding would be visiting Sarajevo in a few days and might wish to meet with me. The UN was now facing a dilemma and beginning to find itself uncomfortably hemmed in. Although its HQ was based in Sarajevo, its mission and area of operations was in Croatia. As such, it had no mandate to engage with the deteriorating situation in Bosnia. Yet here it was, in a city under siege, being shelled by the JNA and unable to move around freely. All the ethnic tensions brought about by suspicion, mistrust and propaganda were coming together in Sarajevo and in their midst was a UN force HQ with no muscle or might. Little wonder Marrick Goulding was coming to visit.

Later that day, the ECMM was to lose one of its monitors based in Mostar. A team was escorting electricity repair workers towards the power plant located about 6km from Mostar in no-man's-land between the JNA and Croat forces. The party came under sustained fire and took cover, but in the midst of the chaos one of them, Bertrand Borrey from Belgium, was killed. They managed to withdraw safely when the fire lifted, and within a few hours Bertrand's body was recovered by his colleagues. It was a sad end to another exhausting day in which, once again, little had been achieved.

Chapter 13

A President is Detained

Saturday, 2 May 1992 was a dramatic day in Bosnia's history. It was on this day that Serb forces succeeded in taking control of the strategically important northern towns of Brčko and Doboj and thus secured the vital east-west corridor from Serbia to Serb-held territory in Bosnia. It was also the day that a concentrated effort was made by the JNA and Serbs to take over Sarajevo by moving on the Bosnian presidency building, the day that the telephone exchange and central post office were destroyed and the day that President Izetbegović was taken hostage. The first indication I had of the events about to unfold was when I received a phone call from the presidential liaison office. It was Hajrudin Somun on the line informing me that there was a problem in the city centre. I asked him what had happened and he told me that it appeared that some Muslims had fired into the JNA officers' club in downtown Sarajevo and three officers had been killed. I told him that these killings must be condemned and a public statement made, before all hell broke loose. He cautioned that it might already be too late and that there was now considerable shelling of the city, some of it directed at the presidency building and the mayor's office. I urged him to issue a statement immediately on television, lest the situation spiral out of control. He said he would do his best to ensure this was done.

I had little time to gather my thoughts when Vitor called me and told me that reports were coming in of fierce fighting in the city. There had, he said, been a number of casualties. I ran up to the office, where monitors were watching live television coverage of events taking place in the city centre. I saw Somun being interviewed. He was giving an account of how JNA officers had fired shots from the officers' club at a passing bus, killing some Muslim passengers. I could hardly believe it. This was the exact opposite of what he had just told me. Why would he do this? I was still shocked and trying to find out what was behind all of this when a radio message came into the ECMM office from one of its monitors in the city. We were told that a convoy of military trucks with troops and weapons was heading towards Marshal Tito barracks. Armed with this information, we continued to monitor the phones and watch developments on television. The reports were giving confusing accounts of what was happening, but one thing was perfectly clear – Sarajevo was under sustained attack by JNA and Serb paramilitary units. Accusations and counter-accusations were being hurled at each other by the different factions, making it impossible to get a clear sense of what was happening. In the light of this, as the situation became more critical, the ECMM ordered its personnel in the city to return to base.

In the presidency building the deputy president, Ejup Ganić, was close to panic. In the absence of President Izetbegović, who was in Lisbon, Ganić was ostensibly in charge, but his security personnel had advised him to leave the building before it was too late. He had been told that there was a series of ancient tunnels under the old government offices which might provide him with an escape route, but he was reluctant to take this option. In the meantime, loud explosions could be heard from the downtown area, and before long we learned that both the telephone exchange and the post office had been destroyed. This was to have serious repercussions for the citizens of Sarajevo, who now faced a future without any contact with the outside world. The siege of Sarajevo had begun. Serb forces had established a sort of front line on one side of the city, effectively cutting it off. The streets were strewn with corpses, many of them lying untouched for days.

Despite their superiority in numbers, weapons and equipment, the attacking forces faced a ragtag army of soldiers, volunteers and members of Sarajevo's criminal gangs who had certain advantages. They used their superior knowledge of the narrow streets and alleyways of the city to fight off the attack that had Ganić pinned down in the presidency building. However, while the attackers came as close as 200m from the building, tanks could not move down these narrow streets and the forward advance was halted. At Skenderija, close to the Miljacka River, the lead tank was immobilized by a shoulder-launched anti-tank missile, thus blocking the Serbs' armoured advance. However, the Serb front line did reach the edge of the city and gave them control of the suburb of Grbavica. In the meantime, members of the Muslim Territorial Defence managed to surround the JNA's barracks in Bistrik, where the JNA's commander, General Kukanjac, was based. By midday the barracks was under siege and several hundred JNA troops were trapped inside.

Vitor handed me his phone and told me that the television studio wanted to speak with me. Despite most of the city's phones now being out of service, the monitor mission had its own communications system which, thankfully, kept us in the information loop. The call was an urgent appeal to the ECMM to find a way of stopping the fighting in the city. With one of our interpreters listening in to translate for me, I chose my words carefully, saying that I had been watching the television news for the last three hours and all I could hear was one side accusing the other of causing this latest outbreak of fighting – yet no one, I emphasized, had talked about trying to stop it. If both Serb and Muslim sides were genuine about wanting to halt this round of fighting, then I would be willing to drive into the city to negotiate a cessation of hostilities. I told the caller to contact me again when both sides were ready to talk.

After I had hung up I wondered if I had made the situation worse. I was still angry about Somun lying to me, felt he had used me and, moreover, suspected he was just doing the bidding of his political superiors. I had suddenly lost any faith in him and would never trust him again. I turned to Vitor and told him that I was going to write a cease-fire appeal, which I would sign on behalf of Lord Carrington. I asked him to have it faxed to the studio for me. Within an hour I was able to see my written appeal held up in front of the studio camera. If I had known my written appeal for a cease-fire was going to be held up in this way I would have tried to make my writing a bit more legible, but it was as much as I could do, and in any event I had little faith that my appeal would make any difference.

Early that afternoon, while all our attention was focused on following the ongoing conflict in the city, I took a call from the presidency. I did not get the name of the caller, but he informed me that because of the fighting in Sarajevo, President Izetbegović would not be returning to the city that day. Assuming this call to be genuine, I thanked the caller, relieved that I would not have to worry about meeting the president; without thinking, I then made contact with UNPROFOR HQ giving them the information and telling them to stand down the escort, which was scheduled to take the president back from the airport. I did not, even for an instant, consider that this call might not have been genuine. It was to prove a serious error of judgement on my part, for which I was solely responsible. In fact, I did not give the matter any further thought as I was concentrating fully on what was happening in the centre of Sarajevo. The situation there had descended into chaos: barricades had been hastily erected and shelling from Serb positions became more frequent. Explosions could be clearly heard. Even the television transmitter on Mount Hum, overlooking the city, was struck. It was surreal watching the unfolding events on live television and at the same time hearing from our balcony the distinctive muffled sound of explosions coming from the city.

It was a few hours later, around 7.00 pm, when I was just finishing a rather meagre snack in the dining room, that one of the monitors came rushing over to my table. He told me that he had just been notified that President Izetbegović had arrived back at the airport, had been taken hostage by the JNA and was now being held by them at their base in Lukavica. I asked the monitor how exactly he had received this information and was told that it was already all over the television. I was up and out in a flash, with a sick feeling in my stomach. I met Vitor just inside the office, and he confirmed that it was indeed true. Who the hell had phoned me and told me that Izetbegović would not be returning? There was no time to consider that now as events were moving too quickly.

It appeared that the president had decided to return to Sarajevo despite his pilot being told that they would be landing at their own risk. I later found out that the JNA commander at the airport had informed the airport's director that Izetbegović would be landing shortly after 6.00 pm. From this I suspected that the phone call I had originally received about the president not returning must have come from the JNA. This was, I assumed, aimed at ensuring there would be no escort for Izetbegović. I later found out that on landing, the small white corporate aircraft had slowly moved along the edge of the apron. The president had expected to be met by the UN escort, but the only people walking out to meet it were a JNA major and the airport director. Izetbegović's daughter Sabina thought it was I who was accompanying the JNA officer and took this as indicating that all was well. As soon as they alighted from the aircraft, it turned and immediately took off again. Too late, they realized it was not me approaching but Jovičić, who had been instructed by the JNA to take the president to his office and await further instructions.

The returning party of President Izetbegovic, his daughter Sabina, Zlatko Lagumdžija and the security officer, Dino Imamović, were escorted to Jovičić's office, where the president demanded he be allowed to return to the city. This was refused by a JNA colonel who said he was acting on the orders of General Djurdjevac, the commander responsible for the airport. He told the president that he had been instructed to take him to the JNA barracks at Lukavica, a Serb-held village on the fringes of the city, about 3km from the airport. On hearing this, Izetbegović demanded to be allowed to contact the presidency, but the colonel told him all phone lines were down. By chance, however, a woman whose daughter was scheduled to depart on an aircraft earlier in the day had managed to put a call through to the director's office to ascertain if the aircraft had departed. Izetbegović took the phone, introduced himself to the lady and, explaining his situation, asked her to contact the presidency or, failing that, the television station. The woman, initially shocked to hear she was speaking with Bosnia's president, duly contacted the studio and repeated what the president had told her. This was the rather bizarre means by which the city found out that President Izetbegović had been detained.

In the meantime, General Kukanjac, surrounded in his own headquarters, was asking Belgrade what should be done with President Izetbegović. Branko Kostić, a Montenegrin and president of the newly-formed Federal Republic of Yugoslavia (consisting only of Serbia and Montenegro), now realized that with Bosnia's president in Serb hands there was an opportunity to use his detention as a means of lifting the blockade of the JNA HQ. Back at the airport, the presidential party was ordered into two cars and driven under heavy guard to Lukavica. The president of Bosnia was now a hostage. We continued to follow the unfolding events on television, which became the conduit for all our information. The television news desk became the only way in which Ejup Ganić, on a phone line not routed through the destroyed post office, was able to speak with Izetbegović. The entire population of Sarajevo must have been listening in to this quite bizarre episode in current affairs broadcasting. Ganić demanded that the president be immediately released, but this was refused. The JNA countered by accusing the government of ordering the Muslim Territorial Defence to surround the Bistrik barracks, thereby laying siege to the JNA. It gradually became evident that some sort of deal would have to be worked out that would facilitate the release of the president and the lifting of the siege of the barracks.

I took two calls late that evening. The first was from General Lewis MacKenzie, UNPROFOR's chief of staff, who told me that as the UN had no mandate in Bosnia he could have no direct involvement in sorting out the mess. He did, however, arrange a meeting between Ejup Ganić and General Aksentijević the following morning at UN HQ in an attempt to solve this crisis. He asked me to chair any negotiations which I agreed to do, albeit with a certain trepidation. I told him that I appreciated his help and that I would like him to be present at the next morning's meeting, to which he agreed. I then mentioned the phone call I had received earlier from what I had believed to be the presidency. He reckoned that I had been set up, either by some rogue element within the presidency or by the JNA at Lukavica.

That I would be charged with negotiating a hostage exchange at such a high level was something I had never even contemplated, and yet here I was facing exactly that. I took some time to think about what I might have to do and how I might tackle the task. The basic idea would seem to be pretty straightforward, the exchange of a president for a general, but it was the peripheral issues that might prove more problematic. It had been a sharp learning curve, but I had discovered over many months that in Bosnia nothing was as it seemed.

The second call I received that evening was almost equally dramatic. I was contacted by a woman appealing to me for immediate help. She spoke fairly good English and I wondered how she had been able to contact me by phone with so few connections possible (as a consequence of the destruction of the post office). She explained that she was a doctor and had been attempting to bring a newborn baby back to hospital for essential treatment, but had not been allowed to pass through a barricade. She told me, in no uncertain terms, that the baby would die if it could not reach the hospital and appealed for my help in achieving this. It was a heartfelt plea, and I felt I had to do something for her, so I quickly asked her where the barricade was located and promised I would do my best. I then told her I would try to make a TV appeal, so she should stay close to her television. The studio was still showing live coverage of the ongoing conflict, and after successfully getting through to the station I asked if I could be given a few minutes of airtime. When this was granted, I made my appeal, repeating what the doctor had told me. I was careful to say that I had not asked the doctor whether she was Serb, Croat or Muslim, nor had I enquired as to the ethnicity of the child. I emphasized that it was of the utmost importance that she be given immediate passage through the barricade so she could save the child's life. I then mentioned where the barricade was located and hoped that my appeal was heard. Later that night, the duty officer took a call from someone wishing to thank me for my help, but I never did find out for certain the outcome of my appeal and have often wondered about both doctor and child.

I spent a very restless night thinking over the day's dramatic events. I felt I was running on nervous energy and seemed to be on a permanent adrenalin rush. I slept fitfully if at all. At around 8.30 am the following morning I arrived at UNPROFOR HQ to meet General MacKenzie before the arrival of Ejup Ganić and General Aksentijević. I was not aware of what might have transpired the previous night in discussions between the presidency, the JNA and Izetbegović, who must have spent a most uncomfortable night in Lukavica. However, I presumed the discussions would have centred on exchanging the president for Kukanjac. MacKenzie agreed that we should concentrate our efforts on seeking a solution to this question. I was still at a loss to know who had contacted me about the president the previous day and wondered if anything might come out of the discussions to enlighten me.

Ganić arrived first and he was clearly quite nervous. I could identify with that as I felt exactly the same. The fact that President Izetbegović had announced publicly on television that he was appointing Ganić to take over if anything happened to himself seemed to weigh heavily on his shoulders. I made it clear to him that he would have to stand over any deal that was concluded. However, he told me that in the event of an agreement being reached he would have to clear it with the other members of the presidency. This was something neither MacKenzie nor I were prepared to accept, though we had both suspected he might take such a line. I told him that whatever was decided upon, he must take responsibility for it. The collective presidency, I told him, was no longer viable, and as President Izetbegović had appointed Ganić to act for him in his absence, then his agreement to any deal would be on behalf of the entire presidency. Both MacKenzie and I stressed that this was a very dangerous situation, in which the life of Bosnia's president was at stake. Ganić seemed taken aback by my firm approach, but having been given little option he just nodded and silently seemed to accept it.

General Aksentijević arrived soon afterwards, and I also explained to him that he alone would be the decision maker with regard to the JNA, though I had no doubt that he would have consulted with General Kukanjac in advance of our meeting. He agreed, but cautioned that he would have to contact Kukanjac to inform him of any agreement reached. MacKenzie looked over at me from his side of the table and nodded agreement. As the meeting proceeded, I suggested that each of them gave an opening statement so we would be clear as to what each side's expectations were. Ganić started by condemning the JNA for kidnapping the president of a sovereign state and demanded his immediate and unconditional release. Aksentijević countered by accusing the Muslims of carrying out an unprovoked attack on the JNA and of surrounding its headquarters. He then demanded the immediate lifting of the siege of the Bistrik barracks. Both MacKenzie and I had expected little else, but we felt that permitting each to let off some steam might render the subsequent negotiations more reasonable.

Within an hour we had more or less reached an agreement. It was envisaged that the UN would provide a convoy escort which would report to the JNA base at Lukavica. Izetbegović would then get into one of the UN armoured vehicles, and with General MacKenzie leading in his French VBL (light armoured vehicle) the convoy would head for the besieged barracks in Bistrik. Once there, Kukanjac would meet with the president and after a short time both would get back into the UN armoured vehicle. The convoy would then drive to the Bosnian presidency and Izetbegović would be allowed to enter his office as a gesture to show that he was no longer captive. Within a few minutes he would get back into the armoured vehicle and be driven back to UN HQ, where we would continue negotiations jointly to effect the release of the remainder of Kukanjac's troops. There was no discussion, at that stage, of lifting the blockade of the barracks. We assumed this would be for further negotiation, as would the question of Kukanjac's troops.

Contact was made with Lukavica, and Ganić informed President Izetbegović that a deal had been concluded. He then handed the phone to Aksnetijević, who informed the Lukavica base commander about what had been agreed. In the meantime, I contacted Vitor suggesting he send an ECMM team to the area of the besieged barracks to monitor developments. He agreed and said he would go himself and keep me updated. I had borrowed one of the mission's two-way radios earlier that morning to have as a communication back-up. As soon as both Ganić and Aksentijević made contact with their respective leaders, Ganić left, on foot, to return to the presidency. MacKenzie then suggested we drive to the barracks to oversee the release of the president. We both climbed into a UN French VBL and headed for the JNA base. It was a very small vehicle, and I was squatting in the rear, with MacKenzie sitting up front. As soon as we reached the entrance to the base we were met by a crowd of demonstrators in front of the locked gates. Thinking these were Muslims protesting at the detention of the president, MacKenzie told them that we were here to help and that we must be given entry or they would 'not get their sons back' and their 'wounded will die'. His words were translated by a Canadian who was one of the protestors. However, what MacKenzie did not realize was that, far from demanding the president's release, they were baying for his blood. The demonstrators were, in fact, Serbs not Muslims. Fortunately for me, I had stayed in the back of the VBL and was not visible to the mob. After a short wait the gates were unlocked and we were waved through.

MacKenzie decided to find out where Izetbegović was being held and went off to search for the base commander, while I stayed near the vehicle assuming the president would shortly appear. I waited and waited, but there was still no sign of Izetbegović or MacKenzie. I began to fret. Some journalists came over to interview me and asked if everything was in order; I responded by saying that we had reached an agreement and that if we were left to do our job all would be fine. Despite my words, however, I wasn't too confident. Finally, MacKenzie reappeared, and by his expression I knew something was wrong. He told me that he had been kept waiting for ages to see the president and it was only agreed that the two men could meet after MacKenzie had threatened to leave. He told me that we could now meet with Izetbegović. Before we had the chance to do so, however, we were taken to the office of the base commander, Colonel Milosav Gagović, a most unpleasant character. We had the distinct impression he would have preferred to kill Izetbegović rather than release him. Anyway, when he began to complain to us about how badly the JNA were being treated, I cut him short, demanding that we be taken immediately to see the president. He reluctantly brought us to the room where Izetbegović was being held, and there I was surprised to find the president speaking on the telephone with Kukanjac, persuading him to accept what had been earlier agreed at UNPROFOR HQ. His daughter Sabina and Zlatko Lagumdžija were with him, but there was no sign of the security officer, Nurudin Imamović. The president seemed in good spirits, although he had not slept for worrying about his daughter, who had been kept in a separate room. After finishing his conversation with Kukanjac he turned towards us and thanked us for arranging the exchange and providing the escort. It appeared that everything was going to plan.

Just when MacKenzie and I thought everything was working out, the phone rang again. It was Kukanjac. Izetbegović listened and then became agitated. He turned to us and said that Kukanjac was now insisting that his entire staff and troops, numbering around 400, should be allowed to evacuate the barracks as part of the deal. It was obvious that the JNA had decided it wasn't getting enough in exchange for the president and so had insisted that they all be allowed to leave with their weapons. I insisted that this could not be allowed, largely because Ganić would not be aware of this change, nor would the Muslims surrounding the barracks. To proceed would have, in my view, been madness. So I told him that he was going to have to call Kukanjac back to tell him that we had agreed a deal and there could be no changing that. Then I turned on my heel and stormed out, much to MacKenzie's surprise.

Outside I met Martin Bell, who was in the base with his BBC crew, and sat down beside him. He realized I was in a bad mood, listened to my frustration and gave me a few words of encouragement. I was heartened by what he said and suddenly realized that we should simply do whatever both sides would agree to, regardless of what that might be. We had to be pragmatic. We were not, after all, there to find the fairest solution but to go with whatever solution both would accept. Back inside, I talked with MacKenzie and told him we should listen to whatever Izetbegović might have to say, so we both went back and asked for his view. He stated candidly that he was willing to give the general what he wanted and that he (Izetbegović) would guarantee the security of the convoy. I tried to explain to him that while we would proceed with this, if that was what he wished, there could be problems. I explained that the evacuation of a large military unit such as the one inside the barracks was a complicated matter and I asked him how he could guarantee the security of the convoy when those surrounding the barracks might not have been told in time that he had agreed to let all the troops depart in a single convoy. I emphasized, moreover, that Ganić might not yet be aware that the details had been changed and that the Muslims, who were desperate for weapons, might think they were being tricked. I knew that MacKenzie was in full agreement with me. I then asked Izetbegović if he was guaranteeing the security of the convoy. He replied that he was, so I turned to MacKenzie and told him that we would give it a try. I had grave doubts, but having given my views already, kept silent.

I immediately contacted Vitor to let him know of the plan. After giving him the general details I asked what the situation was like in the city centre. He said that it was very tense and that they had come across many destroyed tanks and armoured personnel carriers (APCs) en route. The streets, he said, were littered with debris and burned-out cars, and he had seen many bodies and body parts, most of them from the tanks and APCs. He expressed concern that in such a tense situation the Muslim might be unaware that the original plan had changed. I fully agreed with him and told him that although

I had warned the president, he had given a guarantee on the security of the evacuating troops and we had little choice but to go on.

It was when we were coming down the stairs that I was confronted with another problem. Colonel Gagović, the base commander, suddenly appeared and stopped us. Through his interpreter he demanded to know where we were going with the presidential party. I explained to him that we were moving to the UN escort to commence the exchange. He responded sharply that we had negotiated the release of 'the president and only the president'. The rest, he said, had to stay as they were not part of the deal. General MacKenzie interjected that Izetbegović was in discussion with Kukanjac to verify that his daughter, Lagumdžija and the security officer were to be included in the exchange. The Colonel replied that he was simply following orders. I asked who had given them, but he looked at me without answering. This was a critical moment. I realized we needed to move quickly to get the exchange completed before nightfall, because after that it would be too dangerous. We were both already nervous about what might go wrong, so I turned to the Colonel and asked him if he had any idea of the consequences should this exchange fail. He looked directly at me and, to my surprise, told me that I must stay behind. Rattled, I quickly had to weigh up the options. I agreed that I would remain behind, but only on the condition that he allow the president's daughter and Lagumdžija to go. He hesitated for a moment before agreeing. This meant, in effect, that the security officer and I would be held as collateral.

The UN vehicles drew up outside and we helped the presidential party aboard. I turned to MacKenzie and asked that whatever happened he keep me informed, if possible. I added that I had a bad feeling about Colonel Gagović and that I would appreciate being extricated as soon as possible. The convoy then departed, and I was escorted back inside and brought upstairs to an office where I came face to face with General Djurdjevac, the Sarajevo JNA sector commander with responsibility for the airport and the officer who, I was led to believe, had ordered the president to be taken to Lukavica. I was shocked by his appearance. He was partially dressed, wearing only uniform slacks, boots and a white T-shirt. Unfortunately, there was no interpreter in the room to allow us to communicate, but he appeared to be very incoherent

– in a daze. He seemed to have no idea of who I was, although I had met him on a number of occasions. I simply sat down and ignored him. After a few minutes a female soldier entered the room, administered some sort of medicine to him and immediately departed again, ignoring me completely. I began to wonder if it was Gagović who had ordered the president to be taken to Lukavica rather than Djurdjevac, who was obviously in a pretty poor mental state. If this was the case, it would appear that Gagović was now in control, and this might not be good for me. I realized I could be in some danger. Gagović was unpredictable and, therefore, dangerous. I tried to raise Vitor on my handset, but to no avail.

Eventually, the colonel, accompanied by two soldiers, entered and ordered me out, gesturing that I should walk behind him down the stairs. He paid no attention to Djurdjevac. I began to feel very scared as I was brought outside the building to where a group of about fifty restless and noisy soldiers had assembled. Some of them were gathered round a Serb police car listening to some communication coming over the car radio. They were clearly agitated and looking back at Gagović, who was himself clearly annoyed. Just then my two-way radio came to life. It was Vitor. In a low voice, trying to remain calm, I asked him what was going on. His response scared me. He explained that things were 'very bad': though the convoy had arrived with the president, when they re-emerged they were followed by a large military convoy of trucks full of troops, weapons and equipment. The Muslims seemed unaware of what the latest plan was. As soon as they saw all the trucks they started shooting at them. Someone drove a civilian car through the convoy, splitting it in two. There had been much shooting and some troops had been killed. The Muslims were taking all the weapons. As I sat there I silently cursed, suddenly understanding what was causing the agitation among the soldiers around me. At that moment, Gagović looked at me and drew his pistol. I felt a cold shiver running through me and my mouth was suddenly very dry. He started shouting and randomly pointing the pistol in my direction, so I turned to the interpreter for a translation. I was told the news that I had feared, that many JNA soldiers were dead and others had been stripped naked and tortured. This was becoming a nightmare, but I knew I had to say something so I asked the translator to tell Gagović that the information coming over the car radio was inaccurate. Yes, I acknowledged, the convoy had been attacked, but there had been no torture or soldiers stripped naked. I assured him that I was in contact with the ECMM and was getting a true picture of the situation. Gagović, however, continued to wave the pistol at me, shouting that I was responsible for the fate of his men.

I had often wondered how I might react as a soldier if faced with something like this, never thinking for a moment that it would actually happen. Although I was in great fear I turned towards Gagović and told him that I had negotiated a deal that his people had broken, and that it was he who had demanded the release of all the troops. As a soldier, I told him, he should have known that there would not be sufficient time to inform those surrounding the barracks that all the troops were to be released. I went on to tell him that he should have realized how desperate the Muslims in Sarajevo were for weapons, which his people had taken away from them months ago – this was his fault, not mine. My voice was trembling but I continued, stating that if he continued to point his pistol at me I would have him arrested for threatening the life of Lord Carrington's personal representative. I must have sounded really panicked, but, remarkably, it seemed to have an effect. He hesitated, then slowly put his pistol back in its holster and led me back inside. I was taken back to the room which Djurdjevac occupied and the door was slammed behind me. The general seemed oblivious to my presence, and I just sat there trembling but feeling lucky to be alive. It was the first and only time I genuinely thought I would die in Bosnia.

Chapter 14

An Angry General

I tried to make contact with Vitor and after several attempts got through. I asked him what the position was with the convoy, and he told me that the streets outside the barracks were now deserted and all that remained were bits of personal belongings, files, some weapons that were useless and burning trucks. The convoy had been split, with one half of nearly 200 troops taken prisoner, but he had no idea where they had been taken. The other half, including General Kukanjac and General MacKenzie, were on their way back to Lukavica. I asked him about Izetbegović and was told that he was safe and had been transferred into another armoured vehicle heading for the presidency. I enquired whether Vitor might know who had ordered the attack on the convoy, but he said that it was too early to tell. I decided not to say any more on that point and finally asked if he had any information on casualties. He gave me a figure of seven soldiers. What a mess.

I was left for another thirty minutes or so in the same room as Djurdjevac and tried on a few occasions to make conversation with him but got nowhere. Communication wasn't made any easier by not having an interpreter, but I still found it hard to fathom his demeanour. He had made no attempt to attend to his unkempt appearance and seemed in another world. I found it alarming that he had been completely ignored by Colonel Gagović, as if he didn't exist. I felt sorry for him. Then Gagović came back into the room with his interpreter to announce that Kukanjac and MacKenzie had just arrived back at the base. He appeared a lot calmer than before and he beckoned for me to accompany him. As we walked down the stairs I demanded to know the whereabouts of Nurudin Imamović, the president's security officer, who had been held along with me as collateral. I had not seen sight of him since my arrival. He told me that he was being well looked after and would be released in due course. Having taken the chance earlier to confront this arrogant officer I had no problem about doing so again, so I told him that I held him directly responsible for Imamović's safety. However, given that 200 JNA soldiers were now being held prisoner somewhere in the city I thought it better not to press the issue too aggressively.

The returning troops were jumping down from their trucks as I arrived outside. When I saw MacKenzie appear with Kukanjac I suddenly felt a whole lot better, and while it was a great relief to see them back it was evident that Kukanjac was not in the best of moods. He immediately headed for his office, and I presumed his priority was to ascertain the fate of his missing troops. I went over to welcome him back and to assure him that I would do everything I could to ensure that his troops were released unharmed. The attack on the convoy, I added, should not have happened. What I would have liked to say to him was that, given the tension and unease that Sarajevo had suffered during the previous twenty-four hours, the chances of the convoy making it out uninterrupted had been almost negligible. I wanted to tell him of Gagović's part in the whole debacle but decided against saying anything. He nodded but said nothing, his mind no doubt focused on other matters, which I could understand. I went back to join MacKenzie, and in due course he gave a quick brief on what had happened when the convoy left the besieged barracks. Our fears that the convoy might come under attack from the Muslim Territorial Defence had been realized, but whether this was because there had been insufficient time to warn them of the change of plan, or was a deliberate decision to attack, we had no idea.

MacKenzie explained that the convoy was much longer than had been agreed, and its route was through very narrow streets which slowed progress. About 1km into the journey some shots were fired, and he jumped out of his VBL and started to run back towards the sound of gunfire. By the time he neared the scene the shots had become bursts of machine gun fire. Members of the Muslim Territorial Defence were sticking their weapons through the windows of civilian cars in the convoy and shooting the occupants. He could see blood spattered over the windscreens. It was just as he reached the scene that someone drove a car across the road, splitting the convoy. The Muslim soldiers were threatening to throw grenades into the back of JNA trucks if the troops inside did not surrender their weapons, so in an attempt to stop the shooting MacKenzie shouted that the president had guaranteed the security of the convoy.

A reply came from one of the gunmen: 'We gave no guarantee of security. The president is dead or kidnapped.'

MacKenzie then asked some of the Muslim soldiers to follow him, and as he walked back with them he explained that Izetbegović was in the leading APC. He then asked the president to open the top hatch of the APC and stand up. When the soldiers saw him they were astonished and stood silently for a few seconds before clambering on to the APC to greet him. Kukanjac, who was beside the president, was shocked to hear that some of his troops had been killed. It took some time before some semblance of order was restored. It seemed that nearly 200 JNA soldiers had been taken prisoner, with most of their weapons and military equipment taken by the Muslim Territorial Defence. A short distance further on, the president and his daughter Sabina were transferred into another armoured personnel carrier and driven to the presidency building. Kukanjac was beside himself with anger at the thought of having had so many of his men taken prisoner and others killed. MacKenzie then transferred him to his own vehicle and proceeded back to Lukavica.

There was much speculation about who might have ordered the attack on the convoy, but I had no doubt that it was the Muslim side, though at how senior a level I could not be sure. I had my suspicions but no proof. The chances of this operation ever succeeding without incident were never good, but our hand had been forced, and while we could argue that we were simply acting as go-betweens in an impartial manner, our military training and experience led us to believe otherwise. MacKenzie asked if things had been quiet at the Lukavica base and I told him they were tense but fine. I did not mention the incident with Gagović.

There was tension in Lukavica for some time after the convoy incident. It did not take much to realize that we were being held responsible for not guaranteeing the security of the convoy and that it was believed we had not kept our promise. There was little use in arguing the point. MacKenzie was worried about the safety of his troops, about a dozen of whom, mostly Swedish, were with him. I suggested that we should leave. I had had enough of Lukavica, it was getting dark and I was concerned for our lives after all that had happened. So I asked if we could be given a JNA escort to take us to the edge of the Serb-controlled area of Sarajevo. A JNA captain who understood we had not been responsible for the fate of the convoy volunteered to guide us. I climbed into the ECMM car that Vitor had sent me, and with MacKenzie and his soldiers in tow in two APCs we departed the base.

About 1km down the road we were confronted by a roadblock. The JNA officer went forward and spent some time talking to the guards. We stayed where we were, and when he returned he told us we would not be allowed through. When we asked why, he said that those manning the checkpoint knew who we were and believed that we were to blame for the death of the JNA soldiers. We decided to return to Lukavica but somehow, in the dark and being unfamiliar with the route, we ended up back again at the same roadblock a few minutes later. This time we were approached by its senior Serb commander and I distinctly heard the sound of AK-47 assault rifles being cocked. The commander came close and shone a torch in our faces. Trying to look calm, I asked him if he knew who we were. The JNA captain translated and the response came that, yes, they knew exactly who we were. Now we were suddenly surrounded by a number of Bosnian Serb irregulars, who indicated that the uniformed UN drivers should drive the APCs into a nearby yard. For some reason my car was allowed to remain where it was. The UN personnel were then ordered out of their vehicles and stripped of their weapons and flak jackets. I was left in my car. The commander then spoke, giving me an ultimatum. He said that as I had made the arrangements for the exchange, it was my responsibility to get their soldiers back. He told me he would be holding the UN soldiers until such time as the JNA personnel were released unharmed. The soldier told MacKenzie the same thing, to which he responded that, as a UN commander, he could not desert his troops and that he would have to stay with them. However, this tactic failed to work, and he was pushed towards my car and shoved into the back. He turned to his aide, Major Steve Gagnon, and told him that he was 'in charge now'. As we prepared to leave I addressed the Serb leader, telling him that when I returned to Lukavica I would issue a demand on television that the JNA troops who had been captured should be released unharmed. I told him to make sure he watched the TV for an assurance that I was doing everything I could to have them freed. I was sorry for MacKenzie, who must have felt pretty bad about having to leave without his troops or weapons. No commander would want that. Back at Lukavica, Kukanjac was still in a foul mood. We explained what had happened with MacKenzie, warning him that if any of the UN troops were harmed, his face would be all over CNN and the BBC. MacKenzie further added that if he wanted the truth about the attack on the convoy to come out he had better get his people back to him sooner rather than later.

When I realized that we might have to negotiate our way past the same roadblock later that night I asked if I could be put in touch with Sarajevo TV. Luckily, the phones from that part of the city had been unaffected by the destruction of the post office and I was able to be put through fairly quickly. News transmissions on the dramatic day's events were still being screened, and a hastily arranged interview was set up for me. Within a few minutes I was on air explaining the guarantee that had been promised by President Izetbegović on the convoy and my demand that JNA soldiers who had been taken prisoner must be released unharmed and without delay. I also mentioned that General MacKenzie would be in contact with the Bosnian presidency the following morning to negotiate the release of the JNA troops. I decided to say nothing about Izetbegović's security officer, having discussed this with General MacKenzie before giving the interview.

MacKenzie and I were taken into the base conference room, where some officers were having a meal. With a few exceptions, their attitude to the UN seemed to have softened, and we were handed drinks. It was a somewhat strained atmosphere, none of us wishing to discuss the day's events. Additionally, I was still feeling the effects of my earlier ordeal and had no desire to talk to anyone. It must have been particularly difficult for General Kukanjac, who had lost nearly 200 of his troops and had no idea as to their whereabouts or condition. About an hour later the door opened and to our surprise and relief MacKenzie's aide, Major Steve Gagnon, and the other Swedish UN soldiers walked in. They were all freezing but otherwise none the worse for wear. MacKenzie could have jumped for joy. A large tray of meat and fresh bread was brought in for them. We still, however, had to get back to our accommodation and I was anxious to get moving. MacKenzie managed to find someone wearing civilian attire who agreed to escort us back. The route was not to be through the roadblock this time but across a minefield, which had been laid by Serbs. I had no particular wish to be walking through it at night with no idea of the layout, but the volunteer assured us he would get us safely through. MacKenzie and his soldiers mounted the UN vehicles and I got into my ECMM car. We then followed our guide, who had a two-way radio on his lap, out of the base. We approached the minefield very slowly and stopped at its edge; after a lot of conversation on the radio a few individuals emerged from the side and began moving some of the mines off the road. Once through the minefield we bade farewell to our guide and, despite some shots fired in our direction, made it back safely to familiar territory.

Back at the hotel I had a reception committee waiting for me. The ECMM monitors, the press and hotel staff welcomed us back. I was surprised and frankly flattered by their concern for me. A bottle of whiskey was produced from somewhere and I was handed a large measure. It had been a long and dramatic twenty-four hours, during which I had helped negotiate the release of a president, been held as collateral in Serb-occupied territory, threatened with a pistol, endured detention at a checkpoint and been confronted with a minefield. For the first time I had thought I might be killed. No wonder I felt drained. The adrenaline was still pumping, and I didn't sleep a wink.

It was MacKenzie who took up the negotiations the following day, having received a call from the presidency requesting his help. He had alongside him Antonio dos Santos, who had returned from home leave. They met with the Bosnian Minister for Defence, Jerko Doko. MacKenzie made it clear what he was after and said that he believed that the Muslim side had 'captured these soldiers by breaking a promise of safe passage'. This, he argued, had put the UN in a very difficult position. He said that he wanted those JNA soldiers back without any concessions being demanded in return. MacKenzie agreed that in return for the released soldiers he would arrange for the release of Nurudin Imamović. There were a few twists and turns to the story of their release, but eventually the deal was accomplished. Throughout, I contacted Cutileiro on a regular basis to keep him informed. He conveyed Carrington's appreciation of our efforts to secure the release of Izetbegović and assured me that the dramatic television news reports were being avidly watched. He added that he was relieved to be 'listening from the rear' and was sympathetic to my position 'reporting from the front'. He added that I should make sure I stayed safe and that I would know myself when it was right to leave Sarajevo.

Marrick Goulding, the UN Under-Secretary General for Political Affairs visited Sarajevo on 5 May 1992. He had been flown by JNA helicopter to Pale and was due to be escorted to Sarajevo by UNPROFOR, but the escort was held up due to heavy fighting in the city. Finally, the Force Commander himself, General Satish Nambiar, insisted on leading the escort, which eventually succeeded in getting Goulding to the city later that evening. Part of the original plan agreed on the exchange of Izetbegović was that the blockade on the military headquarters should be lifted and that both sides should gather at UN HQ for further negotiations aimed at easing the stand-off between them. The events that transpired rendered this impossible at that time, but I was determined to get the presidency and the JNA round a table to come to some sort of agreement and break the impasse.

It has been suggested that the Serbs should have been included in the talks I chaired the following day, but that, I believe, demonstrates a lack of understanding of the immediate situation prevailing at the time. Firstly, the Serbs represented by the SDS were now firmly established in Pale; none of them were willing to come to Sarajevo for talks. Secondly, the crisis over the previous two days had been caused by conflict between the Muslim defenders of Sarajevo and the JNA. It is true that most of the shelling of the city was perpetrated by the Serbs, but the political talks had been and were continuing under the auspices of the EC Conference. My role was to secure any agreement which would alleviate the suffering in Sarajevo, and I could hardly refuse to chair cease-fire negotiations just because the Serbs were not represented.

Having been given the 'good offices' of the UN to convene the talks, I managed to persuade representatives of the presidency and JNA to convene at the PTT building. The presidency was represented by two of its members, Fikret Abdić, a Muslim, and the Croat Stjepan Kljuić. The JNA was represented by General Aksentijević. Major dos Santos attended for the ECMM. I was surprised that Abdić was in attendance. Although a Muslim member of the presidency, he had rarely been seen in Sarajevo since he had extensive interests in the northern Bosnian town of Bihać. His sudden appearance on television during the dramatic public exchanges between Izetbegović, Ganić and Kukanjac on 2 May was equally surprising. There were rumours in some quarters that he had a close association with the Bosnian Minister of the Interior, Alija Delimustafić, and it was even suggested that both were agitating for a change in the party leadership. That Abdić should suddenly arrive in the city during the hostage crisis was viewed by some as suspect.

Attempting to establish reason in the negotiations was challenging. As usual, they commenced with each side accusing the other of reneging on the original agreement that we had reached in discussions to secure Izetbegović's release. I had become used to this and let them have their say without much comment. Then we came to deciding on how best to move forward. I reminded them that Sarajevo was in chaos: bodies still lay on the streets, there was no free movement and food and medical supplies were urgently required. We spent many hours that day searching for any progress, but it was a case of two inches forward, one inch back. However, at about 7.00 pm that evening we reached an agreement. I reminded both sides that whatever accommodation was reached required the commitment of each to be effective, because I was well aware of the numerous previous cease-fire agreements that had been broken within minutes of being signed. By 7.30 pm we had the signatures. The agreement stated that under the sponsorship of the personal representative of Lord Carrington and the head of the EC Monitoring Mission Bosnia-Herzegovina each side would 'fully respect a cease-fire to take effect immediately in Sarajevo and effective from 20.00 hours elsewhere in Bosnia-Herzegovina on 5 May 1992'.

Agreement was also reached that lists containing the names of captured and wounded would be exchanged, that each side would be permitted to remove all dead bodies and that the free flow of food and medical supplies to hospitals and military installations should be allowed. Hotlines were to be established between the two sides and negotiations would continue at UNPROFOR the following day. After I had outlined the general terms of the cease-fire to the assembled media, Martin Bell took me aside and asked me how I rated the chances of things improving. I told him that I had little faith they would do so and that we might need to have our bags packed for a 'quick exit'. It was something we had joked about a few weeks earlier when discussing the signs that would indicate the need for a hasty withdrawal. I had told him that I would give him the nod when I thought that time had come.

I had the clear impression that because of what had happened over the previous few days the JNA was very anxious to get out of Bosnia. Most of its armament had been handed over to the Bosnian Serbs, including tanks, artillery, mortars and heavy machine guns. There seemed little reason for them to stay, now that the presidency and the Muslims saw them as the enemy. I said as much to Marrick Goulding when I met with him the following morning at UN Headquarters. He was well aware of my role, having been briefed by my good friend, Commandant Dermot Earley. Dermot was, at that time, the Assistant Military Advisor to the UN Secretary General in New York and reported directly to Marrick Goulding. The UN were fortunate to have him.

The cease-fire we had worked so hard on was, indeed, another wasted exercise. Within an hour of its being signed two mortar shells exploded just outside the UN headquarters while we were still talking. The explosions could be heard as Marrick Goulding was in the middle of an interview, having just arrived from Pale. Even MacKenzie vented his frustration, describing cease-fires in Sarajevo as simply 'a term'. I had to agree with him. If a cease-fire were only to last long enough to pick up the dead bodies one could argue that it had achieved something, but even that short period of time seemed beyond us.

Another significant event of that day was the departure of most of the ECMM personnel. The decision had been made to withdraw them from Bosnia to the Croatian town of Split, where they had a regional centre. The situation in Bosnia had become untenable for the monitors. There was little to gain in keeping these unarmed observers in harm's way, given that their safety and security, as well as their freedom of movement, were no longer assured or respected. I suggested to Antonio that a public statement be issued giving security concerns as the reason for their withdrawal, stating that it was important to convey that the monitors were not simply abandoning Sarajevo. The public should be assured that they would return when conditions allowed. However, I did not want to interfere any further in the ECMM's affairs, so left it at that.

Throughout the country ethnic cleansing was now rampant, and in Sarajevo the security situation was out of control. The cease-fire had not taken hold, and the Serb siege blocked movement in and out of the city. Sarajevo was now fractionalized. Barricades and checkpoints were everywhere, snipers ruled the rooftops and inter-ethnic hostage-taking was prevalent. Passage through the city was perilous. Those controlling both Muslim and Serb checkpoints had become nervous, suspicious and aggressive. I was even receiving appeals from JNA families asking for my help in getting them out of the city. In the meantime, the media attention was ever-increasing, with requests for interviews raining down on me.

It was during our continuing negotiations with the presidency and JNA on 8 May 1992 that I realized the direction of the talks had markedly, and irreversibly, changed. From a position where we had been concentrating on cease-fires, prisoner exchanges and food supplies, the talk almost imperceptibly moved to withdrawal. I was suddenly all ears. What had happened in the intervening two days to cause this change? I was unaware that Belgrade had announced at this time its intention of withdrawing all non-Bosnian members of the JNA from Bosnia. In addition, a few days later came news of a military purge of thirty-eight generals, including Kukanjac, Aksentijević and Djurdjevac, thus completing the transition which had begun some months earlier. The JNA had previously moved key armament factories from Bosnia to Serbia, fearing they might fall under Muslim or Croat control. It was obvious that instructions were being issued from Belgrade to the JNA in Bosnia to seek a way of withdrawing the balance of troops from the country.

From my meeting with Marrick Goulding it emerged that UNPROFOR would be moving its headquarters from Sarajevo to Belgrade. This was not surprising considering how unpredictable and dangerous the military situation in the city had become. It was not possible under the prevailing conditions for their HQ to look after its troops deployed in Croatia in 'protected areas', defined as locations within Croatia where there was an absolute Serb majority, essentially most of the territory claimed by the 'Republic of Serbian Krajina'. They would be demilitarized, and the armed forces of both sides withdrawn or disbanded. The UN troops would ensure the demilitarization was assisted by the ECMM, all part of the Vance plan. For the moment, though, this information was understandably to be kept under wraps. It seemed that everybody was anxious to leave Bosnia as soon as possible.

Our negotiations with the presidency and JNA continued. The talks now centred round how to effect a dignified and orderly withdrawal of the JNA from military installations throughout Bosnia, the disposal of its armaments, mines, explosives and equipment, its routes of withdrawal and the security and safe passage of JNA family members. There was also much attention given to Sarajevo airport. With the city now almost completely under siege, it was obvious that the airport might become the only means of bringing in humanitarian supplies. Given the JNA's stated intention of pulling out of Bosnia, the significance of the airport became ever greater. These talks continued over the next three days, and the presidency members were joined by the Defence Minister, Jerko Doko. In the end, most issues had been addressed and agreed upon. How and when any agreement might be put into effect was, however, quite another matter.

It was on Monday, 11 May 1992 that Antonio dos Santos informed me that all remaining ECMM personnel were to withdraw from Bosnia the following day. The message had come from the ECMM HQ in Zagreb. Antonio told me that his remaining monitors would be moving to Zagreb by way of Split. I had taken it for granted that once the ECMM withdrew I would have to leave as well, and I had very mixed emotions about that. I had hoped to conclude the agreement on the withdrawal of the JNA, yet there was not much more we could achieve. The long hours of persuasion and cajoling of each side to agree to and then comply with cease-fires had failed. I felt we were banging our heads against a wall, and while all sides may have given the impression of wanting to reach agreement, the reality was quite different. None of them had the slightest intention of sticking to what they promised. It was all an exercise in futility, with the citizens of Sarajevo bearing the brunt of the pain and suffering. I was frustrated, annoyed and sad.

That afternoon, the ECMM began moving much of its logistical equipment and files to UNPROFOR HQ. General MacKenzie promised that he would arrange its carriage back to Belgrade in UN transport. I received the instruction that, rather than leave with the ECMM, I would be flown by JNA helicopter direct to Belgrade early the following morning from Lukavica. I cannot recall who made this decision, but I was surprised. The last thing I wished for was a free flight out of Bosnia at the hands of the army that had become such an enemy to most of its citizens. In any event, I sought out General MacKenzie to thank him for his support and help. We shook hands and parted. Back at the hotel I said my goodbyes. Many of the media had already departed – Sarajevo had, after all, become a very dangerous place. I had never got to know any of the hotel staff well since its Muslim element left, and those that worked there now were less than friendly. I packed my bag and before retiring walked out on to my balcony to view the night sky. The sporadic shelling and sounds of machine gun fire could clearly be heard, and I had a sudden urge to weep, although the soldier in me refused to give in to it. I was reminded of what Carrington had said to me when he briefed me in London: that peace talks might achieve little or nothing.

I was driven by the UN to Lukavica very early the next morning and welcomed at the base by General Aksentijević, who told me he would be joining me on the flight. I had a high regard for him as a soldier, and I believed him to have been honourable and professional. He explained that he was one of thirty-eight JNA Generals being 'retired' by Belgrade and that Kukanjac was also on the list. When I offered him my sympathy he just smiled, shrugged and said that it was 'Time to go home – we soldiers must do as ordered.' We lifted off from the helipad at around 10.30 am. Aksentijević told me that we would be flying via Pale, where a badly wounded soldier was to be picked up. This was an interesting diversion, as we flew over most of the Bosnian Serb military positions on the hillsides overlooking the city. I saw rows and rows of tanks, artillery, mortar and heavy machine guns all aimed at the city and all now under the control of the Serbs. It seemed that Karadžić finally had his Bosnian Serb Army, and I shuddered at the thought of what might be in store for the thousands of innocent civilians trapped in the city below. I avoided looking at Aksentijević, but was sure he must have felt something similar. Our stop at Pale was very brief. As the helicopter touched down, the badly wounded soldier was carried aboard on a stretcher and placed on the floor beside us; within a few seconds we were airborne again. I could not see the man's face as he was covered in bandages, mostly bloodstained, and for the duration of the flight he never moved. As we approached Belgrade airport General Aksentijević held out his hand. I shook it warmly and wished him well. He was first to leave the aircraft, walking straight to a waiting staff car. Before he stepped into it he turned and honoured me with a salute.

Chapter 15

An Invitation to Dinner

I had no idea what was to happen to me after I landed in Belgrade, but was happy to see an ECMM car parked beside the helipad. Mike Chandler, the head of the Belgrade Regional Centre, introduced himself and invited me to climb aboard. A former British Army officer, he had been appointed to head the Belgrade centre some months previously. The centre operated monitor teams on the Serbian side of one of the four United Nations Protected Areas (UNPAs). He informed me that he had some instructions for me, among them that Carrington wished to see me in Paris in two days' time. He also said that a press conference had been set up for me at the hotel and that the media were waiting – and that wasn't all. Meetings with the JNA Chief of the General Staff, Admiral Miroslav Simić, and with Serbia's Foreign Minister, Vladislav Jovanović, had also been arranged. I groaned inwardly. I was exhausted, and it wasn't what I would have chosen, but it seemed I had little choice in the matter.

When we arrived at the Hotel Jugoslavija, located on the Danube, I was brought directly into the room set up for the press conference. I had no time to prepare, so it was a case of giving an update on my last few days in Sarajevo and evacuation from the city. The room was packed and I recognized many reporters who had left Sarajevo a few days previously. Questions ranged from my opinion on the convoy incident, the futility of cease-fire negotiations and the future intentions of the JNA, to what my future role would be. Someone wanted me to confirm if it was true that I was to meet Admiral Simić and asked what the topics of discussion might be when I met with Serbia's foreign minister that evening. I answered as honestly as I could and ended the press conference by telling them that I would be meeting with Carrington in Paris within two days.

I checked into my room and tried to get some sleep, but instead found my mind wandering over the events of the previous few weeks. So much seemed to have been happening that I had hardly had time to give thought to the reasons for (or consequences of) what had happened in Bosnia. I wondered if what we were attempting to achieve had just been a sideshow. It was certainly the case that we had made little progress; each side seemed determined to pursue its own agenda regardless of the efforts of the international community or mediators on the ground. While my distrust of the Serbs remained strong, I was increasingly disappointed by the Muslim side, which appeared to place all its hopes on some sort of military intervention. I regarded this as hopelessly misplaced.

I had not slept properly for many weeks and needed a break. I made contact with Grainne and we planned to take a few days together in London. I would fly there from Paris after meeting with Carrington and hopefully would be able to relax for a while until it was decided what part, if any, I was to play in future peace negotiations. In the meantime, I informed Cutileiro of my plans and he agreed with them. He was keen to have my report on the meeting with Admiral Simić and asked that I be ready to brief Lord Carrington and his Peace Conference team when we met up in Paris. Following this discussion, I booked a flight from Paris to London for the following Thursday.

Mike Chandler provided me with an ECMM car to take me to Admiral Simić's office that afternoon. He offered to accompany me, but I decided to go alone, suspecting that discussion would be about withdrawing the JNA from Bosnia and thinking it best to keep this strictly within the Peace Conference circle. I was welcomed into the office by an English-speaking officer and introduced to the Chief of Staff of the JNA (and also the Acting Federal Secretary of Defence), Colonel General Blagoje Adžić, and his colleague, Chief of the General Staff of the JNA, Admiral Simić. As I had expected, the conversation was focused on the desire of the JNA to execute a dignified withdrawal from Bosnia. Both were aware of the talks we had been holding in Sarajevo on a withdrawal plan, and they asked for my view of the feasibility of such an operation. I told them that the decision to withdraw the JNA from Bosnia only related to those who were not natives of

Bosnia (which might be as few as 20 per cent). The other 80 per cent were transferring into the Bosnian Serb Army. I made it clear that they could not expect to be allowed to freely transfer all the tanks, artillery and weaponry over to the Bosnian Serbs. I also stressed that JNA military installations in Sarajevo were under blockade by the Muslim Territorial Defence and that such a blockade would continue unless heavy weapons in and around Sarajevo were withdrawn. General Adžić then asked how the JNA could be expected to agree to withdraw from Bosnia with any dignity while their military installations were surrounded by armed Muslims. I responded by stating that as long as the Bosnian Serbs continued to shell Sarajevo with heavy artillery and mortar weapons (which they received from the JNA), they could not expect the Muslims to lift their blockades.

At this stage I suggested that UNPROFOR might be able to assist. I told Adžić that if he appealed to General Mladić to stop the bombardment of Sarajevo, something might be achieved with UNPROFOR's help. The heavy weapons in the army barracks might be placed under international control or monitoring, I added, and it would be very helpful if UNPROFOR were to be provided with details of the numbers, locations and weaponry of all JNA troops to be withdrawn. Adžić asked if I thought UNPROFOR would be prepared to carry out these tasks, and I told him that I would need to discuss this directly with the UNPROFOR leadership. I cautioned, however, that nothing could be achieved without negotiating with the Bosnian presidency – only through them, I argued, could the security of JNA troops be guaranteed – but that, given the situation in Sarajevo, gaining the support of the presidency for such a plan might be difficult. With that discussion at an end, I mentioned to them that I appreciated the cooperation and assistance I had received from Generals Kukanjac and Aksentijević during my period in Sarajevo and asked that they be given my regards. Knowing that both had been placed on the list of officers to be purged, I doubted that my regards would be passed on to them. I left the building convinced the JNA wanted out of Bosnia. How this could be achieved without their losing face was the challenge.

After a short rest I headed into the city later that evening with Mike Chandler to meet with Serbia's Foreign Minister, Vladislav Jovanović. When

I walked into the Metropol Hotel, where we had arranged to meet, the desk manager told me that the minister was walking in the nearby Tašmajdan Park and had left a message that I should join him. Leaving Mike in the lobby, I walked to the park and met the minister. We shook hands and introduced ourselves. He gave me a little information on his background, telling me that after graduating from Belgrade University with a degree in law he had been a career diplomat. He had served in Brussels and London and had been Yugoslavia's ambassador to Turkey. I found him relaxed, engaging and easy to talk to. He spoke English well and seemed to know a lot about me. He was aware that I had met with the JNA chiefs that afternoon. As we headed back to the hotel he asked me for my impressions of the situation in Sarajevo and I gave him my candid view, which he seemed to accept without comment.

We had a pleasant meal, though Mike said very little. Most of the conversation was about events in Bosnia. When I was telling him of the stranglehold the Serbs in Pale had over the city of Sarajevo, Jovanović asked whether I had met the Serbs in Banja Luka, which I told him I had. He told me that he believed that the Serbs were very radical there, much more so than those in Pale or Sarajevo. While I agreed with him on that point, I added that Radovan Karadžić was leader of the Bosnian Serbs and therefore called all the shots from his headquarters in Pale, and that I firmly believed that the Serbs of Banja Luka were under his authority.

'They are,' said Jovanović. 'But they can also be very difficult to deal with. We here in Belgrade are not very impressed with what is happening in many parts of Bosnia, particularly in areas controlled by very radical Serbs.'

I asked him how the appearance in Bosnia of radical Serbs from Belgrade like Arkan and Šešelj could be explained. Were they in Bosnia with Belgrade's blessing? I added that the international community was very concerned at the level of support Belgrade appeared to be giving to Serbs in Bosnia. He avoided any reference to Arkan or Seselj, saying that Milošević was doing his best to prevent weapons and armed groups entering Bosnia from Serbia and that Belgrade fully supported the work of Lord Carrington and the peace conference. He added that he believed that any settlement must be reached through negotiation, not war. I told him that I was reassured by this and that I would convey it to Carrington. Having got his message across, he then asked me if I would be returning to Sarajevo or staying in Belgrade. Having no idea myself as to my future, I replied by saying that this would be decided after my visit to Paris. He seemed satisfied. As we were leaving he said he hoped I would return to Belgrade and that I was 'trusted by Serbs as being impartial and fair'. I responded by saying that such a compliment was a good way to finish a pleasant evening and thanked him for his hospitality.

The following morning, I was driven to the airport, where I took the morning flight to Paris. I was met at the airport by Tadeu Soares, the Portuguese Consul-General in Paris, who was also Secretary of the Peace Conference. He dropped me off at the lovely Hôtel St Louis en L'Isle on the Rue St Louis in the heart of the city, very close to Notre Dame. As I got out of the car he handed over a bottle of 12-year-old Jameson, a present from Cutileiro for my involvement in securing the release of Izetbegović. I felt relaxed in Paris. The hotel was small, quaint and very cosy. It had just twenty rooms and the walls were of exposed stone, with old terracotta and oak beams. Although it was early afternoon I decided to take time out and get some sleep. Before doing so I phoned Grainne and we arranged to meet the following evening at Heathrow for some badly needed rest and recuperation.

I felt pretty good the following morning, having enjoyed a sound and undisturbed sleep, probably my best rest in many weeks. Cutileiro picked me up on schedule and over lunch explained the agenda for that afternoon. He thanked me for my endeavours and told me that Carrington had requested that I update him on recent events in Sarajevo, particularly the details of what was agreed vis-à-vis the withdrawal of the JNA. I was informed that he might also ask about the meeting the previous day with the JNA leadership and Jovanović. He went on to tell me that there would be forty or so attendees, mostly the heads of the working groups, his cabinet, the secretariat and some ambassadors. As soon as we entered the large room where Carrington and his entourage were assembled, he came over to welcome me. He introduced me as his 'personal representative in Bosnia' and explained that I had been living in Sarajevo and directly involved in the recent dramatic events. I then proceeded to give a brief outline of the main developments since his last visit: the kidnapping and release of President Izetbegović, the shelling of Sarajevo and the tightening of the siege. When asked to give my assessment of what the future might bring, I repeated the concerns of the JNA leadership and the difficulty of getting the remains of its army out of Bosnia. I was somewhat critical of the Bosnian Muslim leadership, saying that as time went on Izetbegović had seemed less interested in cease-fires.

'What they want now,' I said, 'is military intervention, and as long as they continue to blockade the barracks containing JNA units with heavy weapons the impasse will, in all likelihood, continue. While the JNA may be prepared to give up some weapons in exchange for lifting the blockades, the Bosnian Serbs and its army will strongly oppose such a move.'

I added that I believed General Ratko Mladić to be a very dangerous man, unpredictable and determined, and that some sort of UN involvement might be required. I went on to provide details of my meeting with Jovanović, raising some smiles when I repeated that the minister had wanted to assure me that Belgrade was doing its best to curtail the flow of weapons to the Bosnian Serbs. After I had answered some questions from the audience, Carrington thanked me and explained that I was leaving to catch a flight to London.

A taxi dash to the airport followed, and I just about made the flight. Grainne and I spent the few days in London relaxing and seeing the sights. While it was great to walk hand in hand with my wife, I found it difficult to relax, and my mind was never far from Bosnia. Grainne was on a return flight after a short three days. That evening, I met up again with Tony Abbott, my original boss in Sarajevo, who kindly invited me to his house for dinner. I was able to give him an account of the main events which had occurred there since his departure and we enjoyed a few hours together.

The following afternoon, Monday, 18 May 1992, I met with Lord Carrington at his office for an hour. He asked me to join his negotiating team in Lisbon, where talks with the party leaders had been scheduled for the following Thursday. They would be chaired by Ambassador Cutileiro, and he was to be accompanied by Henry Darwin and Tadeu Soares. I was told that the Bosnian Foreign Minister, Haris Silajdžić, would lead the SDA delegation, as President Izetbegović would not be travelling. I asked if there was any specific reason why the president was not attending and was told that, given the Serb aggression on Sarajevo, it was understandable that he did not wish to leave the city. I was told that the talks would have a 'twin-track approach', covering both constitutional arrangements and an effort to improve the situation on the ground.

The Conference Administrator, Jola Vollebregt, met me at Heathrow on the Wednesday with ticket in hand. Upon arrival in Lisbon I checked into the hotel and in the lobby I met Haris Silajdžić, who told me that not only was he pleased to meet me again but that he was 'very relieved' to see me alive.

When I asked him to explain, he responded, 'Did you not know you were to have been killed the day you left Sarajevo?'

I told him I had no idea what he was talking about. He went on to tell me that when I had left Sarajevo by helicopter it was to be have been shot down by the Serbs. I was, to say the least, dumbfounded, and after absorbing this 'news' I tried to make some make sense of it. I asked him why the Serbs would want to shoot down their own helicopter with one of their own generals (Aksentijević) on board.

Silajdžić responded, 'You were the target, not Aksentijević. He had already been dismissed. If you had been killed the Muslims would have been blamed. Killing Carrington's personal representative would have made big news. You can count yourself lucky to be alive.'

I asked him how he had acquired this information and he told me that it had come from 'one of our intelligence sources in Sarajevo'. Later, I tried to make sense of what he had told me and began to wonder whether it was just a fanciful bit of drama and propaganda, or whether his story might indeed have some substance. Needless to say, I was somewhat shaken by it.

Over the next several days Cutileiro attempted to make some progress with the party leaders. The main emphasis was on trying to persuade Karadžić to agree to a withdrawal of the Serb artillery from the hills surrounding Sarajevo. Silajdžić insisted that until such time as the artillery moved back, the SDA saw no point to participating in talks. At one point he indicated to Cutileiro that there was a convoy of Serb tanks on its way through Bosnia (having crossed the border from Montenegro). On hearing this I asked him what evidence he had. He replied that he had received the information only a few minutes earlier. I caught Cutileiro's eye and slipped out of the room.

Within a few minutes I had made contact with UNPROFOR Headquarters, which had recently moved from Sarajevo to Belgrade. I spoke with General MacKenzie and asked him if he had received any reports of a tank convoy alleged to be en route to Sarajevo from Montenegro. He told me he was not aware of such a thing and that the only military movement from that direction was a UN APC convoy on its way to Sarajevo. Back inside the delegation office Silajdžić was still in discussion with Cutileiro, and when the opportunity arose I calmly informed him that I had checked his claims and that the only convoy heading toward Sarajevo was the UN one. Silajdžić just shrugged and said that he must have been misinformed.

Mate Boban attended the talks as the Acting President of the HDZ. The party had undergone much change in leadership and direction. Where we had once been negotiating with Stjepan Kljuić, a moderate, we now had to deal with Boban, a hardliner. The moderate Croat leaders such as Kljuić found themselves caught in a difficult situation between loyalty to Bosnia and ties to the radicals of Herzegovina. Boban was now opposed to Bosnian government efforts to preserve the country as a unitary state, and in his discussions with Cutileiro he seemed more concerned about the situation in Herzegovina than about the siege of Sarajevo.

At the urging of Cutileiro, Karadžić gave the impression of supporting the idea that, under international supervision and control, the heavy artillery overlooking Sarajevo might be moved back. However, I reminded him that we had received such assurances before, when I had been sent to Pale to verify such a withdrawal which did not take place. Unblocking of roads and the question of Sarajevo were also discussed. Cutileiro had hoped that agreement might be reached during the talks which would allow for some arrangement on peacekeeping. This would act as a confidence-building measure, which we badly needed. However, the week dragged on with little progress. And while the parties kept stalling on every point or suggestion brought up in discussions, they were very happy to talk with the media. Every time we took a break and went downstairs to the lobby, we would come upon one of the party delegations giving a television interview. They seemed obsessed with the media. We negotiators would leave the hotel avoiding the media and take short walks. I had not visited Lisbon before, and although we had little free time, it was a relief to get some fresh air and see parts of the city.

The shelling of Vase Miskin Street and the killing of civilians in downtown Sarajevo on 27 May 1992 changed everything. As we were reviewing a talks session just concluded with the Croats, someone stuck their head into the room and told us to turn the television on quickly. The pictures we saw were chilling. Two shells had landed in the middle of a bread queue, killing seventeen and injuring more than a hundred; body parts were scattered all over the pavement. A television crew that happened to be nearby captured the terrible scenes before rescuers arrived to take the bodies away. Within a few minutes of seeing the carnage Karadžić came rushing into the room telling us that the Serbs had not fired the shells. We were convinced he was bluffing and as much as told him so. When Haris Silajdžić appeared at the door, Karadžić walked out, ignoring him. We had expected Silajdžić to come to us and were not surprised at his reaction. He told us that his delegation could not remain in Lisbon after what had happened in Sarajevo. Cutileiro asked him if he was ending the participation of the SDA in constitutional talks. He replied that he was not; his party was committed to the process but there was no way talks could continue until Serb attacks on Sarajevo were stopped. Cutileiro nodded, acknowledging this. They both agreed that the constitutional talks were the only way to bring durable peace to Bosnia and that the alternative was an even more dreadful war than the one already raging there.

When Silajdžić left we considered what effect this atrocity might have on the situation in Sarajevo and on the talks. We knew that Karadžić was rattled and we discussed how we could make some or any headway. We needed something tangible. We looked at each other and almost in concert said, 'The airport'. Henry Darwin, who had an uncanny ability to be a few steps ahead of us, was already calculating the best way to achieve this. We calculated that Karadžić might not know who fired the shells, but he must have been aware that the Serbs would be blamed, given the target and its location. We decided that we should attempt to use the dreadful situation to achieve something positive – something that could stop such awful events from being repeated. I told Cutileiro and Darwin that if the siege of Sarajevo was to take hold then control of the airport would be critical. Whoever held it could control what came in and out of the city – and this, I argued, had to be a task for the UN.

After some further deliberations Cutileiro summoned Karadžić back into the room. We told him that the Muslim delegation had decided to pull out from this round of talks and that he must surely understand why they had done so. Their demand was that the shelling of Sarajevo should be ended, the blockade of cities and roads be lifted and the airport opened. We tried to convince him that were he to offer the UN control of the airport (so as to coordinate the delivery of humanitarian aid), it would go some way towards easing the situation in Sarajevo. Karadžić mulled this over for a few minutes and then asked us to give him time to consider it. He left the room, presumably to talk with Koljević. By the time he returned we had drafted a suggested text, which, if Karadžić agreed, would be released to the media. He informed us that under certain conditions he would be willing to hand over the airport, but the details would need to be worked out with the UN. By the end of the session we had his signature on a document, the main sentence of which read:

> The leadership of the SDS announces its readiness to open Sarajevo airport for humanitarian transports. Until the conclusion of the constitutional talks under the aegis of the Peace Conference, the airport will function under a special regime under the command and control of the UN.

It was the only positive outcome from the talks, and as with so many other promises made and signatures obtained, only time would tell whether it was merely an empty gesture. Cutileiro was anxious to have the UN informed of the agreement as soon as possible, knowing that much detailed negotiation would be required with the Serbs before the 'blue helmets' could take control of the airport complex. In any event, the international community's reaction to the Vase Miskin Street atrocity resulted in the UN Security Council imposing a trade embargo against the Federal Republic of Yugoslavia, and the International Committee of the Red Cross (ICRC) announced a temporary withdrawal from Bosnia. That these followed on from the earlier transferral of UNPROFOR HQ from Sarajevo to Belgrade and the withdrawal from Bosnia of the ECMM added to the agony of Bosnia's already suffering citizens.

There were, and continue to this day, very contentious arguments about who exactly was responsible for what became known as the 'breadline massacre'. Karadžić and other Serb leaders insisted that the explosion did not come from a Serb mortar positioned in the hills overlooking Sarajevo but from a remote-controlled detonating device set off by someone inside the city. They argued that the attack was planned and carried out by Bosnian Muslims and orchestrated to look as though the Serbs had done it. It became normal, after such hideous incidents, for statements to emerge from the Muslims blaming the leadership in Pale or Belgrade, while these would be countered by Serbs charging that Muslims were bombing the people they purported to be defending. What is beyond doubt is that the Vase Miskin Street incident was one of the most despicable acts of the siege of Sarajevo.

Following the decision to suspend the Lisbon talks, Cutileiro told me that Carrington had requested that I return to Belgrade for a few weeks. I was told that it was too dangerous for me to return to Sarajevo, since with neither ECMM nor UNPROFOR in the city I would have no support. So I was to stay in the hotel where the regional centre of the ECMM was based and, while there, act as a conduit for the passing of information to the Bosnian leaders on further negotiations and as an interlocutor with contacts in both Belgrade and Sarajevo. I agreed to this and made preparations to relocate to Belgrade.

Chapter 16

A meeting with Milošević

I was unlucky in selecting 2 June 1992 to move to Belgrade. Because of the sanctions imposed by the UN against the Federal Republic of Yugoslavia on 27 May 1992, Belgrade airport was closed to international flights. The closest airport was Budapest, into which I flew from London. The ECMM had sent a car to pick me up at the airport, and following a five-hour drive I arrived at the Mission's Belgrade base, located at the Hotel Jugoslavija in the Novi Beograd (New Belgrade) municipality. It was my second meeting with the ECMM's Belgrade chief, Mike Chandler, and his small group of monitors, who operated teams on the Serbian side of the UNPA Sector East. After he had given me a short briefing on the role of his regional centre, I assured him that I would not interfere with his operation but would appreciate his help with transport and communications. He seemed relieved.

The hotel was situated beside the Danube, and although it was pretty modern I soon learned that location beside the famous river brought its downside – every time I sat outside I was besieged by mosquitoes. My only formal meeting that first week was with General Nambiar, UNPROFOR's Force Commander, who had been redeployed from Sarajevo with much of the Force Headquarters. However, about one hundred troops were left in Sarajevo under the command of Colonel John Wilson, my former UNTSO colleague. Nambiar appeared relieved to be in Belgrade, from where it was far easier and more practical than Sarajevo to command the force. His head of civil affairs, Cedric Thornberry, was back in Sarajevo attempting to broker an agreement on the opening of Sarajevo airport. On 5 June 1992 the airport agreement was signed. After a few tough days of negotiations the UN had persuaded the Bosnian presidency and Bosnian Serb army to sign an agreement which resulted in the airport being demilitarized and placed under UN supervision for the delivery of humanitarian aid. In addition, agreement was reached to facilitate the evacuation of the JNA personnel from the Marshall Tito barracks in downtown Sarajevo which had been blockaded for weeks.

A few days later, I had an unexpected visitor in the form of Lieutenant Colonel Dimitrijević, my former JNA liaison officer from Sarajevo. While I was pleased to see him again I wondered if the visit had come about by chance or design, so I asked him if he was on social or official business. He told me that he had been ordered to Belgrade to see if he could be of some assistance to me. With that he smiled – I think we both knew the real purpose of his sudden reappearance. We had coffee together and spoke a little about how desperate events were back in Sarajevo. He then informed me that Foreign Minister Jovanović would very much like me to visit him. I told him that this would be fine, though I asked whether there was anything in particular I should be aware of or that he required of me. Dimitrijević merely said that Jovanović knew of my return to Belgrade and thought it would be a good idea to meet. So, the following morning, I was driven to the Ministry of Foreign Affairs and was soon sitting in Jovanović's office. He seemed pleased to meet me again and expressed his relief that I had not returned to Sarajevo. He then asked my opinion on the current situation, which I provided for him. He sought again to assure me that Belgrade had little influence over the Bosnian Serbs and that his ministry was endeavouring to convince them that the only option was to support the efforts of the European Community in negotiating a settlement in Bosnia. I was not entirely convinced by this and suspected he was using me as a conduit to assure the EC of Serbia's support for the peace process. My suspicions were realized when, on leaving his office, I bumped into the newly appointed Minister of Foreign Affairs of Republika Srpska, Aleksa Buha, who was waiting to meet Jovanović. My immediate impression was that both would be embarrassed that I had seen them together.

I was surprised when, the following day, Dimitrijević was back to see me again. This time he seemed rather excited and he informed me that President Milošević had expressed a wish to see me. I had certainly not expected such an invitation and was momentarily taken back. I asked exactly why he might wish to meet with me and wondered why Jovanović had made no mention of it the previous day. I was told that Milošević was aware of my involvement in the crisis in Bosnia, that I had a reputation as a neutral mediator and that he was keen to discuss the situation with me. I told Dimitrijević that I would have to inform Carrington about the invitation but that I would respond as soon as I could. I made contact with Cutileiro immediately and he advised that I wait until he had a chance to speak with Carrington. He also suggested that it was best not to discuss the matter with anyone until I had heard back from him. In any event, having little idea what Milošević might wish to discuss with me, there was not much I could do to prepare for it.

I still needed to have as much information as possible on developments in Sarajevo. After the withdrawal of the ECMM in May the only international peacekeeping forces in Bosnia were a small element of UNPROFOR based in Sarajevo. The fighting had continued, as the factions sought to consolidate their territory. Fighting in Sarajevo had intensified and it was increasingly difficult to find out exactly what was going on. Phone contact was now very infrequent and sometimes it took hours to get through to the presidency from the ECMM office in Belgrade. This became a frustrating task for me, spending so much time just trying to get through. I wanted to make contact with Darko Ivić, who was still working in the presidency and on whom I could rely to give me an honest appraisal of what was going on. It took me two full days to get through to him, whereupon he told me that the situation had become increasingly grim. Among other things, he told me that fighting was continuing and many had been killed but that the airport negotiations were carrying on. In the meantime, the Serbs appeared to be tightening their stranglehold on the city. I thanked him and told him that I would attempt to contact him for an update every few days. While I thought that the UN's taking control of the airport would facilitate the arrival by air of humanitarian aid, I wondered how effective its delivery and distribution might be if the Bosnian Serbs controlled the territory through which delivery convoys would have to pass. I assumed, however, that the UN would be taking this into consideration during their planning process.

On 15 June 1992 I was called to the Portuguese Embassy in Belgrade, where I received written instructions on the conduct of my meeting with

Milošević arranged for the following day. Cutileiro had met with Carrington to discuss the issues which might arise, and a list of topics with suggestions was enclosed. I had not met Milošević in person and was happy to take on board whatever advice was being offered. The written instructions indicated that, if given the opportunity, I should define the role and nature of my mission. I was instructed to seek Belgrade's support in maintaining the current (but unstable) cease-fire in Bosnia, to request their assistance in the handing over of Sarajevo airport to the UN, to help facilitate the unhindered delivery of humanitarian relief supplies and to support the efforts of UN observers to neutralize the artillery surrounding Sarajevo.

When I asked the Portuguese chargé d'affaires if I should have someone accompany me to the meeting to take notes, he responded, 'Mr Jackson, the first secretary at the British Embassy, will accompany you' – though he would not take part in the discussions.

I spent some time preparing to face Milošević. I had been warned to be very careful in any conversation I might have with him and not to bring up any topic outside those contained in the brief. As I had no idea what he might wish to say to me there wasn't too much I could concentrate on. I presumed he would simply be using me as a conduit to pass to Carrington whatever information he might choose to give. Jackson was at my hotel to pick me up promptly at 6.45 pm. On the way to Milošević's office he said that he had not had the chance to meet the Serbian president and that he would simply 'sit quietly and take notes'. Anyway, Colonel Dimitrijević, as ever, was on hand to meet us at the entrance. I introduced him to Jackson and he immediately led us into the spacious building, where the president was waiting in the corridor. He came forward, held out his hand and greeted me in rather good English. He proceeded to say that he had heard a lot about me, knew that I was married with a family and that I was an Irish military officer. He then paid me a series of compliments about how highly I was regarded as neutral and trusted by all sides, but these had no sooner finished than he asked why it was that the world was condemning the Serbs. I wasn't prepared for such a question but responded that an almost universal perception existed that the Serbs were to blame for causing the conflict.

'I don't think we will get along', he then said, before ushering me into his office.

We sat at a low table. No words were spoken while staff brought drinks and coffee, but as soon as they departed I decided to open proceedings by clearly defining my role and the nature of my mission. I called for Belgrade's support in re-opening the airport at Sarajevo and guaranteeing the unhindered delivery of humanitarian supplies. I referred to Carrington's demand that there must be an end to the expulsions of non-Serbs from Serb-held settlements and that those who wished to return must be allowed to do so. There was an urgent need to assist the efforts of UN observers in neutralizing the artillery in the mountains surrounding Sarajevo. I also stressed that Carrington was very anxious for him to use his influence over Serb irregulars entering Bosnia from Serbia and that General Mladić must be directed to cease the shelling of Sarajevo. Finally, I emphasized the importance of getting international agencies back into the city as soon as possible and informed him that the international consensus was that the peace conference should be the only forum in which future constitutional arrangements for Bosnia were negotiated.

Having delivered all these points to the president as instructed, I felt relieved. Taking a sip from my coffee cup I sat back and waited for his response. He had been smoking a small cigar while listening attentively. Jackson was furiously taking notes. The president ignored him and, placing the cigar on an ashtray, addressed me. He started by stating that he believed Lord Carrington was aware that Belgrade was doing its best to support the peace process in Bosnia. He told me that he had pressed the Bosnian Serbs to 'avoid bloodshed' and that he believed that Sarajevo was the key problem; he expressed the view that if the city could be pacified, solutions would be more easily found elsewhere in Bosnia. He added that Belgrade supported the idea of re-opening the airport, placing the city under UN control and removing the artillery from the mountains, and stressed that this had been made clear publicly on repeated occasions. It was now the turn of the UN to take action accordingly, he stated, and he was keen to know when the airport might be re-opened and when Carrington was likely to visit Sarajevo.

Milošević also said that he had strongly endorsed the proposal from Karadžić that UN observers be attached to each unit of the Bosnian Serb forces in order to witness the facts on the ground, before adding, 'We are constantly cast in the role of aggressor, but I can tell you that there is not a single Serb from Serbia fighting in Bosnia.'

Upon hearing this I nearly spilled my coffee, but I let him continue.

He went on to say, 'If there were Serbs from Serbia in Bosnia it would be impossible to keep it secret. Our police are monitoring the border with Bosnia and we have already arrested some 1,300 people who have been in the area, carrying weapons for which they have no licence.'

He also claimed that he himself had personally pressed for the evacuation of JNA cadets from the Marshal Tito Barracks in Sarajevo, even at the cost of leaving heavy weapons behind, and that this appeal had caused much annoyance among Bosnian Serbs.

Milošević sought to point out that Belgrade had, on numerous occasions, vigorously condemned the shelling of Sarajevo, a 'futile and criminal exercise' for which the perpetrators should be punished. He guaranteed they would be subject to legal proceedings if they set foot in Serbia. He then highlighted the activities of the Croats, who had regular troops on the territory of Bosnia in Western Herzegovina, a fact which a French emissary had recently confirmed to him. He rejected my suggestion that it had been the Serbs who had principally benefited from the arms and ammunition abandoned by the JNA, claiming that all ethnic groups had ended up securing a share. That I had personally seen the huge convoy of JNA tanks winding its way to the Bosnian Serbs in Pale gave the lie to his assertion. Milošević continued by stating that Belgrade could not halt its supply of humanitarian aid to the Bosnian Serbs and complained that there had been no coverage by the Western media of a number of Serbian relief convoys which had distributed food and medical supplies to the three ethnic communities in Sarajevo. He agreed that there was no alternative to the peace conference for working out a solution to the crisis, and he stated that he believed that it was impossible for any one side to emerge a winner from war in the republic since there were 'no innocent parties'. He asserted that Bosnia was a state of three equal peoples and that Belgrade would respect any argument based on a tripartite consensus. He also acknowledged that Sarajevo had a large Muslim majority and that Serbs could not bombard it to gain control of the entire city.

'The international community', he said, 'was ill-advised to recognize Bosnia when it did, but we here in Belgrade are doing everything politically to bring about peace. It's in our own interest to do so.'

When I mentioned to him that developments in Kosovo were causing alarm he cut me short, warning me that Kosovo was an 'internal matter' and not open for discussion. Having been quickly put back in my box I decided it was time to leave. I thanked the president for his forthright views and promised I would convey his remarks to Lord Carrington without delay. I also stressed that Carrington would appreciate whatever influence he might have with Karadžić's people to encourage them to negotiate. Finally, I informed Milošević that Carrington was planning to convene a conference in Strasbourg the following week and that, along with Presidents Tudjman and Izetbegović, he might have a chance to meet with him before his next visit to Sarajevo. With that, Milošević stood up, which was a clear signal that our meeting was over. He accompanied me back along the corridor and paused to shake my hand.

The following morning, Jackson was back with the report of my meeting with Milošević, and we spent a while reviewing its content. I was satisfied that he had covered all the points adequately and thanked him for his contribution. As soon as I had signed off the report I headed back to the Portuguese Embassy and handed it over to the chargé d'affaires. On my return to the hotel I made contact with Cutileiro and provided him with a brief run-down of the meeting. He asked if there was anything in particular Milošević was anxious to bring up and seemed surprised when I told him that nothing new had been discussed. In any event, I had some time to consider the tone and content of the meeting over a few days. There was really nothing new in what Milošević had said to me, certainly nothing that I felt would change anything. I never had any doubt but that I was simply the messenger and wondered why he felt it necessary to meet me in the first place. The usual platitudes were expressed: we support the peace efforts, we condemn the shelling of the city, we agree to UN observers, we will help to maintain a cease-fire, and so forth. Then there were the usual denials:

there are no Serbs from Serbia fighting in Bosnia, we are not providing any arms to the Bosnian Serbs and we will not interfere with the delivery of humanitarian aid. I had heard it all before and believed none of it. This did not apply to the Serbs alone; each side had its own agenda and we negotiators had to listen to the different brands of propaganda at almost every session we attended. Separating the wood from the trees was no easy task.

The dilemma over the opening of Sarajevo airport under the control of the UN came to a head towards the end of June 1992. The UN Secretary-General, Boutros-Ghali, had made it clear that the Serbs must allow the UN to take control of the airport and, in addition, must stop their shelling of the city. It was to all intents and purposes an ultimatum. He also demanded that the Serb heavy weapons be placed under UN supervision, as provided for in the cease-fire agreement negotiated by General MacKenzie. A separate incident which contributed to breaking the airport impasse was the sudden and dramatic visit to Sarajevo of the French President François Mitterrand on 28 June 1992. These events, in addition to the tasks undertaken by UNPROFOR, resulted in the Serbs turning the airport over to a UN contingent of Canadian troops the following day. MacKenzie, who had been promoted to major general, would assume command of the operation on his appointment as the Sarajevo Sector Commander. His initial position as UNPROFOR Chief of Staff was taken over by a Danish officer, Svend Harders. The subsequent humanitarian effort to deliver aid would ensure that events in Sarajevo received global media coverage, as did MacKenzie himself.

My role in Belgrade at this time was to facilitate the passage of information to both Izetbegović and Milošević concerning the holding of talks with Carrington in Strasbourg. It was difficult to get messages through to Sarajevo and my fax machine was working overtime to transmit communications to the Bosnian presidency on the scope of these proposed talks. With the airport in Sarajevo still firmly under Serb control, Izetbegović pleaded that, although willing to attend, he could not risk travelling. In the circumstances it was recommended that his Foreign Minister, Haris Silajdžić, attend in his place. As with so many other talks, these ones failed to produce any progress.

The transition of the presidency of the EC from Portugal to the UK in July 1992 also meant that Britain now took over the leadership and control of the ECMM. The new Head of Mission, Ambassador Ramsay Melhuish, visited the regional headquarters in Belgrade and I took the opportunity to meet with him. He informed me that he had been briefed on my role and assured me that I would be given every support in carrying it out. So all would continue as normal, I was assured. On the morning of 1 July Cutileiro contacted me to let me know that Lord Carrington was planning to visit Sarajevo and that he had requested I join him. I was required to get myself from Belgrade to Zagreb, where I would be picked up by Carrington's plane. Ambassador Melhuish was not surprised when I contacted him in Zagreb to ask if I could hitch a lift in one of the ECMM helicopters. After an uneventful flight to Zagreb I was delighted to meet up with two of my military colleagues from Ireland who were well into their six-month tour of duty with the ECMM, Lieutenant Colonels Maurice Walsh and Paddy Curley, who were now working at the mission headquarters. I had some free time with them, and they were able to brief me on developments within the ECMM.

Carrington and Cutileiro arrived on schedule at Zagreb airport. As they stepped down from the aircraft they were met by Melhuish and his deputy, Major General David Cranston, who accompanied them into the arrivals lounge for a brief chat before I joined them for a quick cup of coffee. With hardly enough time to drink it, Carrington was on his feet. He wanted to talk to me about my meeting with Milošević and asked if there was anything in particular he should be aware of before his meeting with Karadžić and Koljević scheduled for later in the day. I told him there was nothing special or surprising in what had been discussed; that I believed that Milošević had simply wanted to stress that he was doing everything to ensure that there were no weapons or fighters being sent to Bosnia from Serbia; and that he was supportive of what Carrington was attempting to achieve through the peace conference. Carrington asked if I believed what Milošević had said. I told him that I did not, but that I had the distinct impression he might be trying to distance himself from Karadžić. He then asked about my impressions of Izetbegović's motives, and I told him that the Bosnian president seemed to be relying on some sort of military intervention and was less inclined to support negotiation.

The first thing we saw as we descended into Sarajevo airport was a large UNPROFOR presence on the tarmac. The aircraft had hardly come to a stop before we were surrounded by UN APCs. They were obviously taking no chances with Carrington's security. He was immediately bundled into the leading APC, Cutileiro and I were directed into a second and we were all quickly whisked out through the airport gates towards the city centre. A convoy of press cars kept on our tail. Our first stop was at the PTT building, which was still in use as the UN headquarters. General MacKenzie gave us the latest picture of what was happening in the city, and it was not encouraging. I had the impression that MacKenzie had grown increasingly suspicious of the Muslims, and he confirmed my own impression that Izetbegović's strategy was to appeal for intervention. Where such an intervention might come from was anybody's guess, but to my mind no such option existed.

We proceeded to the presidency, where Izetbegović was on hand to meet Carrington. There were few smiles and the mood was decidedly sombre. The president was insisting on a cease-fire period before he would contemplate any peace negotiations. About ten minutes into the meeting, the president's daughter Sabina came over to me and whispered that I should follow her out of the room. She stopped outside and told me that there was a woman in her office by the name of Mrs Čerkez, who had insisted upon meeting me. The name sounded vaguely familiar, but I could not recall her. When I entered Sabina's office a middle-aged woman came forward and shook my hand. Speaking good English, she reminded me that we had spoken some months previously about her coming into possession of some important documents. We had arranged to meet at the Princip Bridge, but though I had sent two ECMM staff there, no meeting had taken place. She said that after speaking to me she had become too afraid to leave her house because of the fighting that morning. In any event, she went on to remind me that an officer of the JNA, who frequently attended English lessons in her home, had left a briefcase behind him. When he failed to contact her about it, she managed to open the case in the hope of finding his phone number or address. While searching the contents she came upon some documents which, according to her, revealed detailed plans for the takeover of large portions of eastern Bosnia. She did not know whether the officer had left the briefcase on purpose, but she became fearful when she realized the importance of its contents. It was the following week that she tried to contact me, hoping I would take the documents from her. However, when she could not meet with me she replaced the documents and put the briefcase back exactly where she found it. She went on to tell me that about two weeks later the officer in question contacted her and made an appointment for a further lesson. When he turned up he made no mention of the briefcase (nor did she). She made an excuse to leave the house just before the lesson's end, asking her pupil to see himself out. When she returned, both he and the briefcase were gone.

I thanked her for coming and assured her that I would not mention her name to anyone. I could see she was genuinely scared and thought her very brave to have made such an effort to find me. As there was no tangible evidence that such a plan existed, I decided to keep the information to myself. I was, however, intrigued as to why this officer should have left the briefcase in the first place and why he did not seem to have been worried about it, given that it contained what appeared to be very sensitive documents and particularly since the plan to take over large tracts of territory in eastern Bosnia had come to fruition amid such brutality a short time later.

In the meantime, Carrington had made little headway with Izetbegović, who had indicated to him that an earlier plan devised by Ambassador Cutileiro and his negotiation team, to have Bosnia divided into cantons, was a non-runner. He insisted that Bosnia had to be a unitary state. I could sense Carrington's frustration. General MacKenzie then informed us that the plan to meet the Serbs at the PTT building was not acceptable to Karadžić and that it might be better to meet them at Lukavica barracks in Serb-held territory. Carrington reluctantly agreed, and once again we boarded UN armoured personnel carriers. As we made our way across the airport towards Lukavica some shots were fired in our direction from the Muslim-held suburb of Butmir. However, a few well-aimed bursts from a machine gun mounted on the UN APC ensured our safety and we made it to Lukavica.

The meeting with Karadžić and Koljević was short. While Lord Carrington did not wish to interfere with any arrangements negotiated by the UN on the withdrawal of Serb heavy weapons, Karadžić seemed determined that he could not possibly place these weapons under UN control, particularly since he insisted that the Serbs were outnumbered and he had a responsibility to protect his people. He was quite prepared to ignore the fact that Serbs possessed the superior firepower and held the tactical advantage of controlling the high ground surrounding the city. Carrington was becoming increasingly frustrated. There seemed little reason for Karadžić to oppose placing these heavy weapons under UN control, given the Serb superiority in firepower, but I had long accepted that even the reasonable was unacceptable to these party leaders.

I spoke with Lord Carrington before he departed. As he was flying direct to London I was to stay overnight in Sarajevo and hitch a ride on one of the humanitarian flights returning to Zagreb the following day. He offered me his opinion that there was little appetite for any negotiated settlement and that, for the time being, we needed to concentrate on keeping the airport under UN control to ensure free delivery of humanitarian aid. He added that the conflict might just be in its early days and that an 'acceptable way forward' might be difficult. I acknowledged that, sadly, I agreed with him.

Chapter 17

Back to Sarajevo

As had happened many times previously, the lull in the fighting occasioned by Carrington's visit was of short duration. The morning following his departure it was 'business as usual', with major outbreaks of fighting occurring in the suburbs of Dobrinja and Lukavica. Both sides were guilty of starting it. I had stayed overnight with the UN in the PTT building, where we endured a heavy bombardment between 4.00 and 7.00 am. As I hunkered down in the basement, sharing a space with General MacKenzie, I felt more frustration and anger. I thought back to Carrington's press conference of the previous day, when he had talked about one option being to let all sides fight it out and only then come back to pick up the pieces. I wondered if this was now the only realistic course of action, however lamentable it might be. There seemed to be no appetite for peace. The Serbs were willing to continue grabbing as much territory as possible, while the Muslims were hell-bent on some sort of military intervention, which in my view was never going to happen. Neither dialogue nor a cease-fire was in the interests of either side.

I managed to get a lift aboard a Portuguese C-130 Hercules, which was returning to Zagreb having delivered a cargo of humanitarian aid to Sarajevo airport, one of twelve aid flights that reached Sarajevo that day. The opening of the airport at the end of June 1992 was the only positive news coming out of Bosnia, and the UN deserved credit for its role in achieving this. However, there was concern that opening the airport to humanitarian relief flights might give the illusion that the siege of the city had been somehow lifted, thus removing the threat of international action such as air strikes.

After the withdrawal of the ECMM in May 1992 the only peacekeepers left in Bosnia were the HQ element of UNPRFOR based in Sarajevo. As such, events outside of the city were difficult to assess. Muslims held areas in eastern Bosnia, such as Goražde and Srebrenica, but these had little contact with the Bosnian government, while the Bihać enclave in north-west Bosnia was cut off completely from Sarajevo. The ECMM made efforts to monitor the situation from areas outside of Bosnia, most notably in the north around Bosanski Posavina, which was south of Slavonski Brod. Attempts were made to introduce ECMM teams on to the Serb side from either Belgrade or Banja Luka, but these were continually frustrated by political obstacles.

The ethnic cleansing that had commenced in April 1992 continued unabated. The fear it engendered encouraged many of those in surrounding neighbourhoods who feared they might be targeted to flee. In other areas the cleansing was violent and accompanied by mass killings. Humiliation and sheer terror were widely used, designed to create ethnically pure territories to which Muslims would never return. Further south, an ECMM presence was being reintroduced into Croat-held parts of Bosnia. With the onset of fighting in April, the worsening relations between the Muslims and Croats, both within Bosnia and between Bosnia and Croatia, were, for the most part, overshadowed by the fighting between Muslims and Serbs. The desire among the majority of Croats from western Herzegovina for autonomy (and eventual unification with Croatia) led their negotiators, particularly Mate Boban, to oppose Bosnian government efforts to preserve a unitary state.

Back in Zagreb, I briefed the heads of the national delegations at the ECMM Policy Committee that evening. I painted a rather gloomy picture of Sarajevo, predicting no early end to the fighting and suggesting that the hoped-for return of monitors to the city was a long way off. I gave my view that the Muslims were holding out for military intervention and were less interested in negotiation; the latter, as Carrington had pointed out in his press conference, was not a viable position. The following day, I returned to Belgrade and was met by Mike Chandler, who handed over a bunch of fax messages sent to me from London. I was requested to forward them to the Bosnian party leaders, which was quite a challenge given the poor state of communications with Sarajevo. Carrington was calling the parties to London for further talks in the hope of making some progress. Around the same time the British government announced it was sending its Foreign Minister, Douglas Hurd, to Sarajevo to inform Izetbegović personally that the Bosnian government could not expect any form of military intervention.

I managed to have the fax messages delivered to the party leaders and was assured that each of them would travel to London for talks. Although Cutileiro was relieved to hear this, I was far from convinced that anything positive would result. In truth, I was becoming increasingly sceptical about talks with these people and more convinced that their attendance was purely cosmetic. I was tending towards the view that negotiations were just a rather cynical means for each of the party leaders to attempt to gain political advantage over the others. They were certainly a far cry from delivering a political settlement or putting an end to the fighting. At best, a cease-fire might be agreed, but judging from the fate of previous such agreements I had little confidence in its continued observance.

I joined the parties in London for this ninth round of talks, having been driven from Belgrade to Budapest to catch a plane. With the airport in Belgrade closed because of UN sanctions, my trips out of Serbia were always complicated. It was late afternoon by the time I checked into the Hyatt Carlton Hotel, where the delegations were staying. Lord Carrington had met the party leaders earlier in the day, before leaving Cutileiro to chair the substantive talks. I was included in the talks, though more in the capacity of observer than participant. However, as I had suspected, each of the three parties refused to meet directly with the others, and it was after 1.30 am by the time we had finished meeting separately with the SDA and HDZ delegations. We spent all of the following day attempting to reach agreement on a cease-fire. The Serbs continued to argue that the Muslims had little interest in putting a stop to the fighting and were openly advocating military intervention. For their part, the Muslims refused to consider any cooperation with the Serbs until their heavy weapons were placed under UN control. It seemed to me that we were going round in circles and that even the slightest progress was painstakingly slow. However, by the following morning a draft cease-fire document was circulated to each side containing the phrase 'all parties agree to declare heavy weapons to UNPROFOR' – without agreeing, however, to place them under UNPROFOR control, which was what we would have preferred. None of us were confident that the cease-fire would be respected.

Lord Carrington arrived at the hotel that afternoon and following meetings with Cyrus Vance and Douglas Hurd agreed to attend a press conference. He requested that Cutileiro and I sit on either side of him. I was relieved that no questions were directed at me. Before he departed he drew me aside and asked if I thought I would be safe returning to Sarajevo. We needed 'someone on the ground', he said, and there was no one better equipped for the task. He told me that the decision would be mine and that he would respect whatever I decided to do. To be honest, I had not expected him to bring up the issue of returning to Sarajevo. I had begun to feel frustrated, stuck in Belgrade when everything was happening in Sarajevo, but I needed to find out how Grainne would feel if I were to return, so I told Carrington I would consider his request and give him my reply as soon as possible. I mentioned to him that I had made arrangements to take a short holiday with my wife, but he assured me this would not be affected by my returning to Sarajevo. I contacted Grainne and mentioned my possible return to Sarajevo. She told me that I should 'be sensible and take no chances'. I assured her that our pre-arranged week in Crete would not be affected.

I returned to Belgrade on 19 July 1992 and was informed by the British Embassy that Carrington would be arriving in the city the next day. He was anxious to make contact with senior government officials to ascertain if there were any differing views to those of Milošević on Belgrade's relationship with the Bosnian Serbs. I was invited to lunch with him at the residence of the chargé d'affaires. Also invited was Vuk Drasković, a charismatic Serbian opposition leader, who though himself a nationalist had frequently clashed with Milošević. Formerly a journalist and writer, he had founded the Serbian Renewal Movement (SPO) in 1990 and maintained pressure on Milošević through organized street protests in 1991. Nothing emerged from the meeting to give Carrington any confidence of making headway.

Within a week I was back in London for yet another round of talks. Despite many hours of negotiations there was little chance of any breakthrough. The Muslim leadership appeared to have little interest in reaching agreement and simply reiterated their stance that until Serbs were seen to withdraw their heavy weapons and have them placed under UNPROFOR scrutiny, there would be no cooperation from them. They then concentrated on the widespread reports of ethnic cleansing. However, it was very difficult, without concrete evidence, to know just how widespread this had become. The media were indicating it was rampant, with Serbs mainly to blame. Rumours were circulating of camps being established throughout Bosnia, but it was impossible, without any reliable sources, to verify how savage, intense or systematic it might be. The question again arose as to whether these actions were being carried out with Belgrade's approval.

By Wednesday, 29 July 1992 negotiations were concluded. The only progress made was an agreement that a coordinating committee of representatives of all three sides be established in Sarajevo. This committee would meet on a daily basis at the PTT building in order to solve local issues and keep open the lines of communication and negotiation. Initially, both Serbs and Muslims refused to accept the committee, but after much persuasion by Cutileiro they appeared to relent. Before agreeing, however, they wanted to know who would chair it. When Cutileiro suggested that I might assume the chairmanship, their attitude changed. I was suddenly an acceptable candidate, though I did not know whether to be pleased or worried. Karadžić was immediately supportive of my role, while the Muslim representative, Haris Silajdžić, announced that he would need to contact President Izetbegović back in Sarajevo to seek his approval. The Croat leader, Mate Boban, had no objection, and shortly after speaking with Izetbegović, Silajdžić was 'pleased to support Mr Doyle' as the chairman. I wondered if Carrington had had this in mind when he asked me to return to Sarajevo.

At the concluding press conference mention was made of the coordinating committee and, wishing to avoid talking to the media, I escaped to my room as soon as I could. At this early stage I had no idea how I might manage this committee and whether or not such meetings would achieve anything of substance. I even wondered if setting it up had been some sort of face-saving exercise after the previous three days of what had seemed like futile negotiations. There was also the question of how to get back to Sarajevo, given the intensity of the fighting and shelling within the city. It was the conference coordinator, Jola Volabregt, who gave me some answers a short time later. I was to board an early flight the following morning to Frankfurt and from there fly to Zagreb. I would then be transported to Sarajevo on a British Royal Air Force (RAF) AF C-130 Hercules humanitarian flight. In Sarajevo I would be staying with UNPROFOR in the PTT building, where an office had been created for me. I sought out Cutileiro before he left London and asked if he might arrange that a member of the ECMM be made available to me as my assistant while in Sarajevo. I had been giving this some consideration, aware that I would soon be taking a week off to join Grainne for a much needed break in Crete. If I was away for a few days at least I would have someone to stand in for me at meetings. When he asked if I had anyone in mind, I immediately said, 'Jeremy Brade', a British military officer with the Gurkha Rifles. He had previously served with me during my period with the ECMM, and I had been impressed with his objective grasp of the Bosnian conflict. The ambassador promised to speak with the Head of the ECMM about having Brade seconded to me for the duration.

My return to Sarajevo did not exactly go according to plan. Unfortunately, the flight to Frankfurt was delayed, causing me to miss my connecting flight to Zagreb. At the Lufthansa transfer counter I explained my problem. The official checked flight schedules and told me that there was a Swissair flight to Zurich, from where I could get a connection to Zagreb. I asked about my luggage and was informed that it had already been sent on to Zagreb. Although I queried how this was possible, he claimed that it would indeed be there by the time I arrived. I wasn't convinced. After a relatively short flight I arrived in Zurich and immediately headed for the Swissair connecting flights desk. Having given my name and explained my situation I asked what time the connecting flight to Zagreb was scheduled to depart, only to be told that there was no such flight. Further checks confirmed that this was the case. It was not proving to be a good day.

More checking on the computer followed before I was informed that the best course of action was to take a flight back to Frankfurt, where a seat on a Swissair flight leaving within the hour could be arranged. Back in Frankfurt I headed straight to the Lufthansa desk to face the official who had sent me to Zurich in the first place. As I made my way there I heard my name being called, requesting that I report to the Lufthansa information desk. There I was met by a senior official, who apologised for the inconvenience caused. It seems the Swissair representative in Zurich had contacted Frankfurt on my behalf to complain about my treatment by Lufthansa. There was no sign of the person who had obviously made the initial cock-up. Maybe she had taken early retirement. I was assured that everything would be done to accommodate my desire to get to Zagreb. The official told me that there was no direct flight to Zagreb that day but that I could be put on a flight to Prague. I asked if I could connect directly from there to Zagreb, but was told that I would have to wait until the following day. I asked how close I could get to Zagreb that day and was told that I could reach Ljubljana in Slovenia by late afternoon. I asked him if I might have use of the desk phone and contacted the ECMM in Zagreb and asked to speak with Ambassador Melhuish. When I was put through to him I asked if he would be willing to provide a helicopter to get me from Ljubljana to Zagreb. He agreed. The desk official must have wondered who exactly I was when he heard me on the phone talking about helicopters. However, I just confirmed that I would like a seat on the flight to Ljubljana and said no more. Before leaving the desk I asked again about my luggage, wondering where on earth it might have got to by this stage. It was suggested that if the bags had not arrived in Zagreb by my arrival time I should make out a lost luggage claim and charge the airline the cost of replacing essential clothing and toiletries.

By the time I reached Ljubljana that evening I was, to say the least, tired. Another two hours were to pass before the helicopter touched down in Zagreb. As I suspected, my luggage had not arrived and I had to spend further time making out a lost property report at the baggage counter. I finally got to the ECMM headquarters tired, scruffy and frustrated. Having survived four commercial flights and a helicopter ride in one day in the hope of reaching Sarajevo the following morning, I was disappointed to be told that the C-130 humanitarian flight had been postponed because of heavy shelling in the area around Sarajevo airport. Flying in to the airport was, at the best of times, very hazardous due to the constant danger of coming under fire from either side of the runway. This was bad enough without the added threat of heavy shelling, which was becoming all too frequent. There was little I could do but wait until clearance to fly was granted. The extra day in Zagreb gave me the chance to buy some clothes, courtesy of Lufthansa. I was hardly back from my shopping spree when a message came that my luggage had finally arrived at the airport. At least I would be well off for shirts when I got back to Sarajevo.

Zagreb airport was a hive of activity. It was from here that the humanitarian flights to Sarajevo were coordinated and prepared for their onward journey. Some of the aid arrived from donor countries by road and was stored at the airport before being loaded on to aircraft and flown on to Sarajevo. Some aircraft arrived direct from home airports with aid already loaded. These would report to Zagreb, fly on to Sarajevo and return to Zagreb for further loads. The entire operation was a logistical challenge for UNHCR, but its personnel deserve great credit for the manner in which the airlifts were managed. The C-130 aircraft, better known as the Hercules, is a four-engine turboprop military transport aircraft which has been used in countless military, civilian and humanitarian aid operations. It was originally designed as a troop carrier, a medical evacuation and cargo transport aircraft, and it has had the longest continuous production run of any military aircraft in history. It was in one of these, flown by the RAF, that I was returning to Sarajevo. I was helped aboard by the loadmaster, who informed me that he would let me know when I should put on my flak jacket. Not exactly a confidence-booster.

The only other passenger on the flight was Paddy Ashdown, the leader of the British Liberal Democrat Party, who was making a familiarization visit to Sarajevo and was sitting in the cockpit being given the VIP treatment. The loadmaster helped strap me into my seat, amid the roar of the powerful engines. The seat was not designed for comfort, and as I struggled nervously to tighten the seatbelt, he shouted into my ear that we would be making a 'Khe Sanh landing'. Before I could ask exactly what that meant, he had disappeared into the body of the plane. The flight was uneventful, and I got used to the constant drone of the engines. The loadmaster appeared about forty minutes into the flight holding a flak jacket and indicated I should put it on. He then told the 'passengers' that as we approached the airport we would hear a distinct change in the engine noise and that the drone of the propellers would rise in pitch. We were instructed that upon hearing this we should ensure that we held on tightly to the overhead cable. We might, we were warned, feel our stomachs rising into our throats during the descent, and then as we levelled off we would feel a strong push downwards. As the aircraft's nose suddenly dropped I felt this dramatic pull upwards, my ears became blocked, blood rushed to my head and my stomach began to hurt. I was sure we would plummet into the ground, but at the last moment we seemed to ease up and I felt myself being pulled downwards as if the floor was giving way. As the aircraft mercifully came to a halt and my stomach returned to its normal position, the smiling loadmaster came over and congratulated me on my first Khe Sanh landing. The normal manoeuvre was, I was told, a gradual landing approach to a runway consisting of a constant descent at a shallow angle. However, with the hills around Sarajevo and the high risk of enemy fire, crews were forced to keep their aircraft at a much higher level for longer in order to stay out of range of small arms and present less of a target to the larger-calibre weapons. To do this, the UK pilots were trained to drop the aircraft's nose and put it into a steep dive, levelling out only at the last moment. This technique had been developed by US pilots during the Vietnam War to mitigate the risk of fire at the US base at Khe Sanh.

I saw Paddy Ashdown exiting the aircraft with the pilot and I suspect he was as white as I was. As I approached the terminal, the media appeared. I presumed they were there to interview Paddy Ashdown and prepared to pass them by, but some rushed forward to ask me how long I would be staying in Sarajevo, who would be on the coordinating committee and what it hoped to achieve. I was as vague as I could be in my replies because I just did not have answers to these questions, beyond saying that I hoped for the cooperation of all three sides. I quickly escaped into a UN armoured vehicle and headed to UNPROFOR's PTT building. It seemed that travel by any means other than armoured car was just too dangerous. I asked to see General MacKenzie as soon as I arrived, but was told that he had departed earlier that morning. I had heard some rumblings that MacKenzie's relationship with the Bosnian government had become very strained and that some Muslims were even accusing him of being pro-Serb. He had become a TV superstar, with his natural gift for public speaking. It was reported that he had even warned President Izetbegović that if he didn't improve the public's appreciation of

UNPROFOR then his country hardly deserved any support. Was his recall a directive or did he request it himself, I asked myself? I was sorry to have missed his departure because I had got on very well with him and I knew he had really enjoyed his appointment in Bosnia.

I was able to contact the Bosnian presidency and spoke with Darko Ivić, asking him if there was any chance of meeting with Izetbegovic some time that day. He told me that he would get back to me as soon as possible. I was truly amazed at how upbeat Darko always appeared to be, despite the awfulness of what was happening to Sarajevo. He never seemed down and was always jovial. I asked him how bad things had been since I left the city.

In his characteristic manner he replied, 'Really bad, chief. The bloody Serbs even bombed the Sarajevska Pivnica (Sarajevo Brewery). I think it's time to surrender.'

I took it that he was speaking in jest. I was curious to find out if the president would be prepared to meet with me, particularly as I had been told in London that he was no longer interested in having dealings with the Peace Conference. Darko was back to me a few moments later to tell me that Izetbegović would meet me at 3.00 pm. I told him I would be there.

Jeremy Brade arrived a short time later to join me and seemed very pleased to be back in the city. I told him that I hoped it wasn't remiss of me to have requested his assistance without asking him first. He assured me it was not. I told him that I would be going to Crete for one week with my wife and that the trip had been planned for some time; then I asked him to set things in motion, establishing the names of the party representatives for the committee and deciding on a location and timings.

Travelling into the city to meet with Izetbegović, I could see at first hand how things had changed. Sticking my head out of the APC, provided courtesy of UNPROFOR, I could clearly see where buildings carried the scars of bullets and bombs and windows were shattered, their curtains flapping in the wind. Roofs had gaping holes from shell bursts and roads were pitted with mortar craters. The streets were deadly quiet, with hardly any traffic. We had to negotiate a variety of makeshift barricades, many now abandoned. The wrecks of cars and military vehicles were another reminder of a city under siege. The scene before me was one of stark desolation. I immediately realized I would need my own transport over the next few weeks. Any travel was now extremely dangerous, but I considered I could hardly start demanding that the UN provide me with an APC any time I needed a lift. I also felt it important that I should not be seen to be hand in glove with the UN every time I was on the move.

President Izetbegović looked tired and jittery when we met in his office. There was an armed military guard at the entrance, and he had some armed and uniformed personnel with him. He welcomed me back and wished me success with the coordination committee. I told him that my main aim was to keep the lines of communication open, with a view to finding solutions. Though he said he was hopeful that the committee could get the Serbs to cooperate, he was not optimistic.

'They are', he said, 'continuing to lay siege to this city and are killing our citizens daily. Moreover, the UN has not taken control of their heavy weapons and has failed in its mission.'

Although he did not mention MacKenzie personally, he spoke with bitterness about UNPROFOR. He asked how they could be considered a 'protection force' when they had failed to protect anyone. I told him I would do my best to help and thanked him, before departing.

I called into the liaison office to greet Harjadin Somun, with whom I had had no contact since that day in early May 1992 when he told me about a Muslim attack on the JNA officers club and then said the direct opposite on state television. I wondered what his mood might be. He was cordial in his greeting and hoped I would have success in chairing the coordinating committee, but I detected some coolness in his attitude, which was hardly surprising. He warned me that it was time for me to condemn the Serbs, but I told him that I could not afford do this publicly if I wished to be accepted as impartial.

His response was somewhat troubling: 'Then you must be very careful.'

I had no idea why he said this, but it made me distinctly uneasy and I left the building feeling none too confident. I had a discussion with Jeremy back at the PTT building and, having worked out some practical details with him about the committee, I briefed him about my meeting with Izetbegović and told him of Somun's 'warning'. I also told Jeremy that when I returned to Zagreb I would contact Cutileiro about getting our own transport from the ECMM, since the presidency's critical attitude towards UNPROFOR meant that it would be better for us to have our own vehicle. Jeremy then suggested a solution: the ECMM had, apparently, recently taken delivery of ten armour-plated Mercedes SUVs – perhaps we could poach one of them.

I was back in Zagreb by noon the following day and made a quick call to Cutileiro, telling him of my short meeting with Izetbegović and of my sense that there was growing hostility within Bosnian government circles towards UNPROFOR in general (and General MacKenzie in particular). I then brought up the question of transport and my concern about travelling under UN escort. I told him that what I really needed was my own secure transport and went on to mention the armoured Mercedes jeeps newly acquired by the ECMM, suggesting that if I had one of then I would feel much safer. He told me that he would attempt to secure one by the time I returned from my break.

Chapter 18

Breakfast Reading for Karadžić

It's almost 700 miles by road from Belgrade to Athens and the journey by bus takes about sixteen hours. I had been flown by helicopter to Belgrade from Zagreb that morning, following my brief overnight stay in Sarajevo. I needed to get back to my room in Belgrade to pick up some clothes, documents and passport before heading to Athens to meet up with Grainne. I didn't have much time to spare, and after quickly packing a bag I bummed a lift to the bus station for the long trip to Athens. The bus was pretty old and cramped and there were no toilet facilities aboard. Some time during the night, when I had fallen into an uneasy doze, the bus suddenly swerved and braked. I felt myself propelled forward and heard a crunching noise and a splintering of glass. As I opened my eyes I could make out the driver trying to control his vehicle, which was in a skid. Braking hard, he finally managed to bring it to a halt. There were a few screams from passengers and then silence. The driver, clearly shocked, stepped out to survey the damage. The nearside mirror had been sheared off and must have come through a side window as there were glass fragments all over the floor. Luckily, no one had been struck by the flying glass. I later suspected that the driver might have dozed off himself and strayed into the path of an oncoming vehicle. He had been driving constantly for about ten hours by that stage. Anyway, after some patchwork repairs we continued. Sleep was now definitely off the table both for me and, hopefully, for the driver.

I was greatly relieved to arrive in Athens, tired and with muscles aching but in just enough time to grab a taxi to the airport and meet Grainne coming off her flight. It was great to see her, and after an overnight stay in Athens we boarded a ferry to Crete, where we spent a relaxing week in Sfakia on the island's south-west coast, far away from Bosnia's turmoil. My being away for so long had been hard on Grainne. Military wives have a lot to put up with, destined to share their lives with husbands and partners frequently absent on operational duties or overseas missions. It is on them that the responsibilities for all aspects of domestic life fall, and I counted myself lucky that Grainne was always there to support me when these occasions arose.

The week flew by too quickly, and soon we were on a flight back to Athens. I had been dreading the long bus ride back to Belgrade but I was informed in a phone call to my hotel that Carrington wanted me to join him in Brussels for a hastily arranged round of talks and that I would be flying directly to the Belgian capital. I suddenly realized I had nothing other than holiday clothes with me, so I asked a message to be passed to Jeremy to have him pick up a suit and some shirts from my room in Belgrade before he flew to Brussels. Grainne's return flight to Dublin took off before mine. Part of me wanted to be on the flight with her, but we both knew the reality of our situation. I suspected my period in Bosnia would be coming to an end soon, but how soon that might be I had no idea. After she had gone I sat alone in the departure terminal feeling somewhat gloomy.

When I had checked in to my hotel in Brussels, Cutileiro phoned asking me to join Carrington. On meeting him I tried to explain why I appeared to be improperly dressed, but he brushed it aside with a wave of the hand, saying he hoped I had had a good holiday. He told me that he was hosting a dinner that evening which would be attended by Cyrus Vance (the UN Special Representative) and Douglas Hogg from the FCO. He wanted me to join them to give an account of recent events in Sarajevo. He went on to ask me how I had found the situation in the city, to which I responded that I was not too confident that the coordinating committee would achieve very much. I stressed that the Serbs would argue that it was too dangerous for them to meet in Sarajevo and said that I believed the Muslims had, in any event, lost faith in negotiations. I added that the Croats would probably be supportive but that their delegates did not speak for the Croats of western Herzegovina. He asked if I believed anything could really be achieved, and I told him that if the committee kept the lines of communication open, then that was much as we could hope for. The dinner itself passed off without too many difficult questions being asked. I assumed that Cyrus Vance was aware of how the population viewed UNPROFOR. On the one hand, there was much appreciation and relief when UNPROFOR took over control of the airport and began supervising the delivery of humanitarian aid; yet, on the other hand, it had to suffer criticism, mainly from Muslims who believed the force was not doing enough to counter the Serb siege of the city. It is a maxim in peacekeeping that to be criticised by all sides in a conflict means you are probably doing a good job.

The following day, intense negotiations took place between the leaders of all the former Yugoslav republics, Carrington's team and Cyrus Vance. There seemed little optimism that agreement would be reached. The absence of a credible threat of force in Bosnia clearly reduced the incentive for the Bosnian Serbs, who now enjoyed military superiority, to make any concessions. The Muslim-dominated Bosnian government, meanwhile, continued to view intervention as their main goal, and this made them reluctant to agree to any settlement. It was clear that for most western governments, however, national interests were not sufficiently pressing to justify intervention and the risk of heavy casualties was far too great. It was late into the evening when we heard that the talks were to conclude without any breakthrough. By early the next day most of the delegations had already departed, including Carrington and his advisers.

I decided to stay on in Brussels and arranged a flight back to Zagreb for the following Monday. I received word that I was to be supplied with one of the ECMM's armoured SUVs, which I would take back with me on a return flight to Sarajevo aboard a C-130 Hercules. I was delighted to hear this good news and to know I would have some protection while driving around the city, particularly in and around 'Sniper's Alley' – the main thoroughfare from the airport to the city centre. Indeed, one of the most dangerous and terrifying aspects of the siege was the targeting of civilians by snipers. Hiding in high-rise buildings, the snipers, some of them female, overlooked the front lines and picked off victims on both Serb and Muslim sides. Women, children, soldiers and peacekeepers were all killed by snipers, many with a single shot to the head. Travelling along 'Sniper's Alley' had become a terrifying ordeal for many members of the press, who ran the gauntlet by driving at high speed along the route in the hope of avoiding the deadly fire. Many died in this killing zone.

On the Sunday morning I was passing through the hotel lobby when I noticed a colour photograph on the front page of the *Sunday Times* in the hotel shop. The photograph showed an emaciated and skeletal prisoner standing behind a barbed wire fence in a place identified as Trnopolje, one of many Serb detention camps in Bosnia. This was the first published photograph which showed the horrors going on in Bosnia. I quickly bought the paper and headed for the dining room, where I knew Radovan Karadžić was seated alone at a table having breakfast. As I approached his table I was confronted by his bodyguard, who stood in front of me, arms folded across his chest. Karadžić, recognizing me, nodded to the bodyguard to let me pass. When I reached his table I held out the paper, placed it on top of his plate and said, 'Your breakfast reading, Mr Karadžić.' Before he had any time to react or speak, I turned round and walked out.

A short time later, as I took the hotel lift, I was joined by an individual who knew who I was and introduced himself as 'John Kennedy, British and a former Conservative party candidate'. He went on to explain that he was born in Belgrade and was now an adviser to Karadžić, then inquired if I would be willing to meet with the Bosnian Serb leader. I replied that as the peace talks had been concluded I had no authority to meet him. However, I added that were I to bump into him in the hotel bar, where I would soon be having coffee with a colleague, I could hardly ignore him. He thanked me as we both exited the lift. I wondered what on earth this well-spoken Englishman had to do with Karadžić, and I was intrigued, to say the least. Karadžić appeared with Kennedy about thirty minutes later. I was sitting with Jeremy Brade, having told him about my encounter with Kennedy, when Karadžić approached me and asked if he might sit with us. He appeared anxious. I waited for him to open the conversation, and he asked me why I had given him the newspaper.

I answered, 'I thought you might be interested to see what exactly your Serbs are doing to Muslims in these detention camps.'

He said he did not believe these were Serb detention camps.

I asked him if he was denying that any such camps existed, and he stated that these were 'just holding areas for separating enemy soldiers from civilians'.

I pressed him on this. 'But your Serbs have been ethnically cleansing huge areas of Bosnia – surely you cannot deny this?'

He retorted that his troops were merely defending Serbs, to which I responded that the international community was aware that such camps existed throughout Bosnia and that Muslims were being forced to sign away their homes or risk being killed. He acknowledged that this was illegal, so I asked him what he intended to do about it.

After a quick consultation with Kennedy he replied that he would write a letter to *The Times* publicly stating that Serbs had no right to force Muslims to sign away their property. I told him I would inform Carrington of his promise and that we would watch out for the letter.

He went on to mention that the Muslims had tried to scuttle the talks the previous Friday, but I cut him short: 'Mr Karadžić, I was not present in these talks and therefore have no intention of making any comment about them. I am sure Lord Carrington is quite capable of making up his own mind about them.'

I nodded to Jeremy and stood to leave. As we departed, I told Karadžić that I was looking forward to reading his statement in the newspaper. I realized that I needed to inform Cutileiro about this meeting before he heard of it from someone else, and was fortunate to get him on the phone. After I had told him, he assured me he would let Carrington know. I added that I did not expect to see any statement in the paper.

'Nor do I', he answered.

Both of us were proved correct.

I flew back to Zagreb via Zurich on 17 August 1992 and was very impressed when informed that a Mercedes armoured SUV, compliments of the ECMM, would be in the hold of the C-130 Hercules when I boarded it for Sarajevo the following morning. However, I then learned that all humanitarian flights were grounded after a C-130 had been 'locked on' by a missile when lifting off from Sarajevo airport. One of the hazards experienced by the pilots of the humanitarian aircraft flying in and out of Sarajevo was the threat of a 'lock-on'. This came in the form of portable, shoulder-fired, low-altitude, surface-to-air missiles with a high-explosive warhead and infrared homing guidance, usually fired at an aircraft on take-off or landing. A warning system in the cockpit would alert the pilot to the incoming danger, and releasing 'chaff' (a radar counter-measure in which the aircraft ejects a cloud of small, thin pieces of aluminium) could divert these missiles from their target. It was two days before the aid flights were cleared to resume. In the meantime, Cutileiro contacted me with the news that a major international conference would be convened in London towards the end of the month under the auspices of the UN Secretary General, Boutros-Ghali, and the British Prime Minister, John Major. The purpose of these fresh talks would be to provide a new momentum in the search for a negotiated settlement, and I was expected to attend. It would seem that my stay in Sarajevo was likely to be shorter than planned.

I arrived early at Zagreb airport with Jeremy Brade, and having taken possession of my SUV drove it directly on to the C-130, where it was securely tied down by the loadmaster. Once again I was advised to put on my flak jacket and told that we could expect a 'Khe Sanh landing'. On landing we drove directly to the UN's PTT building, where I was met by Martin Bell, who asked for a quick interview. He had managed to acquire a few empty offices under the ramp leading to the main PTT building, where the satellite dishes and telephones were set up. Soon he had been joined by a plethora of other networks, all anxious to be close to the action. It was like an international press club, and the BBC became known as the 'Bunker Broadcasting Centre'. I came to have a high regard for many of these war correspondents, many of whom lost their lives during the conflict.

I then met Colonel d'Avout of France, who arranged for me to meet the newly appointed UN Sarajevo Sector Commander, General Abdul Razek of Egypt, MacKenzie's replacement. There were now about 1,500 UNPROFOR troops based in Sarajevo, with the task of securing the airport and assisting in the delivery of humanitarian aid. Jeremy and I were assigned a room which overlooked the main highway into the city centre. From its window we could clearly see the destruction caused by the almost constant shelling and mortar fire. Directly opposite the PTT building there was a large apartment block which bore the scars of many shell bursts. A large number of windows were shattered and attempts had been made to replace them with wood and even cardboard. Wrecked cars littered the car park in front. We could clearly see some of the block's inhabitants as they glanced furtively across, and I wondered what they must have thought of us as they suffered the slow strangulation of their city. As we watched we could hear the distant sound of shelling, which was described that day as the heaviest in a month. The area between the Holiday Inn hotel and the Marshal Tito barracks came under intense shell fire, as did the offices of the government.

I gave General Razek an outline of what I was doing and as much information about the overall situation as I could. He was too new to the assignment to have a 'feel' for Bosnia, and I had no idea if he had served previously with the UN. However, he expressed the view that the UN should accept that casualties among peacekeepers were inevitable. My immediate reaction to this statement was to advise him that such a message should not be publicly aired, because it would send out the wrong signals; it could be taken as an admission that it was OK to target UN peacekeepers. He went on to tell me that at a recent US military exercise which he attended some troops were killed accidentally, and he said that this was 'something we should all accept as soldiers'. I agreed, but said that to express this publicly was also not a good idea. Coincidentally, within an hour of our exchange we were informed that a Ukrainian UNPROFOR soldier had been killed by sniper fire. He was hit by a bullet in the head and one in the heart as he walked across the courtyard of the Marshal Tito barracks, where his unit was stationed. He was the twelfth UNPROFOR soldier to die in Bosnia. I wondered how General Razek would react to the news. That evening, he gave his first interview to the media and, when asked for his reaction to the loss of the Ukrainian peacekeeper, acknowledged that UN casualties were inevitable in the Bosnian theatre; I was really astonished to hear him say this publicly and wondered what kind of briefing he had received in New York before taking up his assignment.

At 7.30 pm Razek convened his first staff conference, to which I was (surprisingly) invited. Following his opening comments the senior operations officer gave his briefing on the day's main incidents. Apart from the reported killing of the UN soldier we heard that around thirty artillery shells had hit the Marshal Tito barracks. There was considerable damage to the roof of the main building and eight UN trucks were destroyed. (Throughout the meeting we could still hear the sound of exploding shells from downtown.) Street clashes between Muslim and Serb fighters were also reported. As the operations officer was giving his briefing on the day's incidents, I couldn't help but feel some sympathy for Razek, who must have been wondering what the hell he had let himself in for. Just before the meeting ended one of the staff officers read out an administrative directive which had been sent from Force Headquarters in Belgrade; it stated that the working hours of UNPROFOR were to be from 7.00 am to 4.30 pm. Nobody laughed.

The following morning, after attending UNPROFOR's morning brief, I asked Jeremy to arrange our first coordination meeting for that afternoon. He made contact with the presidency and requested that they inform both Muslim and Croat delegations. Contacting the Serbs, however, wasn't so easy. I suggested to him that this might be done through the JNA barracks at Lukavica, where we knew the Serb leadership were frequently to be found. He eventually made contact and was told that while they would make every effort to be in attendance, there could be no guarantee of their presence, given the serious safety concerns. He then asked if there was any alternative location within the city that might be acceptable but got the impression that attending any such meeting anywhere was not a priority for them. I was not, therefore, surprised that the Serbs failed to appear for the meeting. I had not met any of the Muslim or Croat representatives before and found this a distinct disadvantage. I also had the impression that both Muslims and Croats were present for purely cosmetic purposes and had little real interest in negotiation. Indeed, when I asked them to raise any issues they might wish to discuss I was met with blank stares. Part of me could understand their reluctance. Sarajevo was being pounded to death, mainly by the Serbs, and these people had lost any faith in a third party coming to their relief. The Serbs, who were ostensibly part of the discussions, had not shown up. Convinced this committee initiative would achieve nothing, I was now of the view that the parties only agreed to attend in order to avoid accusations of indifference to peacemaking efforts. I decided that we would not proceed with any meeting the following day but would instead wait until after the London talks to see if the situation improved.

That evening, after giving much thought to my position, I concluded that it was time to consider finishing up altogether. There appeared to be no chance of making progress in any talks while the city was under siege. Movement was dangerous, even in an armour-plated SUV. Trust in the international community, if it still existed at all, was eroding. I confided in Jeremy how I felt and suggested that he might be in a position to take my place.

Saturday morning began with intensive shelling in the city. Mortar fire was reported near the airport and our building was struck by artillery shells. We headed for the bunker underneath and waited for the bombardment to subside. When we made our way back upstairs we could see that little damage had been done to the building, although one shell had detonated just outside our window. About midday the UNPROFOR duty officer informed me that Biljana Plavšić, the former Serb member of the presidency who had presented me with a birthday cake in Pale, had heard I was back in Sarajevo and had asked to meet me. Would I be available to visit her at Lukavica? I informed him that I would and that I would drive to Lukavica that afternoon.

We headed out to the airport in the SUV, with Jeremy driving and an interpreter borrowed from the UN. We needed to cross the airport runway as this was the most direct route to Serb-held Lukavica. I was nervous driving into the barracks, reminding myself of the pretty dramatic events which had occurred on my visit there during the hostage incident. Plavšić had changed little since last we had met. She welcomed me back to Sarajevo and asked if there was anything she could do to help. Not knowing if she was aware of the coordinating committee initiative, I explained my role and then expressed my disappointment that no Serbs had turned up for the initial meeting. She quickly told me that it would be impossible for a Serb delegation to visit the PTT building.

'Besides', she said, 'I fear that nothing can be achieved as long as the Muslims continue to shell our villages and murder our citizens.'

I was getting the same old excuses again: the Muslims were to blame and Serbs were only protecting themselves. It was remarkable how the Serbs continually tried to justify their actions in this way, and I was becoming jaded by it.

This was the same woman who had remarked that in Sarajevo 'Muslims like to live on top of each other. It's their culture. We Serbs need space.'

I asked her whether she understood that Muslims were trying to break out of a city under siege and surrounded by Serb forces, but it was clear that she had no answer to this and she chose to say nothing. I asked her if any Serb representative could attend the discussions, but she said it would be impossible while 'Muslim attacks on Serbs continue'. There was nothing left to say, so I thanked her for meeting with Jeremy and me and we departed.

It was when we were crossing the airport runway that shots hit the vehicle, sounding like 'pings' against the armour-plated passenger door. There then followed a short burst of fire which had a far more audible impact. There was barely time to react. Jeremy just pressed the accelerator and we drove like hell over the open space towards the protection of the terminal building. As soon as we reached safety we got out to view the damage; the bullet marks were clearly visible on the lower part of the door and door frame. Our first thought was, of course, who had fired at us? Our vehicle was painted white, with EC logos clearly visible on the roof and sides, and we also flew the EC flag over both side windows. There could have been no mistaking who we were. The firing had come from the far side of the airport near the Muslim village of Butmir, and at that moment I suddenly remembered Somun's warning to 'be very careful' after I told him I would not publicly condemn the Serbs. I decided not to make an issue of the incident, but it went some way towards convincing me that the time had come for me to leave Sarajevo.

Sunday morning dawned with no easing of the fighting. I attended UNPROFOR's morning brief, at which the situation could be best described as very tense. Mortars pounded the city for the fourth day running, with reports that at least fifty shells had hit the city centre, while a fierce battle was being waged in the Serb-held suburb of Ilidža. It appeared that each side was accusing the other of trying to seize the initiative ahead of the coming international peace talks in London. I told Jeremy that I planned to drive to the airport to see if I could hitch a flight back to Zagreb and suggested that he accompany me. UNPROFOR operations let it be known that the airport might have to be closed at short notice because of mortar and artillery crossfire. Sure enough, when we left the PTT building and at the main turn-off for the airport road we could clearly hear machine gun fire coming from the direction of Ilidža. We reached the airport safely and parked our vehicle close to the UNHCR hangar. Their office was in one corner of the building, the rest being used for storage or living accommodation. The RAF were also in residence, busily engaged in the rapid loading and unloading of aircraft, trying to ensure that they were on the ground for as short a time as possible and so less exposed to shelling, mortar and machine gun fire.

I asked the senior RAF officer if there was any chance of a flight out of town but was told that it would not be possible until the following day. It had just begun to rain, making a bad day even worse. The rain was soon joined by shellfire, so I spent quite a while at the airport taking shelter from the shelling, which seemed dangerously close. I met with Larry Hollingsworth of UNHCR, the 'man with the white beard', a former British Army officer who, throughout the conflict, succeeded in bringing convoys of food and medicine through front lines, across minefields, in snow and mud, to give some element of succour to the most vulnerable victims of the war. He was a recent arrival in the city, having been tasked by UNHCR with running the airlift, and he was determined to 'stay the distance'. His enthusiasm was infectious; mine was waning.

We walked back to the car and headed back to our base accompanied by the distant sound of shelling and mortar fire. I felt deflated but thought how much more difficult life must be for the citizens of Sarajevo, who could not avoid this terrible conflict. I could come and go as I wished, but for them there was no escape. Survival was their one objective, and until this pointless war was concluded they were destined to live like rats in a sewer. It seemed senseless that the UN force on the ground, while valiantly providing humanitarian relief, had been less than effective in protecting anyone. When we eventually got back to the PTT building I had the chance to phone Grainne. After I had given her a gloomy picture of the latest events, she told me of the efforts by some of our neighbours to arrange aid to be sent to Sarajevo. She was still worried about my safety but relieved to hear I was heading to London, with a chance of getting home for a few days. My spirits lifted somewhat.

We were back at the airport the following morning, and the Italians offered me a seat on a flight to Zagreb. This, of course, depended on a continuing lull in the shelling. I bumped into Martin Bell again, who told me he was waiting to meet the UN's newly appointed Special Rapporteur for Human Rights for Former Yugoslavia, Tadeusz Mazowiecki (a former Polish prime minister). He was due to arrive in Sarajevo that morning. Anyway, we were finally given the all-clear to fly out of the city just after midday. We took off a few minutes later, and as I watched part of the city below me I wondered if I would ever return.

Chapter 19

The Final Curtain

Delegates from forty countries and international organizations gathered at the Queen Elizabeth II Conference Centre in London for the peace conference scheduled for 26 and 27 August 1992 under the joint chairmanship of the UN Secretary General, Boutros-Ghali, and British Prime Minister, John Major. Also in attendance were the leaders of each former Yugoslav republic and the Foreign Ministers of the United States, Russia, China and countries neighbouring the former Yugoslavia. The conference was called in a fresh attempt to mediate a solution to the Yugoslav conflict.

The ECMM headquarters in Zagreb had, once again, come to my rescue by giving me a helicopter lift to Graz in Austria, from where I boarded a flight to London via Frankfurt. By the time I reached the Hyatt Carlton Hotel it was close to midnight, and there was a message requesting that I be ready to attend a working group meeting at the FCO the following morning. The meeting, which comprised mostly FCO officials as well as some of Carrington's close staff members, was focused on suggestions for working groups to be put before the conference delegates. During the course of these talks I was taken aside by Lord Carrington and asked for an update on events in Sarajevo, including my view as to whether there was any likelihood of progress with the coordinating committee. Lamentably, I had to paint a pretty gloomy picture, and I added that there was no hope of any movement forward while the city remained under siege. He then asked me to attend a conference with his full staff later in the afternoon.

When I arrived at Carrington's office in Christie's auction house, most of his people were gathered there. There were about twenty of us in total, including his deputy, Ambassador de Beauce of France, Cutileiro, his conference coordinator, Ambassador Henri Wijnaendts, Ambassador

Peter Hall, who was the UK Presidency coordinator, members of his own cabinet, Henry Darwin and officials of the conference secretariat. When Lord Carrington arrived he wasted no time in informing us that he was resigning as chairman. His replacement, he said, was to be another former Foreign Secretary, Lord (David) Owen. The status of the conference was to be changed and the full details would be announced at the end of the discussions. He concluded by inviting us to dinner that evening at the Savoy, where he would give an address.

Hearing Lord Carrington's announcement, I knew it was also time for me to end my involvement with the peace conference. Were the United Nations to become more directly involved, as seemed probable, and since they had over 1,500 peacekeepers as well as civilian staff in Sarajevo, there would seem to be little point in having a personal representative there as well. Although I had been Carrington's representative, it hardly seemed likely that I would be asked to fill the same role for Lord Owen, nor had I any wish to.

Returning to my hotel, I saw Ireland's Foreign Minister, David Andrews, and introduced myself to him. He shook my hand, said he had seen some of my interviews on television and invited me to visit the Irish delegation office at the conference centre. It was while speaking with him that an official came over to tell me that Martin Bell had been injured. This was shocking news. I was told that Martin had been struck by mortar shrapnel while filming in Sarajevo and that he had been evacuated back to London.

Dinner that evening in the Savoy, mixing with lords, ambassadors and under-secretaries in such opulent surroundings, was memorable indeed. Lord Carrington spoke of his disappointment at not having achieved a solution to the crisis, which he said was due not to lack of effort by his officials and advisers but to a complete lack of cooperation by the belligerents. He went on to pay tribute to some of his key people, and I was honoured to be mentioned. He was generous in his praise of my contribution as his 'man on the ground', and he ended by wishing his replacement every success.

Security was very tight both inside and outside the Queen Elizabeth II Conference Centre as the long queue of VIP cars drew up at the entrance to deposit their occupants. I had arrived much earlier with Ambassador Cutileiro in a humble taxi, clutching the accreditation pass which, I was warned, 'must be worn around the neck and openly displayed'. A brief glance into the very large delegate conference room brought home just how big this event would be. A miniature national flag was positioned in front of each delegation, as were flags representing international organizations such as the UN, EC, UNHCR, ICRC, WEU (Western European Union), OSCE, the African Union and many more. There must have been over 200 seats for delegates, with seats behind them reserved for advisers and minders. I made my way to the room allotted to Carrington's team, where I was to be available for some meetings on the periphery of the conference.

John Major opened the conference with a warning to all parties, particularly the Serbs, of what they could expect if they did not cooperate in efforts to end the bloodshed. He insisted that any party who stood in the way of agreement could expect tougher sanctions, which would be rigorously policed. President Milošević claimed that he had little control over Bosnian Serb nationalists, and Radovan Karadžić, for his part, denied that his forces had anything to do with the escalation of fighting in Sarajevo. No surprise there. The conference revealed the great differences between the positions of the participants and, in my view, provided little optimism that any settlement would be reached. Although there were calls by some delegates for military action, it became clear that external powers were not contemplating the use of force to bring an end to hostilities. Without the promise of military intervention I had no confidence that the conference would achieve anything.

I was called in the afternoon to a meeting between Lord Carrington, Cyrus Vance, Karadžić and his deputy Koljević (which Ambassadors Wijnaendts, Cutileiro and Hall also attended). The discussion centred on an attempt to persuade the Serbs to halt the fighting and engage in serious negotiations. Karadžić was, of course, adamant that his people were forced to act in order to protect the Serb population, though he did admit that Serbs were willing to hand back territory and remain part of Bosnia, but only if they were granted full autonomy from Muslims and Croats. He constantly referred to the agreement of March 1992 negotiated by Cutileiro in which each ethnic group was to have its own constituent unit, but said that the Muslims had reneged on it. Secretary Vance asked how this could be implemented without moving populations. Moreover, when pressed by Vance as to the areas Serbs would be willing to hand back, Karadžić was vague, saying that this was not decided, although he went on to say that it could be negotiated. He then accused Muslims of shelling their own people in Sarajevo and claimed that they were responsible for most of the shelling in the city. I countered this by stating that it was the Serbs, backed by the JNA, who had started the fighting in the city, and that while the Muslims might be responsible for some provocations, Serbs bore most of the blame. Carrington suggested that the situation in Bosnia was now critical and the world expected progress, to which Karadžić responded that he was willing to consider any proposal which did not jeopardize the right of the Bosnian Serbs to full autonomy. There was nothing said at the meeting that had not been said before. Karadžić offered nothing of substance.

I spent some time in the main conference room to get a taste of how these negotiations were handled by some of the world's leading politicians and diplomats. I sat directly behind Lord Carrington, who was seated between the UN Secretary-General and John Major. I was amused to observe a public squabble between Milošević and Milan Panić, the newly appointed prime minister of the Federal Republic of Yugoslavia. Panić was a Belgrade-born millionaire residing in California. Though he had been hand-picked by Milošević, the two men soon fell out, arguing about which of them had the right to speak on behalf of the Serbs; this petty squabble demonstrated the difficulty of reaching any agreement, however high-powered the conference might be.

On the second day a statement of general principles was adopted that included calls for a cessation of fighting, an end to the use of force, recognition of the sovereignty and territorial integrity of each state, non-recognition of territory taken by force, compliance with obligations under humanitarian law and adherence to the Geneva Convention. There was also condemnation of forced expulsions, a demand for the closing of detention camps, the safe return of refugees, and that a final settlement of all succession questions should be reached by consensus or arbitration. Having been directly involved over so many months in similar negotiations, I remained very sceptical that any of these high-minded principles would be respected or implemented without enforcement provisions.

During the afternoon session I was slipped a note by a British official; it simply said that Martin Bell was back in London and had been admitted to the Princess Grace Hospital. As soon as I had a break I left the assembly and phoned the hospital. At first they refused to confirm or deny that Martin was a patient, but when I explained who I was and asked if I could visit him, they eventually agreed. I met David Andrews in the corridor and when I told him where I was going, he suggested I call into the Irish delegation office, where I was to request a bottle of Irish whiskey to give to the patient. Martin was propped up in bed and not looking too bad. He told me he had been hit by some shell fragments in the groin but that, luckily, the shrapnel had been near the end of its trajectory. He had immediately been taken to the UN hospital in the basement of the PTT building and, after having had the larger pieces removed, was evacuated to Zagreb and flown to London by air ambulance. He remarked that he couldn't help but contrast his treatment to that of the ordinary citizens of Sarajevo.

I handed over the bottle of whiskey with the compliments of David Andrews and told him, 'I expect you may well be back in Sarajevo before I get there.'

At the conclusion of the talks it was declared that the peace conference would remain in being until a final settlement of the problems of the former Yugoslavia was reached, and that it would be guided by the set of principles announced earlier. The permanent co-chairmen would be the Head of State/Government of the Presidency of the EC and the Secretary-General of the United Nations. A high-level steering committee was to be established, which would include representatives of the Troika of the EC, the Troika of the CSCE, the five permanent members of the UNSC, as well as Lord Carrington's replacement, David Owen. The Conference was to operate in continuous session at the office of the UN in Geneva. There were also to be 'working groups' established in Bosnia concerned with humanitarian, succession and economic issues, ethnic communities and confidence-building measures. Before taking a flight to Limerick, I went back to the conference centre the following day to meet some people. I had a quick word with Izetbegović and asked him if he was satisfied with the outcome of the conference. He shrugged his shoulders and said only that I knew better than anyone that nothing much would be achieved. I told him that I hoped to return to Sarajevo, but I was only being diplomatic.

'You will always be welcome', he replied with a smile.

I met Cutileiro in our assigned office and mentioned that I was taking a few days off to return home. I asked him what the next step would be, now that Lord Carrington had stood down from being chairman, and I suggested to him that the time was right for me to return to home service. He suggested that when I finished my break in Ireland I should return to Zagreb and await developments. I agreed, and so arrived back in Zagreb on 31 August, unsure as to my immediate future. I had thought about returning to Sarajevo to tie up a few loose ends, but this plan was shelved by the shooting down of an Italian G-222 aid aircraft about 25km from Sarajevo, causing an immediate cancellation of all aid flights. On 6 Sept 1992 I drafted a letter which I faxed to Martti Ahtisaari, Finland's Secretary of State for Foreign Affairs, who had been selected at the London Conference to chair the 'Working Group on Bosnia'. In it I gave a brief account of my role in Sarajevo and made mention of the fact that prior to the London Conference I had submitted a progress report to Lord Carrington's office. I also mentioned that I was considering ending my association with the peace conference at the end of September.

Two days later I was telephoned by Ahtisaari. He asked for my views on the coordinating committee which I had hoped to establish in Sarajevo. I gave him my opinion, which was that I saw little chance of it achieving anything; in fact, I had no expectation that all sides would even attend a single session. I knew this wasn't very positive, but I was being realistic. He made no mention of having received my fax or of the future make-up of the Bosnian team, and I did not press him on the subject. Before he hung up he told me that David Owen and Cyrus Vance would be visiting Zagreb within a few days and that he would be with them.

A few days later, the Head of the ECMM, Ambassador Ramsay Melhuish, asked me to accompany him to Zagreb airport, where he was to meet Owen, Vance and Ahtisaari, who were on a fact-finding mission. This would be Owen and Ahtisaari's first visit to the region. There were the usual formalities on their arrival, after which the ambassador made them welcome and a fleet of mission vehicles brought them to the hotel. I noticed that Paul Sizeland, Lord Carrington's private secretary and a member of his cabinet, now accompanied Lord Owen. On arrival at the hotel they were led into the conference room, where they received a briefing from the ECMM operational staff. At the conclusion of the briefing Lord Owen mentioned that he was anxious to get to Sarajevo as soon as possible. It was explained to him that because all humanitarian flights were still grounded due to the shooting down of the Italian aircraft, there was no chance of a flight. He seemed a little annoyed at this and mentioned that John Major had promised him any support he might require. He then asked that 10 Downing Street be contacted, presumably with a view to having the Prime Minister order one of the RAF C-130s to fly him to Sarajevo. I was somewhat taken back when I was asked to make the call to ascertain if the Prime Minister would authorize such a flight. I thought it would have been more appropriate for Ambassador Melhuish to do it.

Lord Owen and his team departed the headquarters soon afterwards, Melhuish having informed him that he would be contacted as soon as a reply was received from Downing Street. I thought Ahtisaari would want to have a chat with me, following our previous conversation, but I reckoned he must have had more pressing issues on his mind and so thought no more of it. Before departing, Paul Sizeland informed me that there was a meeting scheduled to be held in Geneva to discuss the make-up of the new Bosnian team. Lord Carrington had asked Paul to remain in place and assist Lord Owen for a transition period. In any event, after numerous attempts I finally succeeded in getting through to Downing Street and, after introducing myself and explaining the purpose of the call, was put through to an official who asked me several questions. He was obviously unaware that humanitarian flights had been cancelled, and when I mentioned this he asked for my contact number and told me he would get back to me.

He returned my call almost two hours later, to say, 'The Prime Minister is unable to assist Lord Owen in this matter. He is of the view that it would be inappropriate to countermand the advice of the Royal Air Force in grounding all humanitarian flights into Sarajevo, which was obviously made with good reason. Perhaps Lord Owen can find another way of getting into the city.'

I thanked him and said I would pass the message on.

I was relieved that I was not the person who had to tell Lord Owen. I heard later that he did get to Sarajevo by taking a flight to Split in Croatia and then proceeding by road. In the meantime, I was wishing my colleague, Lieutenant Colonel Maurice Walsh, farewell on his departure from Zagreb to Sofia, where he was taking up an appointment as the ECMM's Head of Regional Centre for Bulgaria. A few days later, a British member of the ECMM, Lieutenant Colonel Dudley Ells, who was assigned to the logistics section in Zagreb, came to see me. He gave me the welcome news that my proposal that a service medal for ECMM staff be created could be approved if I was to press the issue using my 'weight' as Carrington's personal representative. I was a bit dubious but thought I might as well try, so I made contact with the commission the following day and asked to speak with the relevant authority. I tried the line that I was speaking on behalf of Lord Carrington and that he was anxious to have the latest information on the medal proposal. It was quite amazing how this seemed to generate action by the commission officials. There was a promise that the matter would receive immediate attention and that a decision would hopefully be favourable. Dudley was delighted, and I told him if that if the result was positive he could take all the credit. Within six weeks approval was received, and all ECMM personnel, both military and civilian, were deservedly awarded service medals.

On 17 September 1992 I received a reply to my letter from Martti Ahtisaari in which he stated that, given the new EC/UN structure established by the London Conference, the coordinating committee was no longer necessary and should be wound up; in addition, there would no requirement for a personal representative in Bosnia. He made it easier by saying that he understood I had come to the same conclusion myself. It was no more than I expected and I was relieved that the matter had been decided. I contacted Cutileiro to let him know. He expressed his appreciation for everything I had done and told me he would be standing down himself. He then gave me the sad news that Henry Darwin, Lord Carrington's special adviser on Bosnia who had worked so diligently on the Bosnian negotiations, had died suddenly that day. It seemed the new broom was sweeping clean. Indeed, the very next day, I was amused when Paul Sizeland phoned to tell me that at the meeting held in Geneva the previous day my name had come up for discussion, and while it was agreed by all that I had played a positive role in Bosnia someone had noted, 'But he is only a major – if he was a colonel we could keep him on.' Having served subsequently in New York at United Nations HQ I can well imagine such comments being aired, although in my naivety I then thought, 'Surely it's the person that's important rather than the rank.'

One of the last requests made to me before I left my post was to give a briefing to the commanding officer and staff of the 1st Battalion, the Cheshire Regiment. Lieutenant Colonel Bob Stewart and his unit were about to deploy to central Bosnia as members of UNPROFOR. Major Jonathan Riley of the ECMM spoke to the group first, giving them a breakdown of the three main belligerent parties in Bosnia. I followed him, warning the officers that most people in Bosnia were very good at twisting the truth to suit their purposes. I gave them my view that the UN needed to take more aggressive enforcement action and should not to be fooled by what the Serbs said, which had little bearing on what they might do.

'Each side will promise you everything without the slightest intention of sticking to anything', I told them, adding that the Croats had their own agenda, which was not necessarily what the Muslims wanted.

Over the next week I wrote some letters thanking people for their assistance and support during my service in Bosnia: Lord Carrington, Ambassador Cutileiro, Mrs Henry Darwin, President Izetbegović, Lieutenant Colonel Dimitrijević of the JNA, Rade Ćosić, my interpreter from Banja Luka, Hajrudin Somun and Darko Ivić of the presidential liaison team. I also made copies of many of the reports which I had sent to Zagreb from Sarajevo when working as chief of the ECMM. I wanted them for no particular reason other than as a record of my service there, and little did I realize that they were to become extremely important documents during my testimony at the International War Crimes Tribunal in the Hague many years later. Ambassador Melhuish hosted a farewell dinner for me which was also attended by his two deputies. He expressed his disappointment that I would not be continuing to serve in Bosnia, and by way of compensation he even suggested that I might consider switching back to the ECMM to take over as head of a regional centre in Hungary. It was most thoughtful of him, but I declined, explaining that after a full year of a most exciting and challenging assignment it was time to go. I had no regrets.

On Thursday, 1 October I returned home, one full year after I had arrived in the mission area. Before leaving I managed to contact Cutileiro in Lisbon and Darko Ivić in Sarajevo, both of whom I wished to thank personally. Cutileiro had been my immediate boss and someone I had really enjoyed working for. He had laboured tirelessly to reach some accommodation with the three sides in Bosnia, something which was never going to be an easy task. I was very appreciative of his support and encouragement throughout my assignment with the Peace Conference. Darko helped me through the good and bad days in Sarajevo. He was there at my every call and never once questioned my methods or decisions. It was impossible to be in bad form in his company – he was just good to have around.

Ambassador Melhuish kindly offered his car and driver to take me to the airport, and I slipped out of the front door of the hotel without anybody seeing me. I thought it was better that way. As we drove to the airport I couldn't help but think of the suffering people of Bosnia, and of Sarajevo in particular, who had no chance of escaping from the city and were sentenced to live in fear, danger and uncertainty for years to come. It was easier for me. I just had to board a plane and sit back. I briefly wondered if the international community had achieved anything in Bosnia over the twelve months I had served there. Politicians, diplomats, negotiators, monitors and peacekeepers seemed powerless to prevent the slaughter, suffering and misery of Bosnia. This war would go on for a further three years at great cost. It would appear that Bosnia was destined to have an outcome rather than a solution.

Chapter 20

Witness for the Prosecution

The first indication that the International Criminal Tribunal for former Yugoslavia (ICTY) wished to speak with me came by way of a letter in June 1995 routed through the Irish Embassy in the Netherlands. This requested that I make myself available to meet with the tribunal as it was believed that I was in a 'unique position to give an insight into the situation' in early 1992. It had been almost three years since I had returned from Bosnia, and although I had closely followed developments since, I was now back to leading, at least ostensibly, a normal life. Adjusting to home after Bosnia had not been easy for me or my family, and it had been difficult to settle back into a normal routine following the emotional and psychological challenges of serving in a city at war. I had been on quite an adrenalin rush and had experienced a whole range of emotions, from excitement to fear, hope to frustration and sadness to anger. I had not fully appreciated the support my wife Grainne and the children had given me, despite the stressful time it had been for them. Now, having resolved these issues, I was being drawn back towards that pivotal year in my life once again.

Resolution 827 of the United Nations Security Council (UNSC) in May 1993 established the organization's first ever international war crimes court. The ICTY was tasked with prosecuting 'persons responsible for serious violations of humanitarian law committed on the territory of the former Yugoslavia since 1991'. Its aims were fourfold: to bring to justice those responsible for violations of the laws or customs of war; to render justice to the victims; to put an end to the crimes being committed on its territory; and to contribute to the restoration of peace by promoting reconciliation. Establishing the tribunal did not, however, prevent further atrocities taking place in Bosnia. The genocide in Srebrenica, which followed the fall of that town to the Bosnian Serb army, did not occur until July 1995. Warring factions continued to fight for territory throughout the summer of 1995, culminating in so-called Operation Storm in Croatia and a Croat-Muslim offensive in central Bosnia. These battles shifted the balance of power and eventually led to the signing of the Dayton Peace Agreement in November 1995. As the fighting continued, and in the absence of international intervention, the UN Resolution was at least seen by many as a diplomatic and humanitarian gesture.

It was made clear to me by my military superiors that while the Defence Forces had no objection to my appearing at the ICTY, the decision to attend or otherwise would be mine alone. I had no hesitation in agreeing to meet the investigators, believing it important that the tribunal should have an accurate account of the events that led to the outbreak of war in Bosnia. Furthermore, I believed that those responsible for atrocities should be held to account. I had been in Sarajevo for the period leading up to the war, which gave me an insight into the causes of the conflict and its terrible consequences. I had retained many documents from the period, including ECMM reports, conference notes, cease-fire agreements and diaries, so I set about gathering all this information, which I would then hand over to the investigators.

Steve Upton, a police officer from New Zealand seconded to the tribunal as an investigator, was to be my interlocutor in the Hague. He phoned me a few days before my departure, giving me details of my flight and accommodation, and I flew to Amsterdam on 25 July 1995. It was to be the first of seven visits to the tribunal. Steve met me at the airport and brought me to the hotel in Scheveningen, a seaside resort and one of the Hague's eight sub-districts. The following morning, I made my way to the tribunal, which was still in its embryonic stages. It had about 100 staff, comprising investigators, prosecutors, lawyers, judges and administrators, all highly motivated and determined. Investigators had been recruited from the police forces of UN member states, and lawyers, prosecutors and judges were being assigned to the many cases under investigation. Steve explained that in order to prepare for the trials they needed to get information from individuals like myself who were witnesses to events and had detailed knowledge of what had transpired. When I pressed him as to what was required, he responded that the court would want an outline of my year in Bosnia; once I had given my witness statement and was satisfied that it was an accurate account, I would be asked to sign it. He told me that some of the staff at the ICTY had asked to meet with me because I was one of the key witnesses living in Sarajevo during the early months of 1992.

Over the next three days I made out what was termed a 'witness statement', which covered the entire period of my service in the former Yugoslavia, both as a member of the ECMM and as Lord Carrington's personal representative in Bosnia. I had the help of my personal diaries which, although handwritten and produced under difficult circumstances, provided me with information on where I was and whom I met throughout the period. I also handed over copies of all my reports and other documents pertaining to the period that might be of use to the tribunal. I was surprised how little information many of the investigators seemed to have about the period. Many were therefore anxious to talk to me about different personalities and events. It did, however, become very clear, during our long sessions, that they were determined to see justice done. Steve emphasized that there were no time limitations on preparing these cases. Each one would be meticulously handled, with a detailed picture of events being slowly and carefully constructed. Thus, by the time the accused were taken into custody the court would have a robust record of what had taken place on the ground, and this, in turn, would allow them to pursue prosecutions if a case could be made.

Over lunch I asked Steve if he believed I might be called to testify. He said that he could not be sure but that it was likely that I would be in the event that Radovan Karadžić was arrested and put on trial. He also added that as I had had a one-to-one meeting with Milošević, there was a chance I might be called to testify at his trial, too, should he ever be arrested. It seemed premature to be wondering if I might be requested to testify, when Karadžić and most of the other main players were still at large and some had not even been indicted. However, Steve said that Karadžić's indictment had been drawn up and was expected to be published the following day. It was evident that, whether they had been arrested or not, the tribunal was continuing to build cases against these individuals.

The initial indictment of Karadžić and Ratko Mladić was issued the following day. The charges were divided into three: part one concerned genocide, crimes against humanity and crimes committed against the civilian population and places of worship; part two related to the sniping campaign against civilians in Sarajevo; part three alleged crimes relating to the taking of UN peacekeepers as hostages. This indictment would be subsequently amended on a number of occasions prior to the commencement of his trial, particularly in relation to the UN 'safe area' of Srebrenica.

For many witnesses, particularly those who had never been outside Bosnia or who had suffered greatly as victims of the war, testifying before the tribunal was a very daunting and painful experience. To assist in making this experience less traumatic, a 'Victim and Witnesses Section' had been established to support and protect people who might fear intimidation or retribution. The section was created as independent and given the specific role of facilitating the appearance of all witnesses when called by the prosecution or defence. It provided counselling, arranged travel and accommodation and did its utmost to ensure the health, security and safety of witnesses. In a further measure to protect witnesses, the tribunal's 'Rules of Procedure' allowed the court to expunge names to preserve anonymity and to prevent the disclosure of certain records which might identify a victim; they even provided for image- or voice-altering devices during testimony. During that first trip to the tribunal I was very impressed by the manner in which the Victims and Witnesses Section operated. They had been vital in establishing that serious crimes were committed throughout Bosnia. I later learned that from July 2000 to July 2001 the Victims and Witnesses Section handled 550 witnesses from 30 different countries, all of whom testified in only eight trials conducted during that year. The Section offered an impressive level of support to victims and witnesses alike.

Having reviewed my witness statement with Steve and being satisfied that it was an accurate account of my period in Bosnia, I signed it in his and a tribunal lawyer's presence. As I was handed a copy of the document, the lawyer asked if I had any objection to it being given to any of the accused's defence teams should they request a copy. I informed them I did not. Before leaving for home I was asked to listen to some audiotape recordings (wiretaps) and say whether I could identify any of the voices on them. While I was able to identify the voices of Milošević, Karadžić and Nikola Koljević, I had no idea about the content of the tapes. One in particular was a heated phone conversation between Koljević and an unidentified official. At the end of the tape I was asked if I had any idea as to the nature and content of the exchange. I told him I did not. Steve then told me that the conversation actually concerned my demand from April 1992 that the Bosnian Serbs comply with their commitment to remove some of their artillery pieces from the hills surrounding Sarajevo. In the recording Koljević is telling his (unidentified) interlocutor that 'Doyle cannot be fooled' and that 'he needed evidence of the artillery being withdrawn'. I suddenly remembered the conversation with Bosnia's acting Prime Minister, Rusmir Mahmutcehajić, on this matter back in April 1992.

Radovan Karadžić was finally arrested in Belgrade on 21 July 2008. He was posing as Dr Dragan Dabić, a specialist in alternative medicine. His arrest dominated the news at the time and put the spotlight, once again, on the ICTY. By then I had retired from the Defence Forces after forty-three years' service, although at the time of his arrest I was on a special assignment for the UN in Beirut. However, RTE's 'Drivetime' programme managed to track me down for an interview. I was asked if I would be called to testify at Karadžić's trial but could not give a response in the affirmative. Although I had previously given evidence in the trials of Slobodan Milošević (2003) and General Pavle Strugar (2004), I was far better acquainted with Karadžić. I had often wondered what it would be like to testify before the tribunal as a witness in the Karadžić case.

This was to be the third trial at which I had given evidence, all of them as a witness for the prosecution. However, I did not necessarily see myself as a prosecution witness, but simply as someone who had seen many of the events which led to the outbreak of war in Bosnia. It was my duty to tell the truth, as I saw it, of what I had witnessed. Whether my doing so would benefit the prosecution or the defence was not, per se, a priority for me. The trials of Milošević and Strugar were very different. Milošević, at whose trial I testified in 2003, had chosen to represent himself, and accordingly, it was he who cross-examined me. The prosecutor in the case, Geoffrey Nice, questioned me for about two hours, taking me through my period in Bosnia along the lines we had discussed prior to the trial. I had the advantage of having my diary with me which had notes on the 'who, when, where and what'. The presiding judge, Richard May, gave me permission to refer to my diary when I needed to verify details. Many of my reports from the period were brought into evidence and none of them was challenged by the defence.

Although Karadžić had been arrested in July 2008 and immediately transferred to the ICTY's detention centre, it was April 2010 before the prosecution commenced presenting evidence. The original indictment served on Karadžić in 1995 was later amended to include the slaughter of thousands of Muslims in Srebrenica, and further amended in 2009, prior to the commencement of his trial on 26 October of that year. The presiding judge was O-Gon Kwon of South Korea, the prosecution was headed by Alan Tieger, an American trial attorney, and Hildegard Uertz-Retzlaff from Germany. As in the case of Milošević, Karadžić opted to represent himself.

A week before travelling to the Hague for the trial I had received from the prosecution a transcript of my testimony at the Milošević trial and had been asked to review it so as not to be in any doubt about what I had said at the earlier trial. As I was preparing to leave for the Hague, Karadžić's legal adviser, Peter Robinson, asked if I would be willing to meet his client prior to giving evidence. I immediately sought advice from the prosecution as to whether this would be appropriate. They responded that it was purely a matter for me to decide and that I should contact the Victim and Witness Section, which was largely independent of the court, with such queries. As a result of speaking with them I decided to go ahead. The conditions under which I agreed to do it (including the caveat that a prosecution representative be present) were readily accepted, and the meeting was scheduled to take place in the detention unit three days before I was due to testify, thus giving the prosecution the interim period for 'proofing'. (This legal term, I quickly learned, meant finding 'evidence to establish truth or to produce belief in its truth'.)

Arriving at Schiphol Airport, I was immediately whisked through customs, courtesy of an ICTY staff official. He assured me there would be no need to show my passport. As soon as I was seated in a staff car, he gave me a few instructions, informing me that thereafter I would be known simply by a reference number – CD3262 – and that I would be checked into the hotel as such. The hotel staff, I was told, would be aware that I was a witness and would know not to use my real name. I was also told that if I was expecting any calls I should give the callers my room number in advance. He then told me that he was originally from Sarajevo and that his parents remembered me well. When he had told them that he would be looking after me, they had stressed to him that he must pass on their thanks and regards. We were then driven at speed to the Marriott hotel, where a female official was on hand in the lobby. She gave me various items, including an assistance card with emergency numbers, a briefing paper on security, my hotel room key, some Euros ('to tide me over') and a contact number I could ring at any time should I feel unwell or in need of assistance. Thereafter, and having made a phone call back home, I headed to the bar for a beer. My thoughts were firmly fixed on my meeting with Karadžić the following day. Frankly, I hardly slept a wink.

Although I got through my three-hour session with Karadžić largely unscathed I was relieved to have had a member of the prosecution accompany me. Although he did not speak throughout the session, I presumed that he was able to get a sense of what Karadžić's line of questioning during the cross-examination might be. We did not talk about this, but I had no doubt he would be reporting back to the main prosecution team on the content of our discussions.

The next three days were all about getting ready for my testimony. Hildegard Uertz-Retzlaff would be questioning me and she went through the details of what her questions might be. I asked her how long the cross-examination might take, and she informed me that it should not exceed two hours. Karadžić's lawyers had, however, indicated that they had been granted fifteen hours to cross-examine me, much to my surprise, since I had understood that the same period of time was to be given to prosecution and defence. Hildegard explained that this was normally the case, but given that I had already testified along the same lines during the Milošević trial, the judges would be provided with a copy of that testimony. There would, I was assured, be no need to repeat these questions at this trial. The fact that Karadžić was representing himself had been taken into consideration by the presiding judge, and he was being given some latitude in the time allowed for cross-examination, which, it transpired, could continue over a three-day period. It might, therefore, be pretty demanding.

Back at the hotel, I spent a long time reviewing my notes, diaries and previous testimony, and although I felt ready I endured another restless night. To give testimony before the tribunal proved a stern test of one's memory. Although I had only spent a year in Bosnia, it had been a pretty hectic one and it had covered a critical period in that country's history. I had witnessed much of the downward spiral towards conflict and I needed to be able to describe the main events, the various players and the efforts made by the international community to effect some sort of order in a country in which the party leaders were seemingly devoid of the ability or willingness to compromise.

I had been advised that a car would pick me up and drive me to the court. While I could walk there in about five minutes, a car was to be provided to ensure that I would not meet anybody en route or discuss any matters with the prosecution. Within a few minutes my liaison from the Victim and Witness Section arrived and drove me the short distance to the ICTY building. I was escorted through a side entrance, security-checked and then led to a witness waiting room, where another official was on hand to offer me coffee or tea, which I politely declined. After waiting some two hours I was finally escorted into the court to commence my evidence. Having previously testified there, I was familiar with the layout of the trial chamber. Karadžić and his defence team were positioned to my left, with the prosecution on my right. The witness stand was directly facing the three trial judges and registrars, and directly behind the witness stand was the public gallery, separated from the court room by a reinforced glass partition.

Presiding Judge O-Gon Kwon welcomed me and requested I make a solemn declaration to 'speak the truth, the whole truth and nothing but the truth'. The Deputy Prosecutor, Hildegard Uertz-Retzlaff, then gave a summary of my previous evidence to the court. Following this, she examined me along the lines we had discussed during our 'proofing sessions'. I responded to her questions about my period in Banja Luka as a monitor with the ECMM, the meetings I attended, concerns expressed by Muslims about Serb intimidation, the arming of the Bosnian Serbs, the withdrawal of the JNA from Croatia, my visit to the prisoner of war camp at Manjača. She then moved on to my period in Sarajevo as Head of the ECMM in Bosnia, the independence referendum and the subsequent 'war of the barricades' in Sarajevo. She questioned me on the reasons why I thought Karadžić was the leader of the Bosnian Serbs and on my view that the JNA were arming them.

Following a short break she moved on to my period as Lord Carrington's representative, and I was questioned on Karadžić's reaction to my view that he was responsible for the shelling of Sarajevo TV station. She then asked what my understanding of the term 'ethnic cleansing' was, what I knew about the expulsion of Muslim staff from Hotel Serbia in Ilidža and what I remembered about negotiations over TV access. She went on to ask me about my presenting Karadžić with a copy of the *Sunday Times* newspaper in Brussels and my involvement in the London Peace Conference. During this questioning the prosecution tendered many of my reports as exhibits. There were no objections by the defence to any of those submitted.

It was close to 1.00 pm by the time the prosecution had completed questioning me, and I assumed the trial would adjourn for the weekend. However, Judge Kwon decided to permit the defence to begin its cross-examination, informing us that we had thirty minutes but that Karadžić could commence with his questions. He began with an expression of gratitude, before going on the offensive. He suggested first that I did not have a detailed knowledge of Bosnia before I was deployed there. I agreed. He then probed me about Muslims refusing to be mobilized for military service – thereby, he implied, refusing the opportunity to be issued with weapons. He did not, of course, ask for my opinion about why Muslims objected to mobilization. As we proceeded, I found myself feeling cautious and a little uneasy about his line of questioning.

Karadžić concentrated on asking me to confirm factual events, which gave a potentially misleading impression. He asked, for example, if it was true that the Bosnian Serbs had ever refused invitations to talks. For the duration of that day, however, he concentrated his questioning of me around the issue of Sarajevo Television. He produced an official (presidential) document which, he claimed, refused Serbs permission to have a separate channel. He asked me if I was familiar with the document. I told him I was not, but that I was surprised that he had not produced a copy of it during my negotiations with Sarajevo Television officials. He responded with the accusation that Serbs had not been invited to that meeting – to which I replied that they had indeed been invited but had chosen not to attend.

I began to realize that I needed to be very careful about the direction and content of his questioning and that I should stick to the facts. However, Judge Kwon then adjourned proceedings until the following Wednesday. By the time I left the court I was exhausted. There was now a break of four days, and the Victim and Witness Section had offered to cover a return flight home. However, the eruption of the Eyjafjallajökull volcano in Iceland meant that an ash cloud descended over Europe and grounded flights for a number of days. I spent the long weekend on my own.

The following Wednesday proved to be another long and tiring day. Karadžić went on the offensive, stating that the erection of barricades in Sarajevo by Serbs was because of the murder at a Serb wedding rather than as a consequence of the referendum results (as I had written in my report). He asked for my thoughts on this, and I told him that in my view the erection of the barricades was a well planned operation and not a spontaneous reaction to a sudden shooting. Then it was back to the television station again, with Karadžić claiming that the Muslims had had a 'special forces' unit inside the building. I reminded him that he had not mentioned this to me on the evening I had tackled him about the reason why the Serbs had fired mortar rounds at the station in April 1992. In response to this he immediately referred back to a meeting I had had with the Serb Minister for Information, Velibor Ostojić, and went on to quote from Ostojić's subsequent report to the Bosnian Serb leadership which stated, 'Mr Doyle was astonished to hear that there was a Muslim military unit at the TV station'; Ostojić then added that the meeting with Doyle went very well and claimed that 'I wrote to Doyle after our meeting'. I countered that I had a very different memory of this meeting and that Ostojić had never mentioned anything about a unit occupying the television station. In any event, the meeting had been far from satisfactory and I never received any subsequent report or letter from him or anybody else.

Over the course of that day's evidence Karadžić produced many documents, including military reports, decisions by the SDS leadership and reports of alleged atrocities against Serb civilians. Most of these I had no knowledge of, and I was unable to comment on the allegations or the authenticity of the documents. There were, on occasion, points brought up by Karadžić to which I agreed. Again, however, the questions were 'leading'. He asked me, for example, whether it was true that General Kukanjac's HQ had been surrounded by Muslims; if some of the Bosnian judiciary had stated that the holding of a referendum without Serb approval would be illegal; and whether it was true that the Bosnian Serbs did not interfere with the referendum vote. To these questions I had to answer in the affirmative. But throughout proceedings Karadžić sought to portray himself as wronged and misunderstood, someone who was simply leading his people as best he could to a future of safety and peace. He argued that the Muslims had 'rejected peace' and that the actions of Serbs had been only in self defence. Why would Serbs attack their own city? He appeared to be in a state of denial, believing he had done nothing wrong. His simplistic narrative ran thus: the Muslims were the aggressors, while we were the victims.

He raised the issue of my presenting him with a copy of the *Sunday Times* in Brussels (with the photograph of emaciated prisoners on its cover). He now claimed that the photograph had been staged and that there was no such camp, suggesting that the prisoners in the photograph were probably 'on a diet'. I was incredulous. I had been given permission by the presiding judge to refer to my work diary when there was a need to verify where I was and who I had met on particular dates. Karadžić seized on this, demanding that the defence be given a copy of it. Judge Kwon asked if I would be willing to allow sections of it be photocopied and given to Karadžić. After some discussion I agreed, on condition that I was permitted to redact any entry of a personal nature and only allowed the portion of the diary covering my period in Sarajevo to be copied. This was agreed.

The following day, Karadžić began his cross-examination by claiming I was both partial and biased. Having studied the diary extracts, he implied that I had met with the Muslim leadership far more frequently than with Serbs, that I had no interest in the Serbs' views and did not care about their concerns. It was at this point I went on my own offensive, reminding him that he had always been invited to talks but that the Bosnian Serb leadership had often refused to attend, citing safety concerns. I further reminded him that the Bosnian Serb leadership moving from Sarajevo to Pale (from where they besieged the city) had made multi-party talks impossible. He asked why I had not engaged with them when I chaired talks on the withdrawal of the JNA from Sarajevo, but I again reminded him that he had refused earlier invitations to talks; in any case, these talks were strictly concerned with the JNA's withdrawal from Bosnia and had nothing to do with SDS. I then turned to the presiding judge and told him that I strongly objected to the way that Karadžić was consistently questioning my integrity and impartiality. I emphasized that – in all my time in Bosnia – I had never been accused of bias. I further requested that this objection be noted. The judge agreed and warned Karadžić that his line of questioning was not acceptable.

Day three followed a similar pattern, with Karadžić producing numerous documents issued by the Serb leadership, the JNA and even General Ratko Mladić, purporting to demonstrate Serb restraint. Once again I testified that I had neither previous sight nor knowledge of any of these documents. When Karadžić was informed by Judge Kwon that he would have to conclude his cross-examination of me by close of business that day, he became quite agitated and accused me more than once of being biased. He alleged that I was anti-Serb and was working for the prosecution. He also referred back to negotiations conducted in Lisbon that I had attended – talks that had been suspended as a consequence of the 'bread line massacre' in Sarajevo. Suspecting that the Serbs would be blamed for the massacre, we had pressed Karadžić to agree to the handing over of the airport in Sarajevo to the UN as a goodwill gesture. Now he was denying the existence of any such deal, saying that he had already offered the use of the airport for the delivery of humanitarian aid. We had, quite simply, no evidence of this.

With the judge's deadline fast approaching, the prosecution was permitted to re-direct. Uertz-Retzlaff used this opportunity to ask my opinion about a document submitted as an exhibit. I was asked whether I had been aware that

Karadžić had given interviews in which he had described Republika Srpska as 'a reality', and whether I had heard such arguments during meetings. I answered in the affirmative. Uertz-Retzlaff then went on to quote further from the interview in which Karadžić had stated that the SDS had a list of the actions and steps to take, but that they had 'always waited for the Muslims to make a mistake, and after they made one, the SDS created a union of municipalities and the Serbian autonomous areas, followed by the regions, and eventually an assembly and, finally, a republic'. Karadžić was also quoted as stating that 'Every time the Muslim and Croat representatives told us we were breaking up Bosnia and Herzegovina we replied that our actions were only in response to their mistakes and their aggression against our political rights.' I was asked if these arguments were consistent with those posited by the Bosnian Serbs during my term in Bosnia. Again, I replied that they were.

At the session's end I felt bruised and embattled. These had been tough exchanges. When my testimony was finally over, Judge Morrison directed his attention to me and asked 'out of curiosity' whether I had ever been an infantry officer. When I told him that I had indeed, he replied, 'Yes, I thought so.' The presiding judge thanked me for my evidence and excused me. As I stood up to leave I glanced over at Karadžić, suspecting that we would not meet again. He caught my eye but remained passive. I wondered what might be going through his mind at that moment.

Back alone in the witness waiting room I felt a huge wave of emotion suddenly hit me. By the time the prosecution team of Alan Tiegar and Uertz-Retzlaff entered the room I was in floods of tears. I couldn't explain it nor could I stop the tears flowing. When Tiegar gripped my arm in support, it was as if he had expected it. He acknowledged that I had had 'a pretty rough time' and told me that the judge had just warned Karadžić that his conduct during cross-examination was not acceptable. In truth, it was not the manner in which he had cross-examined me that had affected me. What kept going through my mind was this question: how could this man justify what he had done, what he had allowed the military under his leadership to do, and yet still firmly believe that he was innocent of any crime? I just felt very sad, and the tears continued to flow. I thought back to my year in Bosnia and with this came the realization that, despite our best efforts, little had been accomplished. The international community, after all, had not succeeded in preventing this brutal war or influencing its outcome, and people like Milošević, Karadžić and Mladić had continued on their course of action with near impunity.

When I phoned Grainne after I returned to my hotel she was not in any way surprised when I recounted to her my emotional reaction. In her calm voice she simply remarked that she had been 'waiting for a reaction like that from you for nearly twenty years'.

Six years later, in March 2016, Karadžić was found guilty of ten of the eleven counts against him, including war crimes, genocide and crimes against humanity. He was sentenced to 40 years' imprisonment. For thousands of people this may have fallen short of what they had hoped for. I never had any doubt that he would receive a long custodial sentence, and I hoped that it would give some small sense of justice and closure to his victims.

Epilogue

When my service in Bosnia finished it took me some time to revert from the physical and psychological challenges of Sarajevo back to routine barrack life. The Irish Defence Forces have, however, a tendency to bring you back to earth pretty quickly. Within a month I had returned to familiar ground, serving as a company commander with the 12th Battalion in Limerick. I was then assigned as an instructor to the newly-established UN School at the Curragh. With their wealth of peacekeeping experience, the Defence Forces had long considered establishing such a school institution. Since its foundation the school has been the focal point of the Defence Forces' effort to standardize preparation for peace support operations, not only for its own troops but for those of other UN member states as well. This has been achieved by bringing to bear the experience gained by Irish troops on the broadest range of peacekeeping missions throughout the world over sixty years.

During this time I also completed a Masters Degree (MA) in International Studies at the University of Limerick. Taking such a course had been suggested to me by the academic director following an invitation to give a presentation lecture to postgraduate students a few months after returning from Bosnia. I enjoyed being a mature student, and my dissertation on the conflict in Bosnia allowed me not only to research it in greater depth, but also to reflect on my own experiences there.

On promotion to Lieutenant Colonel in 1995 I was fortunate to get command of my old Battalion in Limerick. And I was to serve abroad again on two further occasions. In 1997 I commanded the 82nd Irish Battalion in Lebanon as part of UNIFIL. I was very pleased to have command of a unit on overseas service, an opportunity enjoyed by few officers and highly prized by those fortunate enough to be selected. It was a real change for me to be part of a UN force, as opposed to my role in Bosnia, when I was on the outside looking in. The most memorable event of the unit's tour of duty was a visit from our President, Mary MacAleese, the first such visit by Uachtarain na h-Eireann (President of Ireland) to troops serving overseas.

My final overseas appointment was a two-and-a-half-year stint as a Colonel at UN HQ in New York, where I served as Chief of Staff of the Military Division, part of the Department of Peacekeeping Operations. The role of the department is to plan, prepare, manage and direct the organization's peacekeeping missions globally, while the Military Division's main task is to ensure that the most appropriate military capability available is deployed in support of UN objectives. It was certainly interesting to work at UN HQ, despite there being many occasions when I questioned whether our efforts in New York had any positive effect on the various operations on the ground. UN HQ can be a very bureaucratic organization, and at times I found it a bit stifling.

Despite these challenging appointments, my mind was never far from Bosnia, particularly as I had been to the ICTY in the Hague on several occasions. I have often wondered what became of so many people I had known well or had worked alongside. I had made many friends there, be they Muslims, Croats or Serbs. Despite their differences, which were manipulated by nationalist politicians, there was much binding the peoples of the former Yugoslavia together.

While it might not be appropriate for a soldier to question or comment on political issues or decisions, I cannot help but wonder where it all went wrong. Could this dreadful conflict in Bosnia have been avoided? Somehow I doubt it. From the first time I arrived in Sarajevo I had the impression that these three ethnic groups were looking for excuses to separate, and this feeling did not change throughout my period there. As time passed, so the suspicion, mistrust and animosity increased. Events in Croatia only added to this gradual deterioration in relations between the three sides.

The subsequent war posed a very significant challenge to the defenders of European security and the international community. The Yugoslav crisis presented the international community with a host of challenges, including issues of ethnicity, sovereignty, self-determination, borders and diplomatic recognition. It also involved the wider issue of regional stability. While the countries of the EU were debating the merits of deeper integration, Yugoslavia was on course for a break-up. The conflict was a severe challenge in post-Cold War Europe to international solidarity in deterring war. The results were not good. Despite much effort, European co-operative security measures failed and the UN achieved no better. The severity of the conflict was so great that the effectiveness of these institutions was questioned. It would seem that, in relation to Bosnia, Western governments were unable to pay the political or military price of achieving stability. Moreover, there existed no consensus between EC member states with regard to policy on Yugoslavia. In my view, the Serbs understood this and were quick to exploit it.

While it might be easy in hindsight to criticise, it would be unfair to judge Europe's capacity to forge a more effective foreign and security policy on the basis of the Bosnian experience. Bosnia was (and remains) a complex country with many problems, the main one being a mixture of three mutually hostile parties – a challenge to any institution seeking a solution. The EC's mistake may have been that it overestimated its capacity to effectively solve the Yugoslav crisis. I recall Luxembourg's foreign minister, Jacques Poos, when referring to the challenge of Yugoslavia, saying that this was 'The hour of Europe' – but a task as immense as dealing with the dissolution of the Yugoslav state proved to be too big a challenge. While some European countries intimated that they believed the Yugoslav federation was at an end, others held the opposite view. Initially, there was strong support for the notion of Yugoslavia remaining a federation, but as time passed some EC member states came to believe that a break-up was inevitable, and divisions emerged.

Peter Carrington's Peace Conference had the 'carrot and stick' taken away from it by the decision of some European countries, particularly Germany, to give recognition to the republics in the absence of any agreement or cease-fire. Thus a main condition of Carrington's mandate was suddenly redundant, and this, I believe, left the conference greatly weakened. Accordingly, we continued to mediate in Bosnia but with no muscle. Though hardly ideal, there was little alternative to what we were trying to achieve. Cease-fires proved futile in many cases. A return to fighting before the ink on the agreements had dried was depressingly commonplace. Of course, it made diplomatic sense for all sides to attend peace negotiations – if for no other reason than to give the impression that they were supportive of our efforts – but in reality, none of them had the slightest intention of complying with the cease-fires which they had signed. As Martin Bell so aptly commented, 'When a cease-fire is signed, it's time to duck for cover.' My own view was that any time won, however short, was better than nothing at all. At least it gave some respite, even if only to collect the bodies from the streets.

The recognition of Bosnia essentially meant that war was inevitable. The EC had announced that the republic would be granted recognition as an independent state once it had carried out a referendum. The Serb view on this was made quite clear. Their contention was that a declaration of independence without their agreement was contrary to the existing constitution, and they were resolutely opposed to a unitary state with a Muslim majority. Karadžić had made this very clear to me when we discussed the issue. President Izetbegović must have known what the likely Serb reaction would be, yet he chose to ignore it. Perhaps this was irresponsible.

As negotiation and mediation continued on into 1992, the Muslims became less interested in finding a political solution and concentrated their efforts on securing some kind of military intervention. This was an issue which had plagued the international community from the outset. There were no quick or easy means to reverse the military reality on the ground, and even if military intervention was indeed to be initiated, there were no grounds for assuming that it would be more effective than diplomacy had been. The Serbs discounted intervention as a likely course of action and pursued their policy of ethnic cleansing and seizing territory. The more territory they seized the more they might be willing to hand back – and the stronger their hand. They were convinced that the international community had no appetite for military intervention and believed that nothing but the use of force could prevent them from achieving their aims. With the additional backing and support of Serbia they had, therefore, little to fear.

Later, when war broke out in Bosnia, the problem was not how to supervise a peace, but rather how to establish one in the first place. The challenge was about managing rather than preventing war. Despite international outrage at the unfolding events in Bosnia, there simply was not the political will to commit military forces. Europe did not possess the will necessary to perform a military operation on the scale demanded. While the UN deployed a peacekeeping force to the region, it was never going to have the means to stop the fighting. Its mandate was limited to the delivery of humanitarian aid, preventing the conflict from spreading and providing 'good offices' in the attempt to facilitate negotiations. However, the force could not intervene to halt the conflict or contain acts of obvious aggression. Even its Sarajevo commander, General MacKenzie, admitted that the force should not have been called UNPROFOR, as it was not mandated to protect anybody. It was very limited in size, and it is my firm conviction that while the threat of force can be a powerful weapon it is only effective if it is believable. The consequences of its use should be well understood by the warring factions. In other words, do not threaten force unless you are prepared to use it. The problem in Bosnia was that there never was a force to threaten anybody with. This only came to pass when the ineffective UNPROFOR passed its baton to the implementation force (IFOR) after the signing of the Dayton Agreement.

It would be fifteen years before I returned to Bosnia. In 2007, having just returned from serving with the UN in New York, I was presented with the opportunity to visit, having been invited to lecture at a newly established peacekeeping training centre in Sarajevo. I was joined by Grainne, who was visiting the place for the first time. The city had clearly moved on and returned to normal. But one didn't have to look too far to see the legacy of the war – the extensive graveyards, in particular, were still a stark reminder of a bloody and brutal time. I pray that hearts will heal, that a wonderful city and its surrounding hills will blossom again; and above all I hope that Bosnian children, whatever their ethnic or national background, will grow up together never having to experience the scourge of war again.

Index